SEASONAL GUIDE TO THE NATURAL YEAR

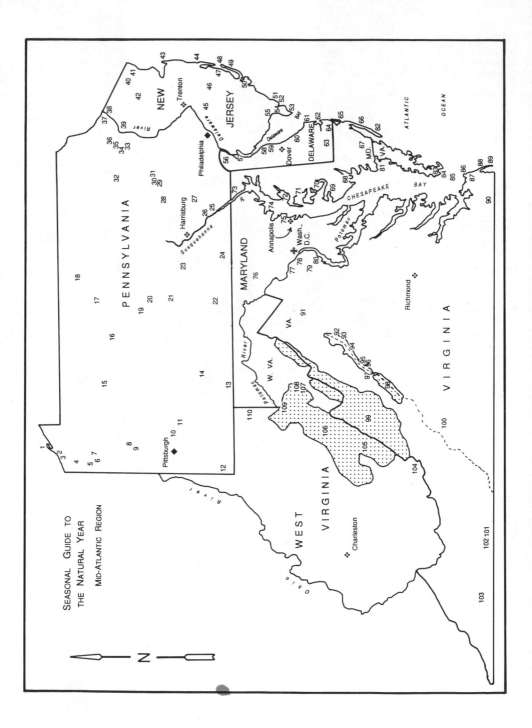

SEASONAL GUIDE TO
THE NATURAL YEAR
MID-ATLANTIC REGION

LIST OF SITES BY STATE

Abbreviations: NA—Natural Area; NF—National Forest (shaded area); NMP—National Military Park; NP—National Park; NRA—National Recreation Area; NRMA—Natural Resource Management Area; NS—National Seashore; NWR—National Wildlife Refuge; SF—State Forest; SP—State Park; WMA—Wildlife Management Area

PENNSYLVANIA
1. Presque Isle SP
2. Walnut Creek
3. Trout Run
4. Erie NWR
5. Pymatuning Lake, WMA
6. Hartstown Swamp
7. Conneaut Marsh
8. Wolf Creek Narrows NA
9. Jennings Envir. Education Ctr.
10. Trillium Trail
11. Guffy Hollow/Braddock Trail Park
12. Enlow Fork NA
13. Mount Davis NA
14. Spruce Flats Bog
15. Cook Forest SP
16. Winslow Hill/Dents and Hicks Runs
17. Kettle Creek SP
18. Fall foliage area
19. Black Moshannon SP/Moshannon SF
20. Bear Meadows NA
21. Canoe Creek SP
22. Tuscarora Summit
23. Waggoner's Gap
24. Gettysburg NMP
25. Shenks Ferry Glen Preserve
26. Conejohela Flats
27. Middle Creek WMA
28. Route 183 Lookout
29. Hawk Mountain Sanctuary
30. Baer Rocks
31. Bake Oven Knob
32. Hickory Run SP
33. Long Pond Barrens
34. Long Pond
35. Promised Land SP
36. Bruce Lake NA
37. Delaware Water Gap NRA

NEW JERSEY
38. Sunrise Mountain
39. Raccoon Ridge
40. Troy Meadows
41. Montclair Hawk Lookout Sanctuary
42. Great Swamp NWR
43. Sandy Hook SP
44. Manasquan Inlet
45. Whitesbog Cons. & Envir. Studies Ctr.
46. Webb's Mills
47. Barnegat Bay
48. Barnegat Light/Eighth St. jetty
49. Long Beach Island
50. Brigantine unit, Forsythe NWR
51. Stone Harbor heronry
52. Nummy Island
53. Cape May
54. Reed's Beach
55. Moore's Beach/Heislerville-Denis Creek WMA

DELAWARE
56. Brandywine Creek SP
57. Pea Patch Island/Ft. Delaware SP
58. Bombay Hook NWR
59. Port Mahon/Little Creek WMA
60. Prime Hook NWR
61. Cape Henlopen SP
62. Indian River Inlet/Delaware Seashore SP
63. Trap Pond SP

MARYLAND
64. Pocomoke/Selbyville/Great Cypress Swamp (Maryland/Delaware)
65. Ocean City
66. Assateague Island NS
67. Pocomoke River SP
68. Elliott Island marshes/Fishing Creek WMA
69. Blackwater NWR
70. Choptank River
71. Wye Island NRMA
72. Eastern Neck NWR
73. Conowingo Dam
74. Hart-Miller Island SP
75. Sandy Point SP
76. Washington Monument SP
77. Great Falls Park/Riverbend Park
78. Scott's Run Nature Reserve
79. Bull Run Regional Park
80. Huntley Meadows Park

VIRGINIA
81. Pocomoke Sound (Virginia/Maryland)
82. Chincoteague NWR
83. Eastern Shore of Virginia NWR
84. Cape Charles
85. Chesapeake Bay Bridge-Tunnel
86. Seashore SP
87. Rudlee Inlet
88. Back Bay NWR
89. False Cape SP
90. Dismal Swamp NWR
91. Linden Fire Tower
92. Hawksbill Mountain
93. Buena Vista Overlook
94. Shenandoah NP
95. Thunder Ridge Overlook
96. Harvey's Knob Overlook
97. Rockfish Gap
98., 99. George Washington NF
100. Blue Ridge Parkway/Skyline Drive
101. Grayson Highlands SP
102. Mount Rogers NRA
103. Mendota Fire Tower

WEST VIRGINIA
104. Hanging Rock Raptor Migration Observatory
105. Cranberry Glades Botanical Area
106. Monongahela NF
107. Dolly Sods Wilderness
108. Bear Rocks
109. Canaan Valley bogs
110. Cranesville Bog (West Virginia/Maryland)

Stretching as far as the eye can see, the salt marshes of Elliott Island are the winter home of short-eared owls and rough-legged hawks.

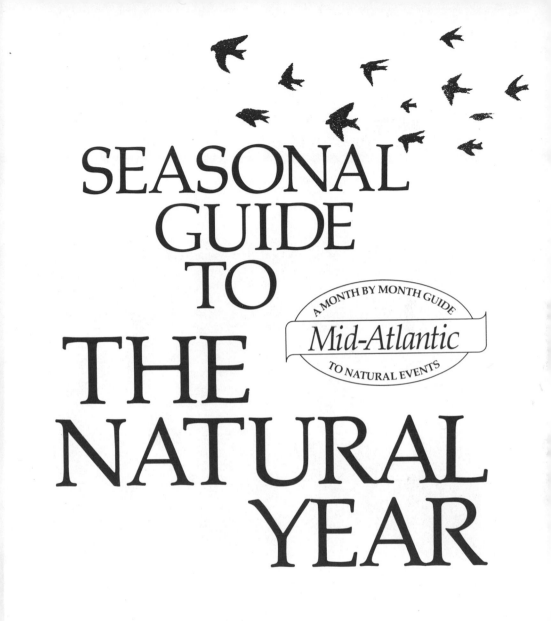

SEASONAL
GUIDE
TO

THE
NATURAL
YEAR

Scott Weidensaul

FULCRUM PUBLISHING
Golden, Colorado

To the memory of the late Ned Smith,
whose skill as a naturalist, artist
and photographer allowed him
to touch many lives

Copyright © 1992 Scott Weidensaul

Cover photo of a Great Blue Heron at sunrise in the Forsythe National
Wildlife Refuge, New Jersey copyright © 1996 Scott Weidensaul
Photographs and maps by Scott Weidensaul
Cover design by Deborah Rich

Library of Congress Cataloging-in-Publication Data

Weidensaul, Scott.
    Seasonal guide to the natural year : A month by month
guide to natural events—Mid-Atlantic / Scott Weidensaul.
        p.   cm.
    Includes bibliographical references and index.
    ISBN 1-55591-105-6
    1. Natural history—Middle Atlantic States—Guide-books.
2. Seasons—Middle Atlantic States—Guide-books.
3. Middle Atlantic States—Description and travel—Guide-
books. I. Title.
QH104.5.M45W45 1992   91-58483
508.74—dc20   CIP

Printed in the United States of America

0   9   8   7   6   5   4   3

Fulcrum Publishing
350 Indiana Street, Suite 350
Golden, Colorado 80401-5093
800-992-2908

CONTENTS

Red-tailed hawks, along with kestrels and rough-legged hawks, are common at a number of sites in the region each winter, including the farmland of southeastern Pennsylvania.

ACKNOWLEDGMENTS

Over the years in which this book was being researched and written, many people contributed ideas, criticisms and suggestions that made it much better than it would otherwise have been, or acted as guides to areas with which they were familiar. It is impossible to acknowledge all of them, but some deserve special consideration. Curator Jim Brett and former executive director Stan Senner of Hawk Mountain Sanctuary in Kempton, Pennsylvania, provided invaluable direction and encouragement in the book's earliest stages, while staff biologist Laurie Goodrich has been a longtime source of information about the northern Appalachians. Paul G. Wiegman of the Western Pennsylvania Conservancy and Elizabeth Johnson of the New Jersey office of the Nature Conservancy made important suggestions about sites within their bailiwicks. Thanks also go to Jody Marshall, Rick Imes, David Moyer, Tanya Parsonage, William Drake of the Pennsylvania Game Commission, Cathy Vivarette, Lynda Richardson, Roger Latham of the Nature Conservancy's Pennsylvania field office, Dr. Scott Shalaway, the office of the executive director of the Chesapeake Bay Bridge-Tunnel, Peggy Wisner, Dave Wolf of the Pennsylvania Fish Commission, Neil Shea of the Fairview Fish Culture Station,

Charlie Conley of DeLorme Mapping Co., and the fine staffs of the region's many national wildlife refuges, who generously shared their information with me.

Finally, special thanks to Jeff Lepore, whose intimate knowledge of the region contributed immeasurably to this project, and to Jeanne Tinsman for unfailing support.

Many of these fine naturalists reviewed parts of the manuscript, catching my mistakes before publication. For those that remain, I take full responsibility.

INTRODUCTION

Every year at the end of May, when the moon pulls the tides to their highest levels of the month, millions of horseshoe crabs swarm out of the depths of Delaware Bay and onto the beaches of New Jersey and Delaware. In gray, almost solid ranks, the crabs jostle for position on the moist sand, where the females dig shallow nests and lay their tiny green eggs by the trillions.

Into this already chaotic scene come tens of thousands of shorebirds. Exhausted by a nonstop ocean flight from the coast of South America, on the verge of starvation, they pour into the bay to feed on the crab eggs, at times obscuring the beaches with their numbers. When they take flight, they fill the air with rushing wings and frantic cries. It is one of the premier wildlife spectacles in North America—but if you are just a week or so too early or too late, you'll miss it.

In nature, timing is everything—the timing of the seasons, of courtship, of migration, of birth. Even though wild animals and plants cannot read the calendar, they respond to the changing length of daylight through the year. Coupled with other, subtle clues we do not fully understand, this signal allows nature to progress at a pace, and with a precision, that surprise many people when they first discover it.

Naturalists take great pleasure in knowing and anticipating these predictable changes in the natural year. Near my home in the mountains of eastern Pennsylvania, I know that the great horned owl chicks will be hatching around March 10, about the same time the tundra swans reach their peak on the Susquehanna River. The pink lady's-slipper orchids will be in full bloom by the end of May's first week, with the mountain laurel following a month later. The second week of October is when I expect the fall foliage to crescendo, at the same time that the sharp-shinned hawk migration is reaching its pinnacle.

Seasonal Guide to the Natural Year: A Month by Month Guide to Natural Events—Mid-Atlantic is a guidebook with a difference—instead of a listing of natural places, it is a guide to natural events, a *when*-to-go rather than a where-to-go approach, with the emphasis on timing rather than geography. Built on a seasonal theme, the book is divided into twelve monthly sections, each covering at least four wild spectacles of unusual interest. What's more, each chapter gives detailed directions to "hotspots" of exceptional quality or easy access, with maps, tips on what to look for and how best to enjoy the experience, and background on the natural history of the spectacle. Breakout chapters in each section provide an in-depth look at one of the month's more unusual features.

The book covers the six states of the mid-Atlantic region—Pennsylvania, New Jersey, Maryland, Delaware, Virginia and West Virginia—and the District of Columbia. This six-state region was carefully chosen because it forms a cohesive natural unit, sharing many aspects of climate, vegetative and wildlife communities. New York, although perhaps a mid-Atlantic state culturally, is not included here because it has more in common with the boreal ecosystems of New England than with the mid-Atlantic states. This region is a huge area, encompassing more than 130,000 square miles, with an incredible diversity of habitat and topography. One of North America's greatest geologic features, the Appalachian Mountains, runs through the heart of it. The Chesapeake Bay, with its thousands of miles of coastline and tidal marsh, is one of the world's most important estuaries, frequently overshadowing the smaller Delaware Bay to its north. Glacial marshes and ponds dot the region's northern sweep. The wide, mild coastal plain and Piedmont, extending inland nearly 100 miles, are home to many plants and animals with southern affinities, while the Blue Ridge and other mountain chains shelter natural communities that hearken back to the last ice age.

In the mid-Atlantic region, convention sometimes stands on its head. Here, it is possible to find cypress swamps, those symbols of the Deep South, that are almost 150 miles farther *north* than the red spruce forests on Mount Rogers, which are emblematic of the North Woods. East and West mix as well, with relict prairies drifting in a sea of forest. It is a rich and fascinating place for a naturalist to explore, and I hope this book encourages you to experience it for yourself.

GENERAL TIPS, CAUTIONS AND SUGGESTIONS

The overwhelming majority of the places listed in this volume are on public land or private property that is routinely opened to public access. In a few instances, auto routes running through private land are given, and in many cases public property and private abut within the same bog or forest. Obey all No Trespassing signs, and treat local landowners with unfailing courtesy and consideration; this is especially important at popular destinations or unusual times of day. The folks who live among the Elliott Island marshes in Maryland, for instance, didn't ask for hordes of bird-watchers to descend on their neighborhood each spring, waiting all night to hear black rails calling, and it is hard not to sympathize with their complaints about noise, lights and trespassers.

While this book contains maps of many routes and places, it is always a good idea to have several detailed maps of the area you are planning to visit. State highway or travel club maps are fine for major roads, but for backroad (or backcountry) travel they leave too much uncovered. The most detailed maps available are U.S. Geologic Survey (USGS) topographic maps; they come in several scales, the most commonly used being 7.5-minute quadrangles, which cover an area of about 6.5 by 7.5 miles. Their drawbacks are high cost, especially if you need information on large areas, and the hassle of handling many big maps in the car or field. A valuable alternative is the state atlases published by DeLorme Mapping Co.; instead of the USGS scale of 1:24,000, the DeLorme atlas maps use a more manageable 1:150,000, and include topographic and forest cover information, all main roads and important dirt roads (with names and route numbers), as well as many trails. At this writing atlases are available for only two of the region's states— Pennsylvania and Virginia—but these two encompass most of the region's land area. I use the DeLorme atlases for general travel and USGS quads when I need more information about specific sites. Addresses for both the USGS and DeLorme are listed in the Appendix.

Common sense is even more valuable than maps or a guidebook. Be aware that hunting is permitted on almost all wildlife management areas and state game lands (which were usually purchased with license fees from hunting and fishing), as well as portions of most state parks and national wildlife refuges. Saturdays are almost always the days of heaviest hunting. Before visiting in autumn and winter, find out if hunting is permitted in the area where you plan to be; a blaze orange cap is never a bad idea. A special concern is spring turkey hunting, a popular sport in much of the region and one many nonhunters are unaware of. In most states the spring gobbler season runs from April through the end of May.

Canoes are invaluable for exploring many of the

hotspots. Wear personal flotation devices even if you are a strong swimmer, and learn the basics of canoe handling before setting out on a wild river or stream.

Finally, just as important as courtesy to landowners is respect for the natural spectacles this book celebrates. Wild animals and plants are not a sideshow staged for human benefit; they have their own lives, needs and purposes, an existence quite separate from ours. Human intervention can be damaging, sometimes dangerously so—thoughtless intrusions can keep nesting birds from their chicks, spook flocks from critically needed food or rest, and trample young wildflowers. Stay on trails and obey all signs restricting access at refuges and parks, for such regulations are rarely imposed capriciously. Remember that the best observers have no discernible effect on that which they are watching.

A REQUEST FOR HELP

The directions contained in this book are the result of (sometimes tediously) exhausting fieldwork. In the time between research and publication, however, things change— roads are switched, bridges are washed out, landmarks removed. Inevitably, readers will find conditions in some places at variance with those described here. To keep future editions as accurate and current as possible, readers are encouraged to send corrections to the author, c/o Fulcrum Publishing, 350 Indiana Street, Suite 350, Golden, CO 80401.

The dozens of wild spectacles that follow are only the tip of the iceberg, for the mid-Atlantic region is an endlessly varied place. If you have suggestions for spectacles that you would like considered for future editions of *Seasonal Guide to the Natural Year,* please send them (with directions and as much background information as possible) to the address above. Bear in mind that the spectacles should be consistent from year to year in time and place, be of unusual interest or exceptional quality, and occur on public land or private land open to the public.

JANUARY

January Observations

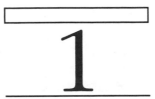

Wintering Bald Eagles

For the novice as well as the seasoned naturalist, few sights can compare to that of a mature bald eagle, its white head and tail flashing in the sun as it soars against a flawless blue sky.

In the 1960s and 1970s, such experiences were rare in the mid-Atlantic region—bald eagles had suffered drastic declines from pesticide contamination, which interfered with their ability to reproduce. By 1962, the Chesapeake Bay ecosystem, which had once boasted a thriving bald eagle population, had but thirty-seven pairs, and few of them were successfully raising young. That changed, starting in 1972 with the banning of DDT, and the subsequent restrictions on related organochlorine insecticides. By the start of the 1990s, more than two hundred pairs of eagles nested in the bay ecosystem, with other concentrations in New Jersey and western Pennsylvania.

As eagle numbers rebounded, birders noticed that predictable concentrations of these magnificent raptors could be found each winter in a few locations. Some, like the Blackwater Marsh area on the Chesapeake Bay, were traditional wintering sites. Others, like the upper Delaware River and Conowingo Dam, were new.

Bald eagles feed primarily on fish and carrion, and

tend to gather where food is readily available. One such place is the tailrace of the Conowingo Dam, just south of the Maryland/Pennsylvania border on the Susquehanna River. A hydroelectric dam, Conowingo funnels the river's water through huge turbines to produce electricity, and in the process sucks in catfish, carp and other fish, which are spit out into the tailrace dead, stunned or maimed. It is an eagle smorgasbord. What is more, the action of the dam keeps this stretch of river relatively ice-free, serving to further concentrate the eagles in the coldest months.

At first, only a handful of eagles took advantage of the provender, but their numbers grew steadily through the late 1980s and early 1990s, probably bolstered by the resurging regional population and perhaps through the eagle equivalent of word of mouth. In any event, a visitor may expect to see up to two dozen eagles around Conowingo—sitting on shoreside trees, rocks in the middle of the river or on the high-tension wires that span the Susquehanna here. As many as forty have been tallied in the area.

First-time eagle watchers are usually surprised to find that many of the eagles are brown, lacking the trademark white head and tail. Bald eagles require five years to reach maturity and their plumage reflects their age. In their first winter, immatures are an almost solid brown, with only a thin strip of white under the wing and small, white "armpit" markings. By age 2, they molt into the so-called whitebelly plumage, with a dark head and chest and plenty of white on the stomach. The dark tail feathers of the first year have been replaced with white feathers that show a wide, brown band. Many inexperienced (and not so inexperienced) birders have confused these subadult bald eagles with young golden eagles, which also have white-based tails.

The final immature plumage, usually acquired in the third year, is the whitest. The bird's chest and upperparts are heavily streaked with white, and there are large patches of white on the undersides of the wings. The next year the young eagle will begin to molt in adult feathers, but the process takes many months, and during the transition phase the eagle can look rather seedy—uneven patches of brown and dull gray on the body, a mix of pure white and brown-banded tail feathers, and a salt-and-pepper head as white feathers replace brown.

Bear in mind, also, that not every big, dark bird is an eagle. At most of the eagle concentration points, black and turkey vultures are common, and both can confuse the unwary watcher. Turkey vultures fly with their wings held in a distinctive shallow V, and may rock gently from side to side while soaring. Black vultures have a much flatter flight profile, but their tails are considerably shorter than an eagle's and they have white patches on the outer flight feathers. Bald eagles soar with the wings held flat, and even at great distances the protruding head seems almost as prominent as the tail, in contrast to the relatively tiny heads of both vultures.

HOTSPOTS

The region has three major concentration points—Conowingo Dam, the upper Delaware River and the Chesapeake Bay. Eagles are also visible year-round at Pymatuning Waterfowl Management Area (WMA) near Meadville, Pennsylvania, where they nest; see Chapter 11 for directions.

Conowingo Dam is one of the most accessible hotspots, and possibly the most convenient for a majority of the region's residents. The facility is owned by the Philadelphia Electric Co., which has expanded its fishing access area below the dam to accommodate growing crowds of eagle-watchers.

To reach Conowingo, take Route 1 to the Susquehanna River; coming from the east, the highway crosses the dam itself, an impressive sight. At the west side of the dam, turn south onto a small road marked with signs for the Conowingo Fisherman Park, which is reached after a twisting descent to the base of the dam (watch for a sharp left turn at a small store). The parking lot is long and ample for even the biggest crowds, and overlooks a wide, shallow expanse of river; there is a wooden observation platform, although almost anywhere near the lot is good for watching.

Look for eagles in flight, and carefully scan the electrical transmission towers, trees on the far bank and rocks in the middle of the river for perching birds. An abandoned railroad bed goes downstream from the parking lot and provides additional views of the river. Remember to glance overhead frequently, since it is not unusual for eagles to soar past at remarkably low altitudes. A release of water through the dam's turbines is the chow bell for the eagles and sparks the greatest feeding activity.

On Maryland's Eastern Shore, **Blackwater National Wildlife Refuge (NWR)** and the complex of fresh, brackish and salt marshes that stretches out far beyond the refuge boundaries form a magnet for bald eagles. More than two dozen pairs nest in the vicinity, with many more arriving for the winter, along with a few golden eagles. The auto loop through the refuge is a convenient (and warm) way of seeing the eagles, which may be found almost anywhere—in the pine trees that edge the impoundments, flying low above the water or often sitting on the mud flats and bars at the water's edge, their heads just visible above the marsh grass. Should one fly past carrying a piece of carp, there may be an explosion of hidden eagles, leaping into pursuit and trying to pirate the morsel for themselves. The sight of six or seven eagles tussling in midair is itself worth the trip.

To reach Blackwater, take Route 50 south through Cambridge; 1.8 miles after coming off the Choptank River Bridge, turn right onto Route 16 West (Church Creek Road). Go 7.5 miles, making a left turn onto Route 335 South, then another 3.9 miles to Key Wallace Drive, another left turn. The visitors' center (open from 8 A.M. to 3:30 P.M., weekdays only) and entrance to the auto tour are 2.7 miles down Key Wallace.

The roughly 4-mile tour starts out in woodland, then crosses open marshes; shortly after entering, take the dead-end spur to the left, which leads to an observation tower. Reenter the main loop and stop at the pull-off to scan for eagles by an artificial osprey nest platform 2.1 miles from the entrance. The tour route loops back to Key Wallace Drive, but instead take a left turn onto a spur 2.6 miles from the entrance; the mile-long spur passes a favorite eagle perch tree and gives good views of the marsh, before joining Route 335. Make a right onto 335 for .3 mile, then another right back onto Key Wallace to return to the visitors' center.

More eagles may be found on the Elliott Island marsh and the backroads that link it with Blackwater; for directions, see Chapter 2.

The **upper Delaware River** has been an eagle hotspot since the 1970s and is regularly censused during a midwinter eagle count. Unlike in Conowingo or Blackwater, the eagles are rarely bunched up at one spot, and finding them usually entails driving from one overlook to the next, but on a good day it is not unusual to see 10 or more. As an added benefit, this is a beautiful region, and even if the eagles do not cooperate, few visitors will leave feeling disappointed.

There are two prime areas, one between the tiny village of Damascus in Wayne County, Pennsylvania, and Port Jervis, New York, and the other downriver, encompassing about 25 miles of water between Milford and Bushkill, in the Delaware Water Gap National Recreation Area. Both can be covered in a day's driving, with plenty of time for stopping and enjoying the views.

Following the route from north to south, take Route 191 north from Honesdale in central Wayne County. Turn east onto Route 371 toward Damascus, a distance of 9.3 miles. To the right of the bridge is the Damascus Access Area, a Pennsylvania Fish Commission facility where you can park and check the river. Crossing the bridge into New York, turn right to follow signs for Route 97 toward Narrowsburg; the small secondary road joins 97 after a short distance. Turn right onto 97 South, which follows the river's wide flood-plain. At 2.7 miles from the bridge, turn right onto a small road marked for Skinner's Falls, which crosses the Delaware at Milanville; a New York access area provides parking.

Back across the river in Pennsylvania, make a hard left .2 mile past the bridge onto State Route 1017, following the sign for Darbytown. For the next 6 miles, the road parallels the river through scenic, boulder-strewn woods, with an overlook just before Darbytown. At the junction with Route 652, turn left and recross the Delaware into New York; follow signs for 97 East, then 97 South (a confusing combination). Route 97 is out of sight of the river for the first 9.5 miles, then rejoins the Delaware above Lackawaxen all the way to Port Jervis, 25 miles farther downriver. There are many places along the way to stop and check the trees for eagles, but be careful to choose pull-offs with wide shoulders and stop completely off the roadway. Eighteen miles south of Lackawaxen the road edges along a high gorge at Hawk's Nest, with breathtaking views of the river below and four scenic overlooks.

From Port Jervis, turn right onto Route 209 South, crossing back into Pennsylvania. Below Milford, the highway enters the Delaware Water Gap National Recreation Area, an important wintering ground (along with nearby reservoirs in New York) for eagles. Over the next 24 miles there are four boat launches off 209 with parking and views of the river—Milford Beach .5 mile south of Milford; Dingman's Boat Launch 8.2 miles beyond Milford Beach; Eshback Boat Launch, a dirt access road 8.3 miles below Dingman's; and Bushkill Boat Launch 3.4 miles below Eshback.

For information on major bald eagle wintering sites in nearby southeastern New York, see *Seasonal Guide to the Natural Year—New England & New York*.

2

Snowy Owls and Short-eared Owls

What sort of owl hunts in daylight, perches on home TV antennas and has a penchant for sitting next to airport runways, beside rumbling jetliners?

It's the sort of owl that makes bird-watchers drool—the magnificent snowy owl of the Far North, a rare visitor to the region and all the more sought-after because of its unpredictability.

Native to the rolling, treeless tundra of the Arctic coastal plain, snowy owls are not migratory, strictly speaking; most stay on their territories winter and summer, hunting voles, ptarmigan and especially lemmings, the mouselike rodents that anchor many Arctic food chains. Unfortunately for the owls, lemming populations are cyclic, running through a boom-and-bust progression that lasts about four years. When lemming numbers are high, the owls respond by producing extraordinarily large clutches of chicks, sometimes as many as ten in a nest. When the lemmings crash, though, the owls are strapped for food. Many starve. Many, especially the young of the year and the more nomadic males, wander south.

This is not a true migration; the owls have no clear destination in mind, nor do they follow predictable flyways.

They simply drift from place to place until they find a spot with lots of food and the look of home—a windswept beach, for instance, or flat, open farmland. Airports are perennial favorites. Farther north, in New England and southern Canada, where snowy owls are more regular winter visitors, certain airports may host as many as two dozen each winter. In the mid-Atlantic region such concentrations are unheard of, but each winter usually brings a smattering of reports. While there is no guarantee that a given site will have an owl in a given winter, certain places (covered in this chapter's Hotspots), consistently attract snowy owls and are worth checking.

Snowies are all but unmistakable; only the smaller, pale barn owl looks similar, and barn owls are rarely seen in broad daylight, perched in the open. Adult snowy owls are nearly 2 feet long from head to tail, and at 4.5 pounds are the heaviest owls in North America. The round head, yellow eyes and white plumage are diagnostic, although each bird displays a varying degree of dark barring— heaviest on juveniles and females, and sometimes completely absent on mature males.

While snowy owls like a perch with a view, they generally avoid trees, so watch for them on top of buildings, TV antennas, water towers, utility poles and the like. In flat country they often sit on the ground, choosing a low hump; at airports, the short runway and taxiway lights are favored perches. Snowy owls are usually quite tame, but avoid approaching them too closely—even a "tame" bird can be harassed by too much human attention.

Unlike the snowy owl, the short-eared owl breeds within the region, albeit in low numbers. The best time to spot this unusual bird of prey is winter, when many more come south to the salt marshes and hay fields. Substantially smaller than the snowy, short-eared owls are about 15 inches long and cryptically colored to match the dead grasses among which they habitually perch.

Short-eared owls are crepuscular—that is, they hunt mainly at dawn and dusk, rather than after full dark, like most owls. Their flight is strangely mothlike and unsteady, with deep, batting wingbeats. In the air, the owl looks pale buff below and darker brown above, with a distinct dark spot at the bend of each wing. The "ear" tufts for which the species is named (actually small clumps of feathers with no role in hearing) are so tiny that they cannot be seen except at extremely close range, so the owl's head looks round.

Like snowy owls, short-ears show an affinity for open spaces, avoiding trees to the extent that they roost on the ground, sometimes communally; it is not unusual for a dozen or more to be flushed from the same corner of an overgrown hay field. Inland they are nomadic in wintertime, wandering in search of food and forming loose aggregations in areas with high meadow vole populations. Along the coast, short-eared owls are much more regular as winter visitors, with salt marshes providing the habitat, food—and best viewing opportunities.

HOTSPOTS

Snowy owls may show up virtually anywhere in the region, from Amish farmland in Pennsylvania to the shores of the Chesapeake, but the most consistent locations are along the New Jersey coast and Presque Isle on Lake Erie. Even there, you'll need luck.

In recent years, snowy owls have shown a tendency to appear at *Sandy Hook* in northern New Jersey, a curved sand spit within sight of New York City's skyline that includes Sandy Hook National Park and the Sandy Hook unit of Gateway National Recreation Area. From the Garden State Parkway take Route 36 East to Highlands Beach, turning north just after crossing the Navesink River. There are a number of parking areas along the length of the peninsula, with access to the beaches and dunes where the owls are most likely.

Snowies have been rare, but fairly regular, visitors to the beaches at **Barnegat Light**, New Jersey. Take Exit 63 from the Garden State Parkway onto Route 72 East. Cross the harbor to Long Beach Island, then go north along the main street 8.7 miles, through such jam-packed beach communities as Surf City and Harvey Cedars. Any snowy owls present will wander widely along the island's northern edge. Start your search at the Eighth Street jetty; after entering the town of Barnegat Light, watch on the right for Eighth Street, a small, dead-end road (the street markers are inconspicuous posts driven in the ground). Park without blocking the driveways and follow the boardwalk to the beach, scanning especially to the left and paying close attention to any white objects on fences and construction equipment. Return to your car and turn north again on Central Avenue, then make a dogleg onto Broadway, following it to the lighthouse parking lot. If lighthouse renovation work permits, scan both sides of the inlet for owls. There are also many side roads that branch off Central Avenue (known as Long Beach Boulevard south of Barnegat Light) with views of the bay shore; watch as well for a perched snowy on water towers or rooftops.

For snowy owls crossing Lake Erie, the windswept beaches and dunes of **Presque Isle** sometimes are irresistible and provide the most consistent hotspot in Pennsylvania. To reach Presque Isle State Park, take I-79 North to Exit 44B (Route 5 West/12th St.). The exit makes a long, sharp curl to the right and merges with Route 5 West. Go .6 mile and make a right turn at the light onto Route 832 North, marked by a sign for Presque Isle. The park office is 4.5 miles from the intersection; stop and pick up a park map, which shows the confusing roads and trails.

For hopeful snowy owl seekers, there are beaches the length of the peninsula, with parking areas every half mile or less. There is no shortcut so you must check each beach area; do not overlook the beach south of Thompson Bay, accessible from the parking lot between the loop road and

Coast Guard Road, as well as the lonely beach around the Bird Sanctuary at the peninsula's far end.

As mentioned, short-eared owls are more abundant and reliable than snowy owls. In fact, almost any large salt marsh will probably have one or two, but for more exciting and consistent viewing, try one of the following hotspots:

Blackwater Marsh and ***Elliott Island*** on Maryland's Eastern Shore are excellent spots for short-eared owls from late fall through the end of March, with peak numbers in midwinter. Together they comprise one of the finest marsh systems still in existence and include Fishing Bay WMA and Blackwater NWR. Start at the visitors' center at Blackwater (directions for which can be found in Chapter 1). Turn right onto Key Wallace Drive and go 1 mile, over the Little Blackwater River, to a stop sign. Turn left onto Maple Dam Road (unmarked) and go .4 mile, then turn right onto Greenbriar Road. Follow Greenbriar for 2.5 miles, past the Harriet Tubman homestead, to a stop sign at Bestpitch Ferry Road. Turn right and follow Bestpitch for 10.4 miles, crossing the small, rickety bridge at Fishing Bay WMA. At the intersection with Henry's Crossroad make a right turn and go 2.1 miles to Elliott Island Road, another right. The marshes appear after about 4 miles and continue for another 9.5 to the village of Elliott.

To return by a more direct route, backtrack along Elliott Island Road to its intersection with Henry's Crossroad and Lewis Wharf Road. Go straight 5.7 miles to the town of Vienna, then take Route 331 north less than half a mile to Route 50.

In Delaware, ***Port Mahon Road*** east of Dover is a short-eared hotspot, with miles of tidal marsh in the Little Creek WMA. From Dover take Route 8 East to Route 9, onto which you turn right. A half-mile south of the intersection is Port Mahon Road (Road 89), which joins on the left. The road runs for several miles through tidal marsh and along the bay beach. Rough-legged hawks, the predictable, daytime counterpart of the short-eared owl, are also found here in good numbers.

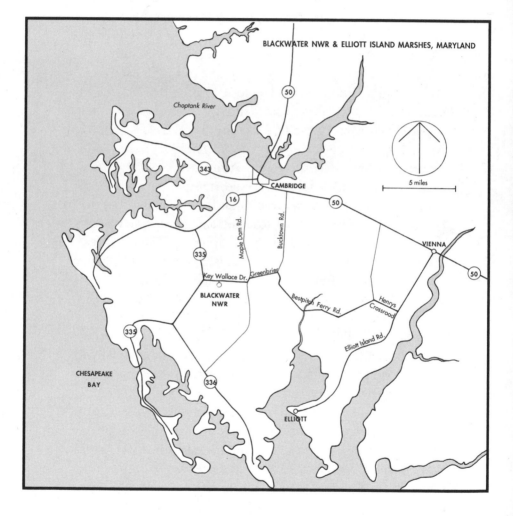

BLACKWATER NWR & ELLIOTT ISLAND MARSHES, MARYLAND

Choptank River

50

343

16 CAMBRIDGE

50

Maple Dam Rd.

Bucktown Rd.

335 VIENNA

50

Key Wallace Dr. Greenbrier

BLACKWATER NWR

Bestpitch Ferry Rd.

Henrys Crossroad

335

Elliott Island Rd.

CHESAPEAKE BAY

336

ELLIOTT

5 miles

Wintering Gannets
and Loons

A large white bird pivots a hundred feet above the ocean, catching the sun on its pointed, black-tipped wings as it turns in the gusty wind. It hangs in the air for an instant, then drops headfirst to the water below, pumping its wings for speed. At the last second the wings fold back over the tail, transforming the bird into a lance that slams into the water with terrific force and vanishes in an eruption of spray.

The feeding plunge of the northern gannet is a breathtaking display of power and control. In summer, it is a sight reserved for the coastal waters of northeastern Canada, but in winter the gannets migrate south, to pass the season on the rough waters off the mid-Atlantic coast. At certain times and places, thousands of gannets may be seen on the seaward horizon, wheeling and dancing like dust motes to the naked eye, but clearly visible through spotting scopes and binoculars—and if strong offshore winds are at work, the gannets may be feeding not far beyond the surf line.

The same cold waters are the winter home of two species of loons—the common loon, whose odd, quavering call is a trademark of the North Woods, and the more strictly Arctic red-throated loon, which nests on tundra ponds in summer. Watching the parade of loons and gannets is a terrific way to usher in the new natural year.

Northern gannets are members of the family Sulidae, which includes such famous, tropical seabirds as the red-footed and blue-footed boobies. Gannets are the biggest of the lot, more than 3 feet long with a wingspan of roughly 6 feet. Adults are gleaming white, save for the black primary feathers on the wings and a touch of ocher-yellow on the head; juveniles are dark above and light below, with increasing amounts of white mottling as they approach their fourth year, when they molt into full adult plumage.

In the air, a gannet looks gracefully pointed at all ends. The head and tail taper almost equally in silhouette, while the wings are long and thin, the typical design for large seabirds.

Gannets are colonial breeders, and the huge nesting colonies on the Gaspé Peninsula and Newfoundland, containing thousands of pairs, are justly famous. They are equally social during the winter, when the flashing white plumage of a diving gannet serves as a visual signal to others of the same species that a school of fish has been located. This is probably not altruism but self-service, since the presence of a large number of diving birds will further confuse the fish and make them easier prey.

Few birds are as proficient at plunge-diving (as the technique is known) as are gannets. Terns also plunge-dive, but rarely do they sink more than a foot beneath the waves. The heavy, streamlined body of the gannet, on the other hand, coupled with its habit of diving from 50 or 100 feet up, helps drive the bird as deep as 30 or 40 feet underwater, where it can catch mackerel and herring out of the reach of smaller, lighter birds. The impact must be bruising, but gannets are protected by a series of buffering air sacs, while specially designed nostrils exclude water. A translucent "third eyelid," the nictitating membrane, allows partial vision while shielding the eye from seawater.

Loons are equally adept aquatic hunters, but they dive quietly from the surface, relying on their powerful legs and webbed feet instead of airborne momentum to propel them. Beginning naturalists are usually surprised—and a little disappointed—to find that the common loons have molted out of their breeding plumage with its intricate checkerboard of black and white, and into a plain pattern of pale gray, noticeably darker above. The red-throated loon takes on a very similar winter plumage, leading to confusion between the two species.

Traditionally, the relative thinness and slight upturn of the red-throated loon's bill made it the preferred field mark, but such distinctions are difficult at best when one is squinting through a spotting scope with wind-blurred eyes. More recently, birders have taken to looking at the sides of the neck, where the light underside and dark dorsal surfaces meet. In red-throated loons the two shades meet smoothly and cleanly, while the common loon's neck shows a faint but noticeable pattern of incomplete light and dark bands that form a deep scalloping along the division between pale and dark gray.

Loons winter much closer to shore than do gannets, sometimes swimming quietly just beyond the breakers, often poking their faces below the surface to watch for small fish. When prey is spotted they give a strong kick with their legs and dive, disappearing with a minimum of disturbance. Once submerged, they may stay down for 15 minutes and swim as deep as 60 feet, although most dives last less than a minute and are much shallower.

In recent years much attention has been focused on the decline of common loons on their breeding grounds in New England, the Great Lakes region and parts of Canada. Acid precipitation and increasing human disturbance (especially speedboats, whose wakes swamp loon nests) are thought to be to blame, but contamination from heavy metals and other toxins, presumably picked up at sea, may also play a role. Fortunately, the decline seems to have been arrested in some areas, thanks to artificial nest platforms and boater education.

Gannets and loons both winter the length of the region's coastline, with loons also present in most of the Chesapeake, where gannets are much rarer. But while loons can be seen in many places, gannets often stay far from shore, and only a few spots consistently produce good numbers at reasonably close range.

The mouth of the Chesapeake Bay is a favorite gannet wintering site, with a couple of options for observation. From the Cape Henry area, just north of Virginia Beach, as many as ten thousand or more gannets have been seen out in the bay, and equally impressive numbers may be seen from the Chesapeake Bay Bridge-Tunnel, which carries Route 13 some 17.6 miles across the bay. Farther south, Back Bay NWR is another reliable spot for gannets.

The *Chesapeake Bay Bridge-Tunnel* (or CBBT) has been called one of the seven wonders of the modern world—hyperbole, perhaps, but few are willing to argue when they find themselves on this thin ribbon crossing the mouth of the bay. For birders, the CBBT is important for several reasons: the four man-made islands that anchor the tunnel entrances act as havens for weary migrant landbirds, and provide a chance for birders to watch species like gannets that are normally found far from land.

Access to all but the southernmost of the four islands is restricted, and naturalists must have a permit from the CBBT executive director's office in order to legally stop on the island (the fourth has a fishing pier, restaurant and— sometimes—good birding). Make a written request for a permit well in advance, providing the date and direction of travel and noting that you wish to watch birds during your stops. The permit will be returned by mail, and is good for the remainder of the calendar year. If time is short, try telephoning the executive director's office directly; the staff may be able to issue a permit in your name and leave it at the security office of the entrance you will be using, for you to pick up on your way. (The address and telephone number are listed in the Appendix.) The administrative and security staff are very helpful to birders, but carefully read the list of regulations they provide and scrupulously follow the rules about where and how to stop.

At the south end of the bridge-tunnel is Cape Henry, dominated by the resort development of Virginia Beach. The quiet oasis of **Seashore State Park**, Virginia's most popular, exists in the midst of the hotels and condos, and its beach is a fine vantage point for seabirds, including gannets. From Route 13, go .4 mile south from the CBBT toll plaza to the exit for Route 60 East and West. At the light, turn left for 60 East (Shore Drive East). Follow 60 across Lynnhaven Inlet for 4.6 miles to the park; turn left to the campground. In the off-season the contact station may not be manned; turn left past the booth and park. The beach is just a short distance beyond the parking area. From mid-September to May 1 the beach is open to the public, but during late spring and summer access is restricted to registered campers only.

South of Cape Henry is **Back Bay NWR**, just north of the North Carolina border, an excellent spot for both loons and gannets. Take Route 60 East through Virginia Beach; after crossing Rudlee Inlet at the south edge of the city the road becomes General Booth Boulevard. Follow General Booth south approximately 5.5 miles to the light at the intersection with Princess Anne Road. Make a left turn onto Princess Anne and go .8 mile to a yellow blinker light; turn left onto Sandbridge Road. Go 2.2 miles to a T-intersection with a stop sign, turning left and following the sign to Sandbridge. After another 3.2 miles come to the village of Sandbridge Beach. Make a right turn at the refuge sign and go 4.3 miles to the refuge entrance; the visitors' center is another 1.4 miles along the road, which cuts through an excellent example of a back dune plant community. The beach is reached by following the Seaside Trail boardwalk, which begins opposite the visitors' center.

Barnegat Light and **Cape May** are the two top loon sites in New Jersey, with red-throated loons a speciality at Cape May, and Barnegat especially good during the early winter migration. For directions to Barnegat, see Chapter 2; the Eighth Street jetty area is a good starting point.

The Cape May area includes the towns of Cape May and Cape May Point, as well as Cape May Point State Park and Higbee Beach WMA. The whole peninsula is one of the best birding spots in North America, with plenty to fill a weekend at any time of the year; in midwinter, for instance, loon-watchers can also find gannets, unusual gulls, sea ducks, winter shorebirds and much more.

For red-throated loons, the Second Avenue jetty, the waters off Cape May Point State Park and the Delaware Bay between the wrecked concrete ship and Higbee Beach are best. Directions to reach them, in that order, are as follows: Take the Garden State Parkway South to its merger with Route 109 South. At Cape May, Route 109 becomes Lafayette Street; stay in the right lane, go straight through the light next to the Acme, then turn right at the T-intersection. Go through another light for a total of .6 mile to the intersection of Sunset Boulevard (Route 606) and Broadway (Route 626). Turn left .3 mile on Broadway, then right .1 mile on Beach Avenue to the Second Avenue jetty at the end of the road.

Return to the light at Broadway and Sunset and turn left onto Sunset (Route 606), going 1.1 miles to Sea Grove Avenue, a left turn. After .5 mile make another left onto Lighthouse Avenue (Route 629) and go .4 mile to reach Cape May Point State Park; scan the waters beyond the concrete World War II bunker. Return to Lighthouse Avenue, going straight .7 mile to its intersection with Sunset, and make a left. Drive west on Sunset .4 mile to Sunset Beach, where an old shipwreck dominates the bay. To reach the bay at the northern end of the area, retrace your steps east along Sunset 1 mile to Stevens Street, a left. Stevens merges with Route 607; go north on 607 about 1.4 miles to county Route 641 (a marked dead end), make a left turn and drive 1.1 miles to the dirt parking area for Higbee Beach WMA. The beach is a short distance through the woods straight ahead. For a map of the Cape May area, see Chapter 36.

In southern Delaware, both species of loons are often seen at *Cape Henlopen*, as well as at *Indian River Inlet* in Delaware Seashore State Park just to the south. To reach Cape Henlopen, take Route 113 South from Dover 17 miles, then turn onto Route 1 South for another 21.9 miles to Route 9 East, which leads 3 miles to Lewes, following signs for the park. Just after entering, follow signs for the fishing pier to the left, then return to Post Lane, making the second left onto Point Road. This ends at a parking area on the cape itself, with fine views of the ocean to the east and Delaware Bay to the north and west.

For Indian River, return to Route 1 and go south through the town of Dewey Beach to the park. From the entrance go 5.3 miles to the bridge over the inlet; cross and go .3 mile, then make a U-turn at the road crossing and pull into the parking lot on the right. Walk to the inlet and follow the sidewalk out along the jetty.

The inlet at *Ocean City*, Maryland, is another favorite wintering site for loons. Take Route 50 East to Ocean City. After the highway crosses the drawbridge, the road splits. Stay in the right lane, then turn right onto Philadelphia Avenue. Remain in the far right lane and go .4 mile, following signs for inlet parking. Park in the large metered lot by the jetty, and scan the inlet from the new boardwalk that parallels it.

4

Gettysburg Vulture Roosts

Legends and biology don't always mix. According to legend, the epic Civil War battle at Gettysburg, Pennsylvania, on July 1–3, 1863, in which fifty-one thousand men and untold thousands of horses, mules and livestock were killed, attracted hordes of scavenging vultures. That may well be. What is impossible is the contention, still voiced by some, that the huge concentrations of vultures that return each winter to Gettysburg are the *same* birds, waiting around and hoping for another battle.

Vultures are long-lived by bird standards, but the maximum life span is only about 30 years—not 130. The big birds congregate at Gettysburg not out of some faint recollection of long-ago feasts, but because the area in its current, peaceful incarnation provides them with roosting sites and food.

There are two species of vultures in the East, and both are found at the communal roosts in Gettysburg National Military Park. The most common by far is the turkey vulture, the familiar, red-headed "buzzard." Turkey vultures are large birds, with wingspans of nearly 6 feet; the wings are held in a distinctive, shallow V in flight, and turkey vultures usually rock gently back and forth while soaring. The tail is long, and the undersides of the flight feathers appear silvery against the blackish-brown of the body and wing linings. High overhead, a turkey vulture may appear headless because the naked head is dwarfed by the feathered neck, giving the head a ruffed appearance.

In smaller, but steadily increasing, numbers are black vultures, a southern species that is spreading farther north each year. Only since the 1970s have they been resident in southern Pennsylvania, and today Gettysburg marks a core area of their range in the central part of the state. Black vultures are smaller than turkey vultures, with short tails, black heads and a flat-winged profile in flight. There is a large patch of white at the base of the primary feathers, but this field mark may not be visible if the bird is backlit against a bright sky.

Vultures have been the butt of rude humor and outright disgust for centuries because of their feeding habits, and there is no way to gloss over the fact that they subsist on carrion, vomit as a defense and cool themselves by defecating on their legs. That behavior does nothing, however, to detract from their beauty. Yes, beauty; a vulture on the wing is extraordinarily graceful, scribing fluid shapes through the air as it seeks out the gentle lift of rising air currents. Fortunately, this is how most naturalists observe them—from a generous distance.

Some of the Gettysburg vultures stay to nest in the park, but many are only seasonal visitors, migrating to the area in late autumn and staying through early spring, forming the most northerly winter roost site known. The farmland around Gettysburg supplies them with food (as do the country roads that exact a toll on opossums, rabbits and other wildlife), while the hills known as the Round Tops afford a place to roost, sometimes by the hundreds. Vulture-watching, coupled with the low number of visitors to the park at this time of the year, makes a trip to Gettysburg in winter an excellent way to combine human and natural history in one excursion.

HOTSPOTS

The largest vulture roosts in the park are on the slopes of **Big Round Top**, the scene of fierce fighting on the second and third days of the battle. The hillock is, now as then, heavily wooded, and the birds spend the night perching on the branches of the large oaks and white pines. They also congregate in several areas around **Big Round Top**, including **Devil's Den**.

The best times for viewing are early in the morning, before the vultures have left, and again in late afternoon, when they are returning from their foraging flights. Throughout the day, smaller numbers of vultures can be seen riding the thermals off Big Round Top's summit.

To reach the park, take Washington Street south from town to the visitors' center, which serves as starting point for the auto tour. The Big Round Top loop trail is between stops 7 and 8 on the tour, at its southernmost end. There are actually two trails: a paved path a quarter of a mile to the summit and a dirt path 1 mile long that circles the hill, beginning on the left about 30 yards up the paved path from the steps. The loop trail has numbered markers that correspond to an interpretive Park Service brochure, available at the trailhead. Return to the car and drive north on the auto tour, making the first left in the saddle between Big and Little Round Tops; turn left again at the T-intersection at Crawford Avenue and park at Devil's Den, where vultures roost in large numbers in the surrounding forest.

Breakout: Owling

Owls are among the most mysterious of birds, hunting as they do through the murkiness of twilight, making the night ring with their weird calls. To most naturalists, an owl is a cipher, glimpsed only rarely—and therefore a prize well worth seeking.

In all, seven species of owls breed in the region; an eighth, the snowy owl of the Arctic, winters here in small numbers each year (see Chapter 2 for more on these rare visitors). The region's home-bred owls range from the great horned owl, a large, powerful predator with a 5-foot wing-span, to the elfin saw-whet owl, scarcely 8 inches from its stubby tail to its round, smooth head. Other breeding species are the long-eared owl, short-eared owl (in small numbers), barred owl, eastern screech-owl and common barn owl.

Because they are most active at night, sound, rather than visual display, is most important to owls in attracting a mate and defending a year-round territory. Birders have long known that owls will respond to a tape recording of their species' call, answering it and frequently flying to a nearby perch where they can be observed. The sport is growing in popularity and known simply as *owling*.

Owling is most effective after midnight, and the top

hours are often the last two before dawn, making owling the perfect pastime for insomniac naturalists. Moonlit nights are best, but more important is the wind—or the lack of it, since a stiff breeze usually keeps the owls silent. Bitter cold temperatures seem to be more of a concern to the owlers than the owls.

What species you'll find depends on the habitat. In north-central Pennsylvania and the Appalachians, where the mountains are covered by an unbroken forest of mixed hardwoods and conifers, barred owls and saw-whets are most common. Farther south and east, where farmland and woodlots share the landscape, great horned owls can be expected, while residential communities with lots of big, old trees are havens for screech-owls. Long-eared, short-eared and barn owls, though found in the region, are usually unresponsive to taped calls.

Owlers usually travel a circuit of lonely backroads that lead through a variety of habitats, stopping periodically to call and listen. Start with the calls of the smaller owls first— the metallic peeps of the saw-whet or the high, descending whinny of the screech-owl; then go on to those of the larger owls. The tape of a great horned or barred owl may scare the smaller species into silence, because the big varieties often kill and eat their tinier cousins.

Play several repetitions of the call, then shut off the recorder and listen. If you are in the territory of an owl of that species, it will probably answer, thinking that it hears an intruder. Play one or two calls again, then wait. Often, the owl will approach, so watch the dimly lit sky overhead for the silhouette of a flying bird. Screech-owls and especially saw-whets are notoriously tame and may sit placidly at close range, ignoring the beams of flashlights and the presence of humans. Great horned owls and barred owls are considerably more cautious, although individuals vary in their degree of tolerance. Move on after several minutes, allowing the owl to get back to its business.

Eastern screech-owls are among the most commonly heard owls in winter and respond well to a taped (or whistled) imitation of their call.

While owling is fun, the sport comes with some significant cautions. Excessive use of taped calls can seriously disrupt an owl's life, especially if the bird lives in a popular park or refuge and is continually bombarded with taped calls. This becomes particularly harmful during the breeding season, when the tape may draw the owl away from nesting or food-gathering duties; it is possible that some owls are even intimidated by calls booming from tape players with the volume jacked high, so keep the decibel level at normal ranges.

Owling is safest if done between late summer and early winter, and it should be avoided completely during the breeding season, which varies from species to species. Screech-owls and saw-whets are courting by March, barred owls by February and great horned owls—the earliest breeding bird in the region—are reaffirming pair bonds by the first week of January.

There are a number of excellent recordings of bird calls on the market, from which you can tape owl calls for your own use. They include *A Field Guide to Bird Songs (Eastern and Central North America)*, which complements the *Peterson Field Guide to the Birds*, and *National Geographic Society's Guide to Bird Sounds*, likewise a companion to the society's excellent field guide.

FEBRUARY

February Observations

6

Winter Hawks

At first glance, the Amish country of Pennsylvania and the tundra of the Arctic would appear to have little in common. One is fertile and lush, dotted with neat farms amid a patchwork of carefully tended fields; the other is harsh and cold through most of the year, a land of stunted spruces and dwarf willows.

But in winter, the farmland of south-central Pennsylvania has the same open, rolling feel as the tundra—horizons of fields and pastures where the wind can bully the snow into drifts, unimpeded by large areas of woods. And it is here that arctic raptors come as well—rough-legged hawks and an occasional gyrfalcon, joining the native red-tailed hawks and kestrels.

Rough-legged hawks are buteos, belonging to the same group of soaring raptors as the red-tailed, red-shouldered and broad-winged hawks. They breed from Newfoundland to Alaska, north of the treeline, building their nests on high bluffs and river cliffs overlooking the tundra. Large hawks, rough-legs have a wingspan of about 4.5 feet—slightly bigger than a red-tail's—but their feet are tiny and weak, since these hawks specialize in catching lemmings, voles and other small rodents.

Their colors vary widely. There are dark and light color phases, with immature, adult, male and female variations of each (see the Peterson Field Guide *Hawks* by Clark and Wheeler for an excellent breakdown of plumages). Generally speaking, however, light-phase birds have a white tail with a dark terminal band; a wide, dark belly band that is much heavier than a red-tail's; and dark "wrist" markings at the underside of the bend of the wing. Dark-phase birds are usually chocolate brown overall, with a light, banded tail and light, black-tipped primary feathers. In flight, rough-legs have a rangy, long-winged look, and they frequently hover with deep, vigorous wingbeats as they scan the fields for food.

Rough-legged hawks migrate south in irregular numbers late each autumn, following the ridge system over what must seem to them to be inhospitable mountains and forests. Some stop in agricultural valleys along the way, but the largest numbers fetch up in the farmland south of the Kittatinny Ridge and in coastal salt marshes. Every few years the lemming population crashes in the Arctic, and exceptionally high numbers of rough-legs make the journey south.

Upon arrival they meet the region's most common wintering raptors, red-tailed hawks and kestrels. Red-tails are the most obvious resident hawks of mixed fields and woodlots, big, husky birds that look chunky and strong sitting fluffed up on a dead snag. At a distance, a red-tail's creamy breast looks stark white (in fact, most erroneous reports of snowy owls start with a red-tailed hawk whose chest catches the sun). There is usually, but not always, a dark, speckled breast band, much less distinct than the rough-legged hawk's; the upper surface of the tail is rusty orange in adult red-tails, but brown with fine, dark bands in young birds, which may make up half of the wintering population.

Kestrels, the third common type of winter hawk, are small falcons, about the size of blue jays. Less aloof than the two buteos, they often perch on roadside utility lines, with traffic whizzing below their feet; this does not mean they are tame, however, and a perched kestrel will usually fly if a car slows down or stops. Kestrels are easy to confuse with mourning doves at first glance—look for the large, round head and squared-off tail of the hawk, very different from the small-headed, pointy-tailed silhouette of a dove. Also, a kestrel often perches at a 45-degree angle to the wire, pumping its tail up and down to keep balance in the wind.

Both sexes are colorful, with a complicated facial pattern and breast spots or streaks; males have blue-gray wings and an orange tail, while the females are all orangish above with black barring. In flight their narrow wings and tail look quite long, especially when the bird hovers—something it accomplishes with far more grace than does a rough-legged hawk.

In summer, kestrels eat grasshoppers and dragonflies, and red-tails take a wide variety of food including snakes and frogs. But when winter comes the raptors' dietary mainstay consists of small rodents, especially *Microtus pennsylvanicus*, the meadow vole. Also known as field mice, meadow voles are tubby little mammals about 5 inches long, including a short tail; the head is round and the ears almost hidden in fur. These are the creatures that cut meandering tunnels through field grass, interlacing runways that connect their globular nests with feeding areas. It has been said, without much exaggeration, that voles are the most important mammals in the region, since they provide food for almost every predator, from tiny shrews to black bears, as well as almost every bird of prey.

HOTSPOTS

In New Jersey, the finest place for winter raptors is the **Brigantine** unit of Forsythe NWR, just north of Atlantic City. With its extensive tidal flats and reed beds adjoining upland fields and woods, the refuge provides food and habitat for a diversity of hawks found in few other parts of the Garden State. Red-tailed and rough-legged hawks are common (the latter's abundance varying from year to year), and northern harriers are almost always in sight, just skimming the horizon. Bald eagles are always a possibility, and in many years a golden eagle or two will winter at the refuge. Other raptors routinely seen here are peregrine falcons (which nest in the hack towers), kestrels and red-shouldered hawks; sharp-shinned and Cooper's hawks hunt the holly and pine woods of the uplands.

To reach Brigantine, take the Atlantic City Expressway to Route 9 North, through Absecon to Oceanville. Immediately after crossing a small, wooden-railed bridge, turn right onto Great Creek Road, following signs for the refuge, about a mile farther. Coming from the north, take the Garden State Parkway South to Exit 48, pick up Route 9 South and drive 5.8 miles, turning left onto Great Creek Road.

For an all-day outing, consider a hawk-finding tour of the **southeastern Pennsylvania** countryside, past bucolic farms and through prime raptor habitat.

> CAUTION: *Much of this tour runs through Amish farmland, and horse-drawn buggies are common. Keep your speed low and be extremely careful in rounding curves.*

The tour starts 13 miles west of Allentown on I-78, where the patches of roadside vetch support meadow voles, and in turn attract red-tails, kestrels and an occasional rough-leg. At the Krumsville exit (Exit 12) turn onto Route 737 North to Kempton; at the intersection with Route 143 turn left, or make a side trip by going straight across 143 toward Hawk Mountain. This valley has a history of producing golden eagles every winter or so.

From Kempton follow Route 143 South under I-78 and through Lenhartsville; beyond Virginville, turn right off

143 onto Route 662 and follow this road to the traffic light at Route 61 at Shoemakersville. Go straight through the light for .4 mile and turn left at the stop; go another .3 mile across the railroad tracks and turn right onto West Miller Street. Follow this 2.1 miles to a T-intersection, turning right toward Centerport; go .6 mile into the village and turn left at the sign for Bernville onto Irish Creek Road (unmarked at this intersection). Follow Irish Creek Road for 7 miles, bearing right at two major splits along the way. At the intersection with Shartlesville Road turn left, go .8 mile to Route 183 South and turn left again.

Follow 183 South for 6 miles past Blue Marsh Dam, an Army Corps of Engineers project surrounded by fields that are excellent for winter raptors, including an occasional short-eared or snowy owl. At Palisades Drive (where a large church and cemetery are on the right) turn right and drive 3.2 miles to Reber's Bridge Road, a right turn. Follow Reber's Bridge for 1.6 miles to a stop, go straight (the road becomes Brownsville Road) and go another 6 miles to Bernville Road, a T-intersection. Turn left, go 2 miles to the junction of Route 422 West and turn right. After 1.8 miles, just past the Conrad Weiser Homestead, turn left on High Street into Womelsdorf. Turn left onto Route 419 South, go 3.9 miles and turn left again onto an unmarked road with a sign for Shady Oaks Campsites. Go straight on this road for 2.6 miles to Route 897 North in Kleinfeltersville, a right.

Go .1 mile on 897 and turn left onto Kleinfeltersville Road, following signs for Middle Creek WMA; the brushy area between 897 and the Middle Creek boundary is often good for red-shouldered hawks. Drive through Middle Creek, paying attention to the dead, standing timber along the edge of the main lake; bald eagles are frequently seen here. Continue on Kleinfeltersville Road another 3 miles, over the turnpike to a stop sign at Mount Airy/Hopeland Road, a right turn. Go .5 mile to the village of Hopeland, turn left onto Clay Road and drive 1.1 miles to Route 322 West, a right turn.

Follow 322 to Brickerville, then turn left onto Route 501 South. Just after you pass through Lititz, look for the Lancaster Airport on the left; this is another good place for rough-legs, snowy and short-eared owls, and it was in a quarry not far from here that two gyrfalcons rocked the birding world by returning two winters in a row. Continue south on 501 to the outskirts of Lancaster, then bear right for Route 30 West, a dangerous merger; pay close attention to the road signs, since 30 breaks off again within a mile. Go 9 miles on Route 30 to Columbia, take Route 441 North to Marietta, then turn onto Route 772 (Mount Joy Pike). This leads approximately 16 miles through Mount Joy and Manheim, back to Lititz. Backtrack on Route 501 North from Lititz; at Brickerville go straight, staying on 501, through Schaefferstown and Myerstown, a distance of 12.3 miles. At Bethel, 8 miles farther, turn left, following signs for I-78. Rejoin the interstate at Exit 3, 40 miles west of Allentown.

As an alternative, continue south through Lancaster on Route 501 to Route 222, then Route 272 South at the far side of town. At the village of Buck, turn right onto Route 372 West and drive approximately 6 miles to the entrance for Muddy Run Reservoir, also good for ducks after ice-out. Continue west on 372, crossing the Susquehanna and turning onto Route 74 North/West toward York. At York, take I-83 North to Route 30 East, cross the river 11 miles later and arrive in Columbia, as noted above.

Many of the same locations given in Chapter 2 for short-eared owls are also good for rough-legs, which are the day shift to the owl's dawn and dusk patrol; the *Elliot Island* marshes and *Blackwater NWR* are especially productive.

7

Tracking

A skilled naturalist is always on the lookout for what generations of woodsmen called *sign*—tracks, scrapes, droppings and the other clues that animals leave to their passage. It may be the squiggle of beetle tracks in the thick dust of a summer dirt road or the pawed-up dirt of a white-tailed buck's mating scrape, but the hunt for sign comes into its own in winter.

With a fresh blanket of snow, nothing that moves on the ground can escape leaving its mark. The naturalist who in summer must be content to find a footprint here or there can revel in long, unbroken trails that lead, not just across the landscape, but also through time and into an animal's life.

Tracking requires a number of skills, some easy to learn, others requiring practice and imagination. The fundamental task is learning to identify the tracks you find, and in this a good field guide is indispensable; the best is Olaus Murie's classic *Field Guide to Animal Tracks,* part of the Peterson series, covering mammals, birds, insects, reptiles and amphibians.

Much harder (and infinitely more rewarding) than merely identifying the track is interpreting its meaning. For this, you must take in all the clues—not just the tracks, but their placement, depth and condition, how the tracks of one animal relate to those of another and to the terrain, the presence or absence of droppings and other sign. A deer trail with closely spaced tracks, bits of broken twigs and neat piles of droppings indicates that the animals were at ease, walking slowly and feeding as they went. Widely spaced tracks with flared hooves, and droppings scattered along the trail, show that the deer were spooked and moving fast; if the tracks are crisp and the droppings warm, you probably scared the deer yourself.

Experienced trackers know never to walk on the trail, in case they need to backtrack to reexamine a section; they also pay as much attention to the surroundings as to the tracks themselves, trying to understand what made the animal do what the tracks recorded. Why would a flock of turkeys suddenly form a tight, milling group, for example, but leave no evidence of feeding? A quick look around might reveal the trail of a red fox across the hollow, which would cause the birds to bunch nervously until the predator passes.

If you lose the trail, mark the spot with a hat and begin spiraling outward until the tracks reappear. Be alert for the smallest clues. A tiny bunch of feathers, caught on a twig, should make you look upwind for more; occasionally, you will find a trail of feathers leading to the branch where a sharp-shinned hawk carefully plucked a sparrow before eating.

HOTSPOTS

The beauty of tracking is that a new covering of snow transforms even a suburban lawn into a wildlife registry, and you can have as much fun puzzling out the amblings of a gray squirrel or the meanderings of a shrew tunnel as following a herd of deer through a remote forest.

Still, there is a thrill in tracking through the big woods, and the Pennsylvania mountains, which get more snow than most of the rest of the region, are an excellent place for a weekend's tracking adventure.

Hickory Run State Park (see Chapter 28 for directions) in Carbon County has large numbers of white-tailed deer and encompasses forest with some of the highest black bear populations in the state. In late winter most of the females are still denned up with their newborn cubs, but the males are already rousing from their torpor, especially toward the end of the month and through March.

Deer, bear, bobcat and turkey are common in *Kettle Creek State Park* in Clinton County, named for one of the state's prettiest trout streams; a careful examination of the banks of the creek north of the park may also reveal the winter snow slides of river otters, which have been reintroduced here and on neighboring Pine Creek. To reach the park, take I-80 to Exit 26, then go east 8 miles on Route 220 to Lock Haven. From Lock Haven, travel west on Route 120 for 33 miles to the village of Westport; turn right onto Route 4001 and follow the signs approximately 9 miles to the park, which includes the Alvin Bush Dam.

In western Pennsylvania, *Cook Forest State Park* in Clarion County combines woodland wildlife with the East's largest stand of virgin white pine, especially breathtaking in winter. Take I-80 to Exit 13 (Brookville), then go 17.2 miles on Route 36 North to the bridge across the Clarion River; at the far side is the park office, and near the Big Trees sign just beyond it, the nature center. The park has more than 25 miles of hiking trails (pick up a map at the office), not all of which will be passable in heavy snow. The most popular area of virgin pine is the Cathedral, or Big Trees, stand, but other old-growth pines and hemlocks can be found along the Baker Trail. There is something magical about following the trail of an animal beneath trees that were alive in the days of the Indians.

Even in the mountains of the Blue Ridge in Virginia, long-lasting snow is the exception rather than the rule, but when a heavy storm covers *Shenandoah National Park* the tracking can be superb—a result of the park's high deer population, good numbers of bear and bobcat, and excellent system of hiking trails. Exercise caution, however, because steep, snowy slopes can be treacherous. The northern entrance of the park can be reached by taking I-66 to Route 340 South, then driving 3 miles to Front Royale and following the signs. From the south, take I-64 to the Blue Ridge Parkway North near Waynesboro. Visitor facilities are limited in winter, so call the park at (703) 999-2266 before your trip. See Chapter 52 for a discussion of the park's deer herd.

8

Lake Erie Steelhead

Tampering with nature can have unexpectedly negative consequences. For every introduction of an alien species that goes well, like that of the ring-necked pheasant, there are usually several more that go sour. The folks who released house sparrows and European starlings in North America thought they were doing a good thing, after all.

So there was some trepidation when fisheries biologists suggested introducing Pacific salmon to the Great Lakes in the 1960s. Sport fishermen welcomed the chance to augment the lakes' game fish populations, which had been decimated by commercial overfishing and pollution. Others wondered if there might be unforeseen problems.

Fortunately, the introductions went smoothly, and the lakes, including Lake Erie, now enjoy a thriving salmon fishery. In fall, the spawning urge brings coho and chinook salmon close to shore and sparks a stampede of boats and shore fishermen. Less well known, but every bit as impressive from a biological standpoint, is the spawning run of Lake Erie steelhead.

Steelhead have always been something of a puzzle. A big, powerful fish native to the West Coast, the steelhead was originally thought to be a sea-run race of the rainbow trout, but it grows considerably larger than landlocked rainbows. Fish of 15 or 20 pounds are not uncommon, and some weighing more than 40 pounds have been caught. The steelhead's name comes from the glossy, metallic gray color of a fish fresh from the sea, but the steelhead quickly takes on a purplish tone that deepens to maroon as it makes its way upriver.

Even though steelhead evolved to live much of their life in saltwater, the ocean is not necessary to their survival, and fingerlings stocked in Great Lakes tributaries took immediately to their new homes. The lakes provide the same essentials as the sea: vast areas of open water in which to school and dense concentrations of small prey fish on which to fatten. In the Great Lakes, two groups of introduced fish, the salmon and trout, were able to control another introduced fish, the alewife, which had badly overpopulated many waters.

Even though the environment is different, the steelhead's life cycle remains essentially the same. The smolts (as young salmonids are known) descend the spawning creeks to the lake, then spend several years feeding and growing. When they reach maturity, they gather just offshore before entering their natal stream—the same process followed by coho salmon. But unlike coho, which peak quickly in October and early November, the steelhead run continues for nearly six months, from early autumn through late winter, in dribs and drabs as the winter weather allows.

In the Lake Erie drainage, steelhead do not travel as far upstream as do the salmon. An even more important difference is survival; while the salmon die after their first spawning run, the steelhead usually survive to repeat the process over the next several years. Still, the upstream run and spawning itself place a lot of stress on the fish, and those that enter the season old or weak are not likely to live to return to the lake.

Even the steelhead's precise place in the family Salmonidae has been open to question. For years, rainbow trout (including steelhead) were classified in the genus *Salmo* as one of the true salmon. Recently, however, biologists have become convinced that rainbows, along with cutthroat and Gila trout, have more in common with Pacific salmon like the chinook and sockeye, and have assigned them to that genus, *Oncorhynchus*. For those who enjoy seeing or catching steelhead, the point is strictly academic.

HOTSPOTS

Almost every stream emptying into Lake Erie supports a steelhead run of one size or another, but the best may be Trout Run, about 7 miles west of the city of Erie; it is also an important salmon stream. Situated on Trout Run is the Pennsylvania Fish Commission's Fairview Fish Culture Station, which nets and artificially propagates steelhead and salmon, a process visitors may be lucky enough to stumble upon on a day of good weather. For directions to the stream, hatchery and other suggestions for salmonid watching, see Chapter 48.

Pelagic Birding Trips

Few people willingly brave the open ocean in the middle of winter, and fewer still do it for fun, paying for the privilege of freezing and fighting seasickness. Those that do, however, can take comfort in knowing they are exploring one of the region's last real natural history frontiers—the mysterious, exciting world of pelagic birds.

For nearly three hundred years, the landbirds of the mid-Atlantic states have been studied, their ranges and breeding seasons noted and minor shifts in their abundance monitored with increasing accuracy. But offshore, out of sight of land, exists another, completely separate community of birds, so poorly understood that a birder taking ship for a pelagic trip never knows exactly what to expect.

For the most part, the pelagic species seen at this time of year are northern birds passing the winter on the open sea—northern gannets, black-legged kittiwakes, pomarine and parasitic jaegers, red phalarope, northern fulmars and several species of alcids, or auks: common murres, razorbills, Atlantic puffins and dovekies. Much rarer is the great skua, a huge, predatory relative of the gulls that breeds in Iceland and Europe but winters over the northern Atlantic, and the Manx shearwater.

The winter ocean may seem intimidating to humans, but it is home for these birds, most of which do not set foot on dry land except for the brief summer breeding season, when biology compels them to come ashore. As harsh as the winter seas are, they provide an abundance of food, mostly in the form of small fish and invertebrates, but the ways in which these birds capture their prey differ dramatically from species to species. The gannet, as already mentioned, is a plunge-diver that seeks fish many feet below the surface. The puffin and murre also take deep-swimming fish but catch them by chasing them underwater, using the wings and feet as though flying—a technique dovekies use in shallow water for finding plankton. Kittiwakes take fish and crustaceans near the surface, while jaegers hunt fish, supplementing their catch with prey pirated from other birds.

The pelagic birds are drawn from many families—the boobies, gulls and auks, to name the most important—but all face a major physiological hurdle: ridding the body of excess salt. Normally, because ocean water has a higher salt content than the bird's body fluids, a bird would have to excrete more water to get rid of the salt than it took in by drinking, a course that quickly leads to dehydration and death. Despite their varied origins, the pelagic birds have evolved similar ways around the problem. A pair of glands on the top of the head between the eyes filters the blood and removes the extra salt, which drips from the beak in highly saline droplets.

Winter pelagic trips have been far more popular on the West Coast than the East, so we still know relatively little about species distribution and abundance in the northern Atlantic. This is one area of ornithology where experienced amateurs can make significant contributions, provided all sightings are fully documented with detailed written descriptions, photographs, sketches or other supporting material.

Pelagic birding requires perseverance, even before you step on board the boat. It can be difficult to find an organized trip and tougher to sign up quickly enough to claim a spot; even then, there is always a good chance the trip will be canceled by winter storms. If everything clicks into place, however, you'll be able to experience the kind of exciting birding denied to landlubbers.

HOTSPOTS

Organized pelagic trips are few and far between, but several operators run trips from Barnegat and Cape May, New Jersey; Ocean City, Maryland; and Virginia Beach, Virginia; addresses and telephone numbers can be found in the Appendix. Also listen regularly to the rare bird alerts listed in the Appendix, on which such trips are usually advertised. For a newcomer to this unusual style of birding, an organized trip with experienced companions is the best way to learn since seabird identification can be difficult.

As discussed in Chapter 44, the other alternative is to sign up for a trip on a fishing party or charter boat, which run virtually year-round and, depending on the type of fish being sought, reach the deep waters far offshore that hold the greatest concentrations of pelagic birds. Check coastal or metropolitan newspapers for trip ads, and tell the person taking the reservation that you want to bird. Some captains refuse to carry nonfishing passengers, while others offer a discount since you won't be using up gear, bait or the first mate's time. On the other hand, don't expect a fishing boat captain to go chasing after an especially rare shearwater for you.

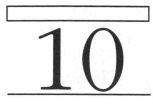

10

Breakout: Exploring Winter Beaches

A winter beach is a good place to lose yourself—in the biting wind, in the way the salt-damp air seeps through your heavy clothes, in the unexpected treasures wave-tossed on the sand.

Scoured free of summer's swimmers, the beach is refreshingly clean and empty, barren even of human tracks. The lifeguard stands are sealed with plywood, the parking lots empty. At first, the beach seems barren of life in general, but the impression is a misleading one; the eye is fooled by the fabric of sand and sea, and misses the subtle clues of winter.

Even the birds are muted by the season. The laughing gulls that made the summer air ring with their calls are gone, for the most part, having retreated to the south for the winter. In their place are Bonaparte's gulls, lithe as terns on the wind and considerably smaller than laughing gulls, riding the sea breezes on wings marked with large patches of white. Herring gulls and greater black-backed gulls are still around, content to wait out the winter on their home turf, but they are more subdued than during the breeding season, as if the cold weather has given them a case of the sulks.

The wind bends the dead dune grass of last September until it snaps, then spins the broken heads, digging circular furrows around the plants. It whistles through the skeletons of beach goldenrod and tickles the caps of gray seed fluff where the flowers used to be. Only the leaves clinging stubbornly to the wax myrtle give the dunes a touch of green. When the wind blows hard, it picks up a skiff of sand and sends the grains skittering along the dunes, shifting the drifts particle by particle.

On the beach the sanderlings run endlessly between the sea and the shore, as though trapped in the narrow band that is soaked by each new wave. This palest of the sandpipers is the same color as the bleached shore, with only the dark tips of the wings and flashing black legs showing any contrast. To many people, sanderlings are a permanent part of the ocean's edge, as much a bird of summer as winter. They never realize that the breeding range of this tiny bird is more than 1,800 miles to the north, on the tundra of the Canadian Arctic. Ever so briefly, the sanderling changes from the ghostly gray of winter to a bright cinnamon plumage for the nesting season, then back to gray before it arrives on the "wintering" grounds once more in late summer.

Trudge down the beach, walking just beyond the reach of the rising tide, where the waves will wash your tracks away before they turn again. In overlapping crescents that echo the last high-water mark, shells sparkle in the low sun—small bay scallops, slipper shells with their pinkish platforms hidden below, the heavy shells of surf clams, the blue triangles of mussels. Here and there are perfect specimens of channeled whelks, but more often than not the big shells are broken and splintered, reduced by the abrasion of sand and waves to a tightly spiraled core around which the living snail once coiled.

The heavy storms of winter are a beachcomber's ally, throwing onto the sand objects that are more rarely seen in summer; there is less competition, and a prize is as likely to be swept back by the next storm as to be hauled off to a mantelpiece. A dead horseshoe crab, upturned like a boat; the bleached carapace of a blue crab, pointy at either side; or the speckled shell of a lady crab grown reddish from the sun. Maybe a stranded dogfish or something truly rare, like the pointy skull of a dolphin or a water-smoothed whale vertebra.

All the time you walk, there are birds in sight. Back along the dune edge, a flickering of movement resolves into a flock of horned larks, snow buntings and water pipits. The larks are seaside birds the year-round, although in winter their numbers are augmented with flocks migrating from grasslands far inland. The buntings and pipits, on the other hand, are Arctic birds during the warm months, only coming south to the beach in winter.

There is even more bird life offshore—loons and sea ducks beyond the surf line, gannets on the horizon, more birds drawn from the Far North. Where the beach ends at a

Left by the tide, a horseshoe crab is the only sign of life at dawn on the deserted winter beaches of Delaware Seashore State Park.

jetty, black rocks slick with spray, a baker's dozen of purple sandpipers hunch against the wind, sheltering in the lee of the big boulders; the only touch of color is a fleck of orange at the base of each bird's bill, like an afterthought. Ruddy turnstones linger nearby, their plumage a somber version of their rusty breeding color, but when they move their orange legs flicker against the barnacles.

Turning back toward the car now, a hint of motion in the wax myrtles catches the eye; a flash of gray becomes a wing, then a hawk. Rising above the shrubs, a male harrier catches the sea wind under his wings, then pivots on air and dives again below the bushes. A thin squeak is cut off abruptly, and the hawk rises with a vole clutched in his bright yellow feet, then vanishes behind the dunes like a memory.

MARCH

March Observations

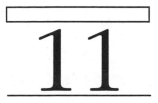

11

Migrating Ducks and Geese

Before the wildflowers and warmth of April, before the equinox balances day and night, long before humans huddling inside their centrally heated homes know it, spring is felt by wild animals. Their clue is the steadily lengthening day, regardless of vagaries of temperature and snow cover. By the beginning of March, the spring migration is under way, and at the vanguard arc the waterfowl—ducks, geese and swans.

No doubt the most treasured moment in the annual northward hegira is the passage of Canada geese, sailing across the sky in wavy strings and sharply formed chevrons. Many years, there comes one day (or sometimes one night) when the geese move as if by command, and the sky seems full of flocks from horizon to horizon, gabbling in endless chorus. More often than not, this biggest push comes with the passage of a warm front and southerly winds, when the overcast is low and the breeze mild, almost as if the geese are towing the first breath of spring behind them.

Although Canada geese may be the most obvious migrants, they are far from alone. Nearly thirty other species of waterfowl pass through the region each spring, some hopping from lake to river on the inland route, others skirting the coastline on their way north. Most drakes are in their full nuptial plumage, and courtship is a constant activity along the way.

Obviously, this is a marvelous time for the naturalist.

Only one species of native swan, the tundra swan, passes through the region (its migration is dealt with in greater detail in Chapter 13). There are three kinds of geese—the ubiquitous Canada, the snow goose and the brant, this last a strictly coastal species. The greatest variety is found among the ducks, which are usually broken into three broad categories. The first are the puddle ducks, or dabblers—birds like mallards, wigeon, teal and pintails that feed in shallow water by tipping up, rear in the air, and grubbing for seeds and roots on the bottom. Diving ducks, exemplified by the canvasback, ring-necked duck and scaup, are more streamlined, with powerful legs. Inhabitants of large lakes and inshore ocean waters, they dive to great depths for their food and, unlike puddle ducks, must run along the surface to become airborne, instead of springing nimbly into the air.

Larger and more powerful still are the sea ducks, whose wintering areas are detailed in Chapter 57. These are generally northern ducks that migrate no farther south than the mid-Atlantic coast and Chesapeake. Finally, there are a few ducks, like the ruddy duck and wood duck, that do not fit neatly into any category, as well as the three fish-eating mergansers, which form a group unto themselves.

Throughout March, almost any body of water is liable to hold transient waterfowl, sometimes only for a few hours while they rest and feed. Other areas produce superb duck-watching each year, with numbers and variety to satiate any birder. The tools of the trade are warm clothing, good binoculars, a field guide and—almost indispensable—a spotting scope mounted on a tripod.

NOTE: *Naturalists with an adventuresome bent should consider this: Strong storms may temporarily ground migrating waterfowl, sometimes for just the duration of the downpour, including sea ducks that pass over inland sites but usually do not stop. By checking large lakes during bad weather, it is possible to find such usually coastal ducks as scoters and oldsquaw hundreds of miles from the ocean.*

HOTSPOTS

In the 1930s, the Shenango River near Meadville, Pennsylvania, was dammed for flood control, destroying one of the largest bogs in the state and creating **Pymatuning Lake** in the process. The result was a waterfowl paradise, and one of the best places in the region for duck-watchers.

Pymatuning is a vast, horseshoe-shaped lake on the Ohio/Pennsylvania border, with habitat that ranges from wooded swamp to grassy marsh and windswept, open water; it thus fulfills the requirements of almost every species of duck that migrates on an inland route, as well as swans, geese and other waterbirds like common loons. The land surrounding the lake is largely state park or state game lands, and the Pennsylvania Game Commission maintains an interpretive museum on Ford Island in the northern arm.

From I-79, follow Route 6 West to Linesville. In town, turn left at the first traffic light onto South Mercer Street (there is a sign for Linesville Spillway) and go .8 mile. On the right is a parking area and the trailhead for a proposed Pymatuning Trail, with a good view of a quiet, stump-choked cove that can be excellent for dabbling ducks. Continue south another .8 mile to the entrance of the Wildlife Museum on the left; the museum itself has wide views of the lake and, on the island to the left, a bald eagle nest at which the adults are often seen in March.

From the museum, turn left again and drive .4 mile to the spillway. This is a popular stop with summer tourists, who feed the mallards and the squadrons of huge carp that rise beneath the ducks to suck down the chunks of stale bread or corn. This sideshow notwithstanding, the spillway area is a good one for other species of ducks, too, with less freeloading habits.

Some 2.3 miles south of the spillway, Route 285 intersects the road at a blinker light. Turn right onto 285 West and drive 3.9 miles to the Pymatuning causeway linking Pennsylvania and Ohio. On the Pennsylvania side of the border, parking is permitted on the south shoulder; drive almost to the Ohio side, turn around in the parking area on the left, and return to the middle of the lake to park. Scan for diving ducks, mergansers, swans and common loons, which often fish surprisingly close to the rocky causeway.

Return to the blinker and turn right. Go 1.2 miles to a white Game Commission building on the left, beyond which are several ponds that sometimes hold good numbers of dabbling ducks. Continue another 3.4 miles to the intersection of Route 322 at Hartstown. Turn left onto 322 East, cross a bridge over the Shenango River and at the far side make an immediate right turn onto a dirt road that circles around and follows a railway bed under the highway. This dirt track, for the next several miles, parallels Hartstown Swamp, a very good area for dabbling ducks.

Four national wildlife refuges within the region are outstanding for the numbers of migrating waterfowl they attract each year—**Blackwater** in Maryland, **Bombay Hook** in Delaware, the **Brigantine** unit of Forsythe in New Jersey and **Back Bay** in extreme southeast Virginia. Directions for Blackwater can be found in Chapter 1, Brigantine in Chapter 6 and Back Bay in Chapter 3. To reach Bombay Hook, take Route 13 to Smyrna, 12 miles north of Dover or 36 miles south of Wilmington. Just south of Smyrna, turn east onto Route 12, which merges with Route 9. Go 4.9 miles on 9, then turn left onto Road 85 (White Halle Neck Road), which leads 2.4 miles to the refuge entrance. The visitors' center and office are just inside the entrance, at the beginning of the 12-mile auto loop.

Another rewarding site for spring waterfowl is **Middle Creek WMA** in southeastern Pennsylvania, owned by the state Game Commission. A 400-acre lake and dozens of smaller ponds and wetlands are the focus for both human and avian visitors; the management area is productive for a variety of puddle ducks, including blacks, shovelers, wigeon and teal. Canada geese are the most obvious migrants, but in recent years substantial flocks of snow geese have also been seen in March—and even more unusual, many have been of the "blue" phase, which is uncommon in the East. Middle Creek can be reached by taking Route 501 north from Lancaster to Route 897 at Schaefferstown; turn right and drive 2.9 miles to Kleinfeltersville, making the first right turn in the village at a sign for Middle Creek. This public road bisects the area and leads to the entrance to the visitors' center. It also passes close to many of the impoundments, but be careful making sudden stops, since it is a heavily traveled road.

In the latter half of March, oldsquaw gather in the upper Chesapeake, preparatory to migrating north. Flocks of more than six thousand are sometimes seen, often out of sight of land but occasionally close enough to shore for observation with a spotting scope. The best areas are along the shores of **Kent County**, Maryland, especially near Swan Point, and farther south near the mouth of the **Choptank River** west of Cambridge.

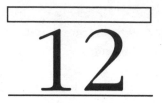

12

Endangered Fox Squirrels

The term *endangered species* has a certain glamour to it, bringing to mind thoughts of noble eagles, stalking panthers or beautiful birds. Not every endangered species is majestic, however. Some are plain, some (to human eyes) quite grotesque and some—like the Delmarva fox squirrel—are simply cute.

This large squirrel, which looks a great deal like an oversized, overfluffed gray squirrel, is native to the Delmarva Peninsula, where it was largely isolated by the Chesapeake Bay from the more widespread eastern fox squirrel. Isolation is often the precursor to evolutionary change, and so it was with the Delmarva fox squirrel, which became even paler than its close relatives across the bay. Given time, it may have diverged so much from its ancestral stock to warrant status as a full species, but for now scientists classify the Delmarva fox squirrel as *Sciurus niger cinereus*, a subspecies of the fox squirrel.

Sadly, it is gone from most of its native habitat, driven out by the logging and agriculture that began to change the face of the Delmarva as early as the 1600s. By the turn of the twentieth century, it was gone from surrounding areas and lingered in Delaware only through the 1930s. When it was formally declared an endangered species in 1967, the Delmarva fox squirrel existed, in small numbers, only in four Maryland counties and one spot in Virginia. The situation looked bleak.

Not long after, however, the federal government, with state cooperation, began transplanting the threatened squirrels to new areas. A few pairs were moved, for instance, to the protection of Chincoteague NWR in Virginia, where they found the lush, mixed pine forests to their liking and have since thrived. Indeed, the most visible colonies are on public land on the Delmarva, and early spring—before the hardwoods have leafed out, but when the squirrels are active after winter's passing—is an excellent time to see them.

There is a great deal of controversy over the exact taxonomic position of the fox squirrels of the mid-Atlantic region. The dustup stems from mankind's tendency to pigeonhole everything—and nature's refusal to follow such hard and fast rules. Species are split from one another on the basis of physical characteristics, differences that can sometimes be minute and open to disagreement. To some mammologists, the only fox squirrels that can be considered true Delmarvas are those found on the peninsula, with those from southeastern Pennsylvania classified as eastern fox squirrels, *S.n. vulpinus.* Other specialists, examining old skins found in museums, believe the Delmarva subspecies was found as far northwest as the Susquehanna River and the Kittatinny Ridge.

The point is not as academic as it might seem, for fox squirrels have been extirpated from southeastern Pennsylvania, and any reintroduction effort that might be undertaken to restore them should use the right subspecies (one misguided effort by the Pennsylvania Game Commission a few years ago brought western fox squirrels—demonstrably the wrong type—to the region).

Meanwhile, biologists have been coddling the remaining Delmarva squirrels, with some notable successes.

Since second-growth forests rarely have enough mature den trees, a simple, effective technique is erecting special wooden nest boxes in the forests—oversized birdbox-style homes, which provide the squirrels with nest sites and shelter.

Fox squirrels spend a great deal more time on the ground than do gray squirrels, foraging for nuts, which constitute the bulk of their diet. Although active all day, fox squirrels are most conspicuous in the early morning, often retiring to their dens at midday; there is a second, lesser period of activity late in the day.

Size and color help distinguish the Delmarva fox squirrel from gray squirrels. The fox squirrel is substantially bigger, with an overall length of 18 to 28 inches and a weight of up to 3 pounds, compared to the gray squirrel's 15- to 20-inch length and maximum weight of about 1.5 pounds. Ironically, the Delmarva fox squirrel is grayer than the gray squirrel, with none of the latter's rusty coloration on the sides and flanks—just a coat of pure, battleship gray.

HOTSPOTS

Probably the best place in the region for watching Delmarva fox squirrels is **Wye Island Natural Resource Management (NRM) Area** in Queen Anne's County, Maryland, just southeast of the Chesapeake Bay Bridge. All but a few parcels of this large island in the Wye River are owned by the state Forest Service, which has dotted the woods with squirrel boxes.

To reach Wye Island, take Route 50 east from Queenstown; 3.1 miles past the Route 50–301 split, watch for the sign for Wye Island NRM Area on the right. Turn right onto the small unnamed road, which crosses a bridge to the island after 5.2 miles and reaches the entrance to the management area another 1.1 miles farther. Just after the entrance, the road enters a rich woodland of oak, pine and beech, with many squirrel boxes hung in the trees; this is a good place to stop and quietly observe.

Continue a total of 1.4 miles from the entrance to the Wye Island Nature Trail on the right, a short loop that runs through a magnificent forest of white oak and pine, prime habitat for the fox squirrel. (The trail passes along the edge of East Wye River, where the waterside trees are the occasional hangout of bald eagles, and where in early spring such diving ducks as bufflehead and scaup may be seen.) The dirt road continues another 1.9 miles, past the Holly Tree Trail, before dead-ending at the Ferry Point Trail. Both the Holly Tree and Ferry Point trails may yield squirrels, but the nature trail is by far the surest bet.

Three national wildlife refuges on the Eastern Shore also have sizable fox squirrel colonies, although the mammals are not as easily visible as at Wye Island. *Eastern Neck NWR*, on the Chester River about 10 miles north of Wye Island, is actively managed for the squirrel's benefit, including hedgerow maintenance and control of the deer population, which would otherwise compete with the rare squirrels. Fox squirrels may be seen almost anywhere on the island refuge; watch especially along fencerows and hedgerows bordering the refuge roads. The Wildlife Trail, which begins along the main refuge road 1.7 miles from the entrance, provides the best chance of seeing these big, pale squirrels. To get to Eastern Neck, take Route 20 south from Chestertown to Rock Hall, then make a left turn onto Route 445 South. After 6.1 miles the road crosses a wooden, one-lane bridge linking the mainland with the island.

The dedicated squirrel-watcher can easily combine stops at Eastern Neck and Wye Island with a side trip to *Blackwater NWR*, south of Cambridge, for a weekend excursion. The presence of fox squirrels is immediately noted—if not by spotting the squirrels themselves, then by the large road signs with stylized silhouettes and the words *SLOW—Endangered Species*. (For directions to Blackwater, see Chapter 1.) Another colony exists at *Chincoteague NWR* on the Virginia tip of the peninsula. The mixed pine forests around the visitors' center, Wildlife Drive, the road leading from the causeway to Swan Cove and—especially— the Pony Trail are all good places to look. To get to Chincoteague, take Route 13 south from Pocomoke City about 10 miles. Turn left at the traffic light onto Route 175 and go east another 10.2 miles to the town of Chincoteague. Follow the signs for the refuge, which lead you left onto Main Street for .4 mile, then right on Maddux Boulevard 2.2 miles, across Chincoteague Channel and onto Assateague Island, the site of the refuge and national seashore.

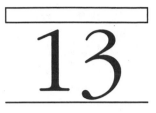

13

Tundra Swans

The call of the tundra swan is unmistakable—a weird, quavering yodel that rises and breaks like a high-pitched bark or whinny. It is the signature call of the Arctic coastal plain, where the swans breed—and of the lower Susquehanna River, where thousands gather each March on their northward migration.

Tundra swans (formerly known as whistling swans) are magnificent birds. Adults are pure white, with black legs and bills and a tiny spot of yellow in front of each eye; juveniles are grayish, with a flesh-colored base to the bill and no yellow. At any age they are large—about 4.5 feet from beak to tail, with a wingspan of nearly 7 feet and weighing up to 20 pounds. Their breeding range extends from the islands of Hudson Bay to western Alaska, in a narrow band that hugs the coast of the Arctic Ocean and Bering Sea, a region where summer comes late and does not linger. In fact, the swans do not wait for it, arriving well in advance of the warm weather and depending on their fat reserves to get them through the incubation period. The female lays up to five eggs, and the male defends a proportionately much larger territory than is usual for waterfowl.

Family groups of adults and cygnets stay together on

the fall migration and on through the winter, which the flocks pass on the Chesapeake and along the Atlantic coast from New Jersey to North Carolina (western populations winter in California and the Southwest). In the East, tundra swans prefer quiet, brackish coves, although they are sometimes found on freshwater lakes or salt water.

The tundra swan is one of three species in North America. The mute swan so often seen in parks, with its gracefully curved neck and orange beak knob, is a European import that is causing concern among wildlife experts as it spreads in the wild, aggressively supplanting native species. The trumpeter swan, once native to most of North America, was virtually annihilated by market hunting in the eighteenth and nineteenth centuries, and barely survived in a few remote western locations. The tundra swan also took a beating, frequently shot for its feathers and meat during the same period. It took a further blow in the 1930s when its favorite food, the aquatic plant called eelgrass, all but disappeared because of blight. In the past two decades the swans have adopted a trick from Canada geese, however, and have begun foraging in harvested fields, picking up corn and grain missed by the machines. This new food supply, coupled with protection, has brought on a renaissance for the tundra swan.

In late February, and sometimes earlier if the weather turns mild, the swans begin to filter north, many of them following the Chesapeake to the Susquehanna. For most of its length, the Susquehanna is a wide, shallow river, and nowhere is this more evident than in the nearly 50 miles of river from Harrisburg, Pennsylvania, south to the Maryland border. Except where hydroelectric dams have backed up large impoundments, the Susquehanna is perfect for dabbling ducks, geese and swans, providing sandbars, shallow waters and plenty of food in and near the river. The swans use the river as a staging ground, their numbers building through early March. In a normal year, by the first or second

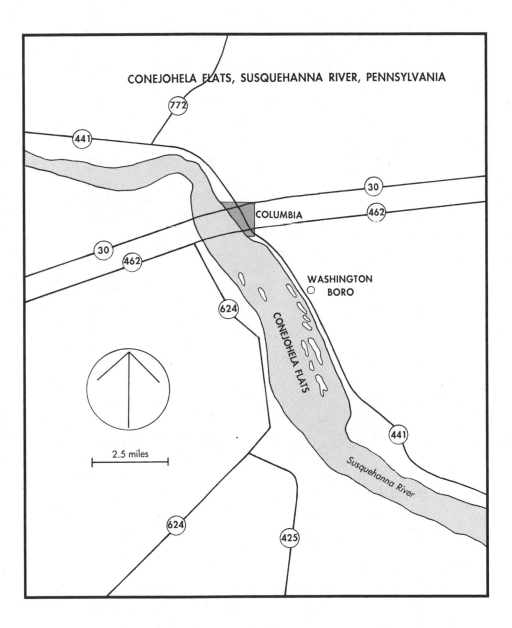

CONEJOHELA FLATS, SUSQUEHANNA RIVER, PENNSYLVANIA

weekend of the month up to twelve thousand swans may be resting and feeding along the river and nearby lakes, waiting for the right moment to fly north.

It is a sight worth seeing, especially if you can arrive early in the morning. Most days, an hour or so after daybreak, the swans begin stirring and head out to the surrounding countryside to feed. They flap laboriously into the air, running heavily along the surface of the water, pumping their wings. The birds are low, sometimes barely clearing the electrical lines overhead—often so close one can hear the rhythmic *swish-swish-swish* of their wingbeats.

The timing of the swan peak is dependent upon the weather; in an exceptionally mild winter, there may be a few swans present as early as New Year's, while a cold, ice-choked February may keep them away until the floes clear out. Weather, too, seems to be the signal that sends them north, often en masse with the passage of a warm front, heading back to the Arctic for another season of renewal.

HOTSPOTS

Wildlife populations are dynamic, and that fundamental rule has been exemplified in recent years by the changing habits of tundra swans in the lower Susquehanna valley. Traditionally, the major staging ground was on the river itself in the island-studded *Conejohela Flats* south of Columbia, but since the late 1980s, increasing numbers of swans have been forsaking the river for *Middle Creek Wildlife Management Area*. Fortunately for visiting naturalists, the two sites are fairly close to each other and can be easily enjoyed in a day.

To reach the flats, take Route 30 to Columbia, then go south on Route 441 for about 3 miles toward Washington Boro. Near Washington Boro United Methodist Church at Rockfish Road is a nice parking area on the right (which should not be used on Sunday mornings); just offshore is a narrow channel that will offer the closest views of swans, if they are present. Another .3 mile south, opposite Penn Street and the Lion's Community Park, is a second parking area with a fine view of the flats to the northwest.

CAUTION: *The only way to observe the flats is to stand along the Conrail tracks, which are extremely active even on weekends. Keep a watchful eye and ear for approaching trains, and retreat to the road side of the tracks (instead of the steep, dangerously loose slope along the river) until the train passes.*

Even on mild March days the ever-present wind that cuts across the river is cold, so dress warmly and if possible bring a spotting scope mounted on a tripod.

No one is quite sure why the swans have been moving to Middle Creek in growing numbers each spring, but totals

Stopping on their way from the Atlantic coast to the Arctic, tundra swans by the thousands rest for several weeks on the lower Susquehanna River.

have exceeded five thousand, up from a mere handful just a few years before. The largest flocks form on the central lake, easily visible from the two-lane road that skirts its edge. (For detailed directions to Middle Creek, see Chapter 11.) The management area loop road, just north of Willow Point, is a good spot for watching swans in flight, since they frequently fly over this corridor on their way to feed. In most years, however, the loop road does not open until the middle of the month.

An intriguing new possibility for tundra swan-watchers is the chance (admittedly slim) of seeing a trumpeter swan as well. In recent years trumpeters from the Rockies have been transplanted to Ontario and the Great Lakes states, and there have been a few reports of individuals along the lower Susquehanna. The two species look very much alike, but the trumpeter is larger, with no yellow on the base of the adult's bill, a longer bill and flatter head; in addition, the tundra swan's neck usually rises straight up from the breast, while the trumpeter's neck often has a crook at the base. Do not assume that an adult swan without yellow on the bill is a trumpeter, however, because many tundra swans also lack that field mark.

A smaller group of several hundred tundra swans also appears each March in the cranberry bogs at **Whitesbog Conservation and Environmental Studies Center** in the New Jersey Pine Barrens. See Chapter 31 for directions.

14

Rare and Unusual Gulls

Gulls suffer from a bad press. Beach-goers dislike their pilfering habits, shoreside residents resent their splattery, whitewash droppings and, perhaps most ignominiously of all, they are denied any recognition as individual species. Instead, they are all lumped together as *sea gulls*, a term usually spoken with disparagement.

Naturalists know better. They know, for instance, that there is not just one kind of gull in North America, but twenty-two, ranging from the almost obscenely common herring gull to the rare, pinkish Ross' gull of the Arctic. Naturalists also know that gull identification is confusing, but for those with patience and a taste for winter weather, this is the best time for finding rarities.

Each winter, gulls congregate by the tens of thousands—sometimes the hundreds of thousands—at several locations in the region. Most are of three species—herring, ring-billed and Bonaparte's gulls, with smaller numbers of the great black-backed gull, a coastal species that has been spreading south from New England. The great flocks, massed white on the water or swirling chaotically in the air, are a spectacle in themselves, but for many naturalists, the real lure is the needle-in-a-haystack hunt for the oddballs.

Among the most sought-after species are the so-called white-winged gulls, a generic term for several large, pale varieties including the glaucous, Iceland and Thayer's gulls. These birds breed in the Arctic and winter along the northern coast (the Thayer's normally in the West, but usually showing up in the East a few times each year). Another attraction is the possibility of one or more European gulls, such as the lesser black-backed, little and common black-headed gulls. All three of these vagrant species have begun to breed in North America, and in the past decade sightings of lesser black-backed gulls have become so routine that many birders no longer report them.

The hardest part about watching rare gulls is picking them out of the crowd and then knowing what you're looking at. Gull identification can be frustratingly difficult, given the number of species and the fact that each has a unique series of plumages between hatching and adulthood; some gulls take four years to achieve their final plumage, with a slightly or radically different appearance every few months. Obviously, the subject is too complex for detailed discussion here—study one of the in-depth field guides such as National Geographic's *Field Guide to the Birds of North America* or *The Audubon Society Master Guide to Birding*. An invaluable resource is *Advanced Birding* by Kenn Kaufman, one of the Peterson field guide series; it greatly simplifies the daunting task of putting a name to a strange gull.

HOTSPOTS

The lower Susquehanna River in Maryland and Pennsylvania, especially in the vicinity of **Conowingo Dam**, is traditionally good for large gull flocks, and lesser black-backed gulls have become a virtual certainty each winter; use a scope to carefully compare size and mantle color of the gulls resting on the dam abutments and rocks. When water is released through the turbines, chewing up fish and creating a bonanza of food, gulls pour in from upriver and down, converging into a roiling white storm below the breast, sharing their airspace with bald eagles. For directions to Conowingo, see Chapter 1.

The *Manasquan Inlet* at Point Pleasant, New Jersey, is a good spot for unusual gulls, although the numbers are not as overwhelming as at Conowingo. Bonaparte's gulls, which breed along lakes in the boreal forests of Canada and Alaska, winter here abundantly, and their ternlike grace makes them easy to distinguish from the heavier ring-billed and herring gulls. The Bonaparte's also has a distinctive white wedge along the leading edge of the flight feathers—but look closely at all "Bonaparte's" gulls for one with the same general pattern and shape but somewhat larger, with darker undersides to the primaries and a red, not black, bill. This is the common black-headed gull, a European species showing up with increasing frequency along the East Coast. Manasquan is one of the places where it is most often spotted, and is also good for white-winged gulls.

To reach the inlet from the south, take Route 37 east from the Garden State Parkway, across Barnegat Bay to the resort community of Ortley Beach, then follow Route 35 north to Point Pleasant at the north end of the island. Route 35 bears left; instead go straight, following the sign for the beaches. Go 1.7 miles, passing an amusement center (the boardwalk affords views of the surf). The road becomes one-way, turning left at the inlet. Park and walk along the inlet and jetties.

Narrow *Rudlee Inlet*, at the southern edge of Virginia Beach, Virginia, is well known for the gulls that gather at its mouth, including several white-winged species, common black-headed, lesser black-backed gulls and black-legged kittiwake. Take Route 60 south through Virginia Beach; after the road crosses the inlet it becomes General Booth Boulevard. There is access on both sides, including Old Rudlee Road on the south shore.

Presque Isle in Lake Erie, known for its waterfowl and songbirds, is also a major wintering site for gulls, with more than half a million recorded in exceptional years. Obviously, among so many gulls there are bound to be some rarities, and the naturalist with patience to sift through the chaff of ring-billed gulls is all but certain to find some worthwhile species. For directions to Presque Isle, see Chapter 2; pick up a park map at the state park office, and check the protected areas like Misery and Thompsons bays, Marina Lake and Big Pond, as well as Presque Isle Bay itself, where schools of gizzard shad have been known to attract as many as ten species of gulls, mostly ring-billed, Bonaparte's, herring and great black-backed. Rarities often encountered at Presque Isle are glaucous, Iceland, lesser black-backed, little and Thayer's gulls.

15

Breakout:
"Accidental" Species

Animal migration generally follows predictable patterns—
the sort of patterns on which much of this book is based, in
fact. While naturalists obviously appreciate this almost
clockwork regularity, there is also a thrill in finding something where or when it shouldn't be. Most often the lost soul
is a bird, and if it strays far enough from home, it may set off
shock waves among the bird-watching community, making
the rare-bird hotlines hum.

Such wayward birds are known variously as
accidentals, vagrants or extralimitals. Often, they are migratory species blown off course by storms or strong winds, or
suffering from a faulty sense of navigation—flying the
correct distance but going southwest instead of southeast,
for instance, or overshooting their destination. Overshooting appears to be the origin of some of the tropical fork-
tailed flycatchers that regularly appear in the mid-Atlantic
states. That the species shows up here at all is remarkable,
since it breeds no closer than southern Mexico. What is even
more remarkable is that the individuals sighted in the region
are usually of a race native to *southern* South America.
Ornithologists theorize that when these birds migrate north
from Argentina toward their wintering grounds in Colombia

and neighboring countries, a few miss the mark and continue to the United States, more than 2,500 miles beyond their intended destination. These arrive in our spring, while others, which apparently migrate in the opposite direction from that which they are supposed to go (a sort of reverse migration), show up during the Northern Hemisphere's autumn, having flown north instead of south.

Gulls have frequently been the cause of all this fuss. In 1974, a Ross' gull—rare even in the Arctic—unexpectedly showed up in Massachusetts, drawing birders from across the United States and Canada hoping to add the species to their North American life lists. A cherished birding tradition, the life list is a compilation of all the species seen in a birder's lifetime; many divide their lists by continents and states, so that a bird seen in, say, Europe would not count for the North American tally, nor would a white pelican seen in Montana count on a New Jersey list. Thus, from the standpoint of strict inventory, a vagrant can be a valuable addition, especially if an experienced birder has already checked off most of the native species.

Some bird species seem to have a propensity for wandering—shorebirds, ducks and gulls, all being strong fliers, are among those most often seen out of range. The displacement may be fairly slight, like a great black-backed gull at an inland site instead of along the ocean, or it may be more extreme. In the late winter of 1990, for instance, birders at the Georgetown Reservoir in Washington, D.C., noticed a gull that didn't look quite right. With good reason—it was a yellow-legged gull, the Mediterranean race of the herring gull, which had only been recorded in North America once before.

Not every bird seen far from its range is a true vagrant. An Egyptian goose that appeared with hordes of freeloading mallards at a municipal park in Pennsylvania in 1991 was more likely an escapee from captivity than a vagrant from the wild, North African population. This is the probable origin

of many odd, out-of-range waterfowl, and reports of unusual ducks like Baikal teal from Asia are generally greeted
with suspicion by those who keep the official records. Other
species are more problematic, like barnacle geese, which
breed in Iceland and sightings of which may be either
escapees or true vagrants. Experts often go by the condition
of a bird's feathers, which may show excessive wear from
rubbing against cage wire, and its general temperament; a
bird that acts wary of humans is much more likely to be wild
than one that begs handouts.

The appearance of a vagrant is generally ephemeral;
the bird may linger a few hours or a few weeks, but once
gone it rarely returns. This is not always so, however. In the
winter of 1970 a Barrow's goldeneye, an Arctic species
rare in the mid-Atlantic region, was discovered on the
Shark River estuary in northern New Jersey. It returned
each winter for the next fourteen years, setting something of an ornithological record for fidelity to an adopted
home, before finally failing to show up, its fate unknown, in
1984.

Most sightings of accidentals are one-shot affairs, but
on rare occasions they presage a major range extension. The
first brown pelicans to be seen in the region in the early
1980s were dismissed as oddities, but their numbers quickly
grew, and each summer they penetrated farther and farther
north—along the Virginia coast, then Maryland and Delaware, eventually as far north as New Jersey. Meanwhile,
pelicans were settling in to breed in Virginia, and today there
are thriving colonies at Fisherman's Island NWR, Virginia,
near Ocean City, Maryland, and at a number of other
locations along the coast.

Much the same thing has happened in recent years
with European gulls. Lesser black-backed, little gulls and
common black-headed gulls were sighted in increasing
numbers, and each has since been proven to be breeding in
small numbers in North America. All three are sure to

become steadily more abundant, and they may well establish themselves as some of North America's newest "natives."

NOTE: *For a list of telephone numbers for regional rare-bird alerts—the best way to find out about accidentals—see the Appendix.*

APRIL

April Observations

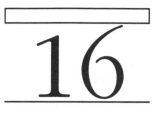

16

Bluebells and Early Spring Wildflowers

The Virginia bluebell, or mertensia, is the showiest member of the forget-me-not family of wildflowers, and is one of more than forty species of bluebells in North America and Eurasia. It is also one of the most fleeting; its wide leaves sprout quickly in late March, producing columns of drooping, pink buds by the beginning of April. With the arrival of warm weather the buds swell and open into flaring trumpets of sky blue. The floral show lasts only a week or two, and by midsummer the plant has withered and died back to the root, leaving no trace of its presence.

Bluebells like their soil rich, with plenty of limestone beneath their roots. They are found as far north as southern Canada, but are most common from southern Pennsylvania through the Piedmont, where they form stands that may include several hundred plants.

Occasionally, though, conditions will be just to the bluebells' liking, and they respond enthusiastically, carpeting acres with their pendulous flower clusters. Coming as they do in spring's earliest days, the bluebells are doubly welcome, since they provide color where there recently was only winter's brown.

One of the finest floral displays anywhere in the

region, in fact, occurs each April in a sheltered creek valley within sight of the Susquehanna River in south-central Pennsylvania. Here, in the Shenk's Ferry Glen Wildflower Reserve, more than seventy-three species bloom through the spring, summer and fall, but the highlight is the staggering profusion of Virginia bluebells and the unusual white phase of the red trillium, which quite literally turn the hillsides into a solid sheet of blue and white. Tremendous numbers of bluebells are also the attraction at Bull Run Regional Park in Virginia, just west of Alexandria.

At Shenk's Ferry, the bluebells and trilliums alone would be worth the trip, but look past the masses of these species and you'll find dozens of other wildflowers indicative of rich, alkaline woods—squirrel corn, Dutchman's breeches (including some deep pink specimens), both the common yellow and the much rarer white trout lilies, cut-leaved toothwort, blue cohosh, a host of violet species, abundant spring beauties, blue phlox and wild columbine. Somewhat earlier in the season, bloodroot and hepatica can be found; a bit later, wild geranium, jack-in-the-pulpit, wild ginger and puttyroot.

Many visitors mistakenly assume that the white trilliums that carpet the glen are large-flowered trillium (*Trillium grandiflorum*), when in reality they are red trillium (*T. erectum*), usually a deep crimson but here white with a slight tinge of green; this species is highly variable, and a patch on the southern side of the glen, where the trilliums grow in almost pure stands, shows a wash of pink.

The bluebells and trilliums usually hit their optimum around the end of the second week of April, although the timing obviously depends somewhat on how warm or cool the spring has been.

HOTSPOTS
To get to **Shenk's Ferry Glen**, take Route 324 South from Lancaster toward New Danville. After about 9 miles, the road enters a short tunnel under a railroad embankment;

.9 mile beyond the tunnel, turn right onto River Road. Go 2.1 miles and turn left onto Shenk's Ferry Road, where there is a sign for the reserve. Follow Shenk's Ferry 1.1 miles to a stop sign at a T-intersection, turning left onto Green Hill Road, which becomes dirt and descends toward the river. At the railroad tracks take the left road at the Y and go another .3 mile to the dirt parking area by Grubb Run.

The main walking path up the glen, an old railroad bed that supplied a nineteenth-century iron furnace, starts on the other side of the small bridge and goes just a few hundred yards back into the woods. It may take a wildflower buff hours to cover that short distance, however, since there is so much to see. The trail continues past a cutoff utility corridor, but the best bluebell displays are between the road and here. For other wildflowers, pay particular attention to the small spring that comes in from the left.

Obviously, such a small, heavily used site is at risk from human abuses. Picking or digging flowers is strictly forbidden, and visitors should restrict themselves to the main trails, since it is almost impossible to leave them without stepping on blooming or sprouting wildflowers.

After enjoying the bluebells at Shenk's Ferry, make a worthwhile detour by returning to Route 324 at River Road. Turn right on 324 (Pequea Boulevard). About .3 mile past the Pequea Creek Recreation Area, the hillside to the right is covered in a beautiful, almost pure stand of Dutchman's breeches. The road is narrow and there is no place to pull off or stop, so enjoy the sight from the car only.

Bull Run Regional Park just north of Manassas, Virginia, has the typical park accoutrements like picnic tables, a swimming pool and a Frisbee golf course. Far more unusually, it also has bluebells in numbers that exceed those at Shenk's Ferry, although the variety of other wildflowers is much more limited. As the bluebells pass their peak and drop in late April, the visitor becomes aware of a secondary carpet of flowers previously upstaged—a low-growing layer

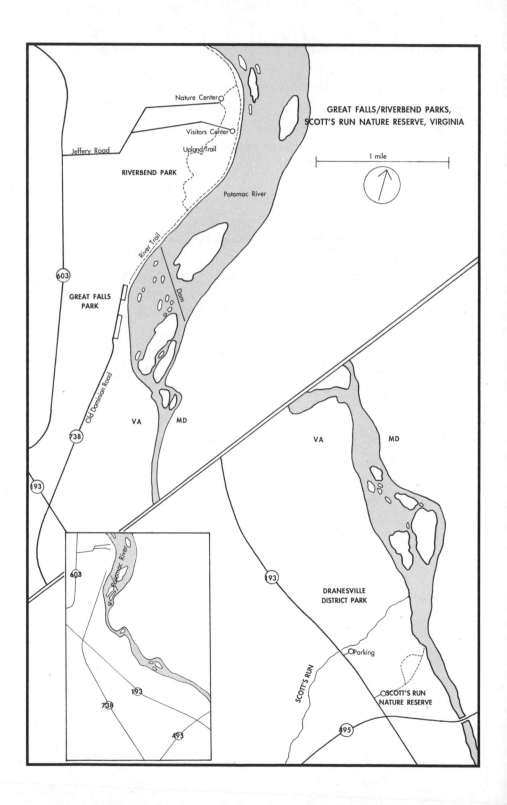

GREAT FALLS/RIVERBEND PARKS,
SCOTT'S RUN NATURE RESERVE, VIRGINIA

1 mile

Nature Center

Visitors Center

Upland/Trail

Jeffery Road

RIVERBEND PARK

Potomac River

River Trail

603

GREAT FALLS
PARK

Dam

Old Dominion Road

VA   MD

738

193

VA   MD

Potomac River

603

193

738

495

93

DRANESVILLE
DISTRICT PARK

SCOTT'S RUN

Parking

SCOTT'S RUN
NATURE RESERVE

495

of spring beauty, both the small, common species, *Claytonia virginica*, and the larger Carolina spring beauty, *C. caroliniana*. The wider leaf of the Carolina species, not flower color, is the key to identification, since both species exhibit a full spectrum from pure white to deep pink.

Bull Run Park is reached by taking Route 66 West from Fairfax. At Exit 12, turn right at the light onto Route 29 South and go 2.2 miles to the left turn (marked by a park sign) onto Bull Run Post Office Road. Follow this two-lane road for 1.2 miles to a sharp left curve, where you bear to the right into the park. The contact station is .9 mile beyond; from there, follow the signs 1.4 miles to the swimming pool and park.

The trail begins across the road from the parking lot, running arrow-straight through the seasonally flooded forest and across a utility corridor. Beyond this, the trail turns left along the stream and the bluebells begin in abundance, mixed with pale violets, mayapples and a few other species. Where the trail forks, follow the yellow-blazed trail to the left, which loops back around to the parking lot, a level circuit of about 1.5 miles.

A third stop for April wildflowers, including some bluebells, is **Scott's Run Nature Reserve**, **Great Falls Park** and **Riverbend Park**, three public areas in close proximity along the Potomac River north of Vienna, Virginia. Visit Scott's Run first to see several fine stands of the strange sessile trillium, which grows in a damp little stream gorge with jack-in-the-pulpit, rue-anemone, star chickweed, Solomon's seal, spring beauty, yellow violets and much more. Then head down the road a few miles to Great Falls and Riverbend, which are linked by a trail that extends north from the falls along the river, then loops back through the uplands, passing through a variety of habitats along the way. In late April as the bluebells fade, their place is taken by drifts of sweetly aromatic blue phlox, accentuated with splashes of yellow from golden ragwort; wild ginger, Dutchman's breeches, early saxifrage, pink lady's-slipper and cut-leaved toothwort can be identified along the trails as well.

To visit these three sites, take I-495 (Capitol Beltway) to Exit 13, turning onto Route 193 West. Less than .2 mile after the turn onto 193, the tiny parking lot for Scott's Run is on the right. Take the trail uphill, straight through an intersecting trail and, when it forks, go right. This leads through dry uplands, ending at a rocky promontory with a fine view of the river. Double back a few yards and take the trail that drops to the right, into the gorge formed by a small creek (no more than a rivulet), then hike upstream. Here are found hundreds of sessile trilliums, or toadshades, with their wide, mottled leaves and curved, brown-purple petals. Make a left when the trail meets a wide dirt path, and then take the next clear right to return to the parking lot.

Leaving Scott's Run, turn right onto Route 193 West once again (you will pass another parking lot on the right beside Scott's Run, another good jump-off point for a botanical hike). Go a total of 4.6 miles and make a right onto Old Dominion Road to enter Great Falls Park, a National Park Service site. Park and see the falls first, if you've never enjoyed the dramatic sight; then walk upriver from the last parking lot along River Trail. Above the low dam, the trail passes from Great Falls Park to Riverbend Park, a county facility. The footpath, often muddy, transverses a typical bottomland forest. Big sycamores lean over the water, providing nest holes for wood ducks and prothonotary warblers, and perches for bald eagles and ospreys; the rich, wet soil is also perfect for many wildflowers.

Past the visitors' center, the blue-blazed river path intersects the green-blazed Pawpaw Passage Trail, named for the odd, flowering tree that grows commonly here; turn left and take this to the nature center, then follow the red-marked Upland Trail back to the river path. In all, the loop covers several miles, with level hiking along the river and some steep inclines on the Upland Trail. A trail map, available at the visitors' and nature centers, makes sorting out the confusing Upland Trail easier.

17

Beavers and
Beaver Dams

At more than 50 pounds, an adult beaver is the largest rodent in North America and one of the heaviest in the world. But this chunky, flat-tailed mammal is even more famous for its feats of engineering than its size, for the beaver is the only wild animal on the continent that actively changes its environment to suit itself.

A beaver is something of a contradiction—an aquatic animal that feeds on trees. Out of water a beaver is vulnerable to attack from bobcats, bears or coyotes, so it brings the water to the forest by damming creeks and streams, usually in several places, forming a series of wide ponds that flood into the surrounding timber.

The dams are works of instinctive art, varying in height and shape to match the immediate need. On a mountain creek that runs through a steep gorge, the beavers will pick a narrowing of the channel and build dams that may be higher than a man's head, but only 30 or 40 yards wide. In a sluggish marsh, on the other hand, the dam may need be only a foot or two high, but it may have to stretch a third of a mile or more in order to seal off the drainage. In other places, all that may be needed is a plug of branches and mud across a road culvert to flood the forest—and, more often than not, the road, too.

This adaptability to local conditions may not be the genius it appears. Experiments have shown that beavers instinctively react to the sound of running water by trying to dam the source, and they may simply work until the water stops flowing. Not that a beaver dam is waterproof; the current still seeps through the breast itself, slowly and quietly. If heavy rains raise the water level, and pressure threatens the dam, the beavers will cut spillways in the breast to vent off the excess. Once the danger has passed, the spillways are repaired with new logs and applications of mud—carried in the paws, not on the tail as is often thought. The odd tail, in fact, plays no role in construction at all, but is a rudder and thermal regulator.

Beaver dams are only part of the construction complex. Somewhere in the middle of the pond, safe from most predators, the beavers construct a conical lodge, only the top of which protrudes above the surface. Hidden below the water are several entrances, which connect to passages above the water level. At the core of the lodge is a central chamber where the kits are born in early spring. Although most of the lodge is heavily plastered with mud for insulation, the very top is made of loose sticks and logs, allowing ventilation to the living chamber. If the resulting pond is too deep (or along man-made lakes where a dam is unnecessary) the beavers may dig bank lodges like muskrats or build a lodge of logs along the shore.

A third aspect of the dam complex, usually hidden from view, is the winter food larder. In early autumn the beavers begin stashing branches by jamming them into the pond bottom, eventually forming a thicket of cached saplings—food for the months ahead when the pond is frozen and the beavers cannot get ashore. Because the beavers can hold their breath for up to 15 minutes while submerged, this causes no hardships. In fact, the thin layer of exhaled breath that collects beneath the ice acts as a gas exchange, becoming reoxygenated and eventually forming a trapped layer of breathable air that the beavers, with their flattened nostrils, can use if necessary.

There are two major periods of activity in the beaver's year—autumn, when the winter larder must be filled, and spring, when the kits are born and the flush of new plant growth in the marsh attracts the adults. Beavers are most active at dawn and dusk, so the naturalist who wants to watch these fascinating animals will have to match their hours, especially if one wishes to see a beaver felling trees.

It is a common belief that beavers eat wood chips. They do not, feeding instead on the tender bark of the upper branches of hardwood trees, and using the bigger logs for building. They fell the trees with their teeth, of course—massive, orange incisors that cut easily through wood, powered by thick, bulging jaw muscles. The beaver stands beside the trunk and cocks its head sideways, working in a circle around the trunk as it cuts an increasingly deep trough, until the tree's weight causes it to topple. Beavers seem to be good at judging where and how a tree will fall but mistakes do happen, and the tree may hang up in others and not come all the way down, or it may even fall unexpectedly and crush the beaver.

As the colony grows, young beavers strike out along the creek, forming new lodges, sometimes making overland journeys of many miles between watersheds. Despite the exodus, the original colony cannot last forever. Eventually the nearby stands of edible trees will all have been cut, and the beavers may have to dig canals to link the ponds with more distant pockets of forest. In time, even these will have been exhausted, and the colony may break up and abandon the dam. The life of a beaver colony may be as short as a few years or measured in decades, depending on the quantity and species of the trees around the ponds. Beavers prefer young aspens, although they feed on a wide variety of hardwoods and in summer switch to a diet heavy with aquatic plants like spatterdock. A colony that is forced to cut pines or hemlocks is probably in its final stages, having used up everything else edible in the neighborhood.

As soon as the beavers are gone, the roots of the cut trees begin sending up new shoots, and in another twenty or thirty years, there may be enough edible species to attract a new pair of beavers. In the meantime, the ponds will slowly silt up and become bogs, providing homes for wood ducks and many other wetland animals.

When looking for beavers, remember that your chances are much better early in the morning and at dusk—especially just after daybreak. Beavers have excellent eyesight and keen senses of smell and hearing, so arrive quietly and conceal yourself behind a screen of bushes. Sit motionlessly and watch. An incautious movement may bring the resounding slap of a beaver's tail, the classic alarm of this species.

Most dams also have a population of muskrats, which superficially resemble beavers. Muskrats are much smaller, however, and usually swim with the long, vertically flattened tail sculling the surface, making the smaller animal look somewhat bigger than it is. A beaver swims with its webbed hind feet, and the head is big and very chunky in appearance. It is possible for a beginner to mistake a muskrat for a beaver, but the reverse almost never occurs.

HOTSPOTS

With the exception of the Chesapeake Bay and Delmarva Peninsula, beavers are widespread in most remote areas of the mid-Atlantic region. Three places in particular, however, offer excellent beaver-watching prospects—Erie NWR and Black Moshannon State Park in Pennsylvania, and Huntley Meadows Park in northern Virginia.

Erie NWR in Crawford County is famous for its beavers, which inhabit most of the streams and ponds in the refuge's two units, together totaling more than 8,000 acres. The larger of the two, the Sugar Lake Division, is the most accessible, with two major streams watering this winding valley set between low, forested hills.

Even the small ponds near headquarters, patrolled by querulous pairs of Canada geese, are home to beavers, and a beaver dam on the nearby Tsuga Nature Trail is crossed by a boardwalk, from the ends of which one can hide behind concealing hemlock branches and watch the show.

From I-79, take Exit 37, turning right at the stop sign onto Route 198 East. Go 16.6 miles to the village of Guys Mills and turn left at the four-way stop, staying on 198. The refuge headquarters is on the right .8 mile later; turn in and park. Early in the morning you may see beavers on the ponds between 198 and headquarters, but a better bet is to take the nature trail, a 1.6-mile loop that begins near the headquarters building, passes one large artificial pond in the open and enters the woods. Here, beavers have dammed the creek; sit quietly and watch the water not just for the giant rodents, but for great blue herons, wood ducks and other wetland animals.

Return to 198, turning left for .4 mile, then making a right just beyond Union Cemetery. The road forks after .6 mile; take the left fork and go 1 mile to the parking area for the Beaver Run Trail, on the right. This trail skirts a field, then comes up on a gully, blocked by a fine example of beaver engineering. The trail continues right, upstream, passing older dams that have been breached. A beaver colony is a finite entity, and this one has nearly used up its food supply.

Return by car to the four-way stop in Guys Mills on 198, this time turning left (south). Drive 2.3 miles to a stop sign and make a left onto Route 27; go .5 mile and turn right onto a dirt road. At the fork go right, and after a total of 1.7 miles from 27, watch for the parking area for the observation blind on the right. The blind overlooks one of several ponds in the Lake Creek drainage.

North-central Pennsylvania is a stronghold for beavers, which are very much in evidence at ***Black Moshannon State Park*** in Centre County and in Moshannon State Forest

BLACK MOSHANNON STATE PARK, PENNSYLVANIA

immediately beyond. From State College, take Route 322 West to Route 22 North. Go 4.9 miles and turn left at the sign for Black Moshannon onto Julian Pike. Follow this road 8.5 miles to the park office, where you should ask for a trail map, then continue straight along the lake to a stop sign.

Turn left, cross the narrow cove and take the first paved left on the other side, West Side Road. Follow West Side 1.2 miles to a paved cul-de-sac and park. At the edge of the lake is the beginning of the Bog Trail boardwalk; from here you can scan the lake, where beavers have been active for years (note the old lodges on the distant island to the left, and among the spatterdock leaves and stumps off to the right).

On a busy weekend the main lake may be too raucous for beavers, so return to the end of the boardwalk. In the woods to the left is the trailhead for the Moss-Hanne Trail, which makes a wide circle of the southwest end of the lake, passing through prime beaver country, particularly in the Black Moshannon Bog Natural Area where the creek passes into the lake. The trail is long and can be quite soggy, but is worth the effort. Fortunately for those without the time or inclination for a wet hike, there is a classic, active beaver dam not far from the northern trailhead. From the cul-de-sac take the orange-blazed Moss-Hanne Trail to its intersection with the red-blazed Indian Trail, turn left and walk a few hundred yards along the path. There are fine views on the north side, but at evening the light is better if you follow the path around to the far shore and settle in among the bushes.

Another dam complex can be found just west of the park, on Sixmile Run in Moshannon State Forest. From the park office go south on Julian Pike to the first dirt right, Strawband Beaver Road. Go .3 mile to the fork and bear right onto Shirk's Road, which is unmarked. Two miles later you will cross the creek just upstream from the Black Moshannon Bog, and beaver sign is plentiful here. Continue another mile to Clay Mine Road, turn right and go 2 miles. Turn left, cross a small bridge and turn left again onto Sixmile Run Road. The dams are about .3 mile farther on the left, but the popularity of this area with fishermen makes it difficult to watch beavers on a weekend. To return to the park, double back north on Sixmile Run Road to Route 504, turn right and proceed to the lake.

Huntley Meadows Park in Virginia is utterly improbable—a 1,200-acre preserve of mature forest and wetland, set within spitting distance of Washington, D.C., and surrounded by neatly tended residential neighborhoods and highway strip development. Inside the park, however, suburban life seems light years away, especially now that an ill-conceived plan to drive a four-lane expressway through the park has been abandoned.

Huntley Meadows' centerpiece is a complex of marsh and pond that has been greatly augmented by thriving beaver colonies—sixteen lodges' worth at last count, and perhaps the most easily observable such colonies in the

With nothing but sticks and mud, a colony of beavers has dammed this small stream in Erie NWR, Pennsylvania, to form a wide, still pond—a feat typical of beaver engineering.

region. Much of the western edge of the shallow marsh has been surrounded by a low, beaver-built dam, which retards the drainage of water flowing into Barnyard Run. An excellent boardwalk and trail system gives access to the impoundment, passing close to several of the big, conical lodges, and an observation tower at the midpoint of the trail loop gives unrestricted views of the area. The park is open from dawn to dusk and, as always, the best times to see the beavers are shortly after daybreak and just before dark. Competing for attention with the beavers will be river otters, great blue herons, wood ducks, blue-winged teal, yellow-crowned night-herons and an abundance of songbirds, turtles and other marsh life.

To reach Huntley Meadows from the west of Washington, take I-95 (Capitol Beltway) to Exit 2B, then to 241 South/Telegraph Road. Follow 241 for 2.7 miles to a light at Route 633 (South King's Highway). Make a left; the small entrance to the 1.2-mile hike-and-bike trail is immediately on the right. Continue on South King's Highway for 1.5 miles to Harrison Lane, making a right turn at the light. Go another mile to a sharp left turn where Harrison intersects Lockheed Boulevard; the main entrance to the park is at the angle. Coming from the east and north, take 95 to Route 1 South (Richmond Highway), then go 3.2 miles to the light at Lockheed Boulevard. Make a right and go another .6 mile to the entrance.

18

The Blue Ridge in Blossom

There may be no lovelier sight for the winter-weary naturalist than the rush of color that spreads over the forest in early spring. Weeks before most of the trees have leaves, they bring forth a profusion of flowers—in fact, a cascade of blossoms appears overhead well before most of the wildflowers everyone expects on the forest floor.

Across the region, one of the earliest, surest signs of spring is the blooming of the red maples, turning stream valleys and swamps crimson with their globes of blood-red flowers. Other flowering trees are more subtle—the small, greenish blooms of the spicebush and sassafras, or the drooping catkins of aspen or birch, for instance.

Three species of wild trees, however, put on a show that stretches from the earliest days of spring to the middle of May, depending on latitude and elevation. They are the shadbush, redbud and flowering dogwood—and there is no finer place to see their spectacular display than in Virginia's picturesque Blue Ridge Mountains, which stretch from the North Carolina border to the northern terminus of Shenandoah National Park.

The shadbush is really a group of closely related species in the genus *Amelanchier*, and for a small tree, it has a multitude of names—serviceberry, sarvisberry and Juneberry, to name a few. The names are rich in pioneer history; it is thought that *service* (and the corruption *sarvis*) may have referred to the early spring blooming period, which coincided with the opening of the mountain roads, letting circuit preachers make their first rounds of the year. Juneberry, on the other hand, focuses on the ripening of the small, sweet purple berries, an important fruit for both Native Americans and European settlers.

Two species—the Allegheny serviceberry and the more southerly downy serviceberry—are found in the mountains, with the Allegheny more tolerant of higher elevations. Both are smooth-barked, smallish trees, rarely growing taller than 30 or 40 feet, with elliptical, serrated leaves that are fuzzy underneath in the downy serviceberry. Like the redbud and dogwood, the shadbush is an understory tree, growing in the shade of the taller oaks and ashes, and it makes its best show at the edge of forest openings where it can grow without competition for light. It is the first of the Blue Ridge trio to bloom, opening clusters of thin-petaled, white flowers in March at the lowest elevations, but reaching its peak in April.

The redbud (*Cercis canadensis*) is one of the most unusual of eastern trees. It is a member of the huge legume family, as a close look at its small flowers will make clear—the lower "slipper" and three flaring wings look much like a pea blossom. The color is uniquely its own, however, for there is no other shade of pinkish-purple quite like it in the woods.

An exceptional specimen of redbud may grow to more than 50 feet, but most are half that size, scraggly little trees with dark red-brown bark flaking into scales, and glossy, purplish twigs that in April become covered with tightly packed flower clusters. Where the airy blooms of the shadbush fill the gaps between branches to form smoothly rounded crowns, the redbud flowers merely outline the meanderings of the tree's haphazard shape, and only where many grow close together, as along a road, does form become lost amid color.

The redbud is probably a relative newcomer to the slopes of the Blue Ridge. During the last ice age, just eighteen thousand years ago, the mountains were covered in spruce forests like those in northern New England and Canada today, and only gradually were replaced over the next ten thousand years by hardwoods as the climate warmed. Redbud is primarily a southern species, uncommon north of the Mason-Dixon line; even today it is most abundant at the middle and lower elevations of the Blue Ridge, leaving the higher reaches to the hardier shadbush.

Flowering dogwood (*Cornus florida*) may be the most famous of the mountain's blooming trees. It is also the latest of the three, opening only when spring is assured. Shadbush may shine in the barren, empty forest, but dogwood is at its best against a filigree of new green leaves.

The white "flowers" are not blossoms themselves, however, but large bracts, or specialized leaves, that frame the small, greenish true flowers at the center; it may be that the showy bracts serve as an advertisement and landing platform for insect pollinators. The four bracts start small and green, growing quickly in the mild spring weather. Most turn pure white with a touch of brown at the notched tip, but a rare few have a pale pink shade, more delicate than the cotton-candy hue of domestic pink dogwoods.

Tragically, dogwoods by the millions are dying in the Appalachians, victims of a disease known as dogwood anthracnose. First discovered in New York and Washington state in 1978, it has spread rapidly through the Northeast and Appalachians, killing dogwoods—especially those that grow in damp woods at elevations of more than 2,000 feet, like so many of the best mountain stands. The fungus, *Discula*, can be controlled with chemical fungicides, but this is obviously impractical (as well as environmentally risky) on a massive scale. Moreover, dogwoods that grow in sunny, warm spots and have ample supplies of water seem to be resistant to the blight, so many roadside trees (as well as those in backyards) are safe. Even more inexplicably, the fungus does not kill every tree in a stand, since some specimens seem to have a natural resistance. Botanists hope that these trees will live to repopulate ravaged areas, and have experimentally re-planted resistant saplings in Maryland's hard-hit Catoctin Mountains to test the theory. Even with help, though, it may be generations before the dogwood can completely recover in the worst-affected regions.

HOTSPOTS

More than 330 miles long, the ***Blue Ridge Parkway and Skyline Drive*** (as the road is known in Shenandoah National Park) offer an outstanding opportunity to see spring come to the Blue Ridge. Twisting and winding its way

Overlooking fertile valleys far below, a shadbush provides the earliest color in the Blue Ridge Mountains' spectacular spring-time display of flowering trees.

over mountains, threading gaps and plunging through tunnels, this two-lane road is virtually empty on weekdays, and even weekend crowds in April are a shadow of the hordes that come in summer and autumn.

It is difficult to single out any given stretch of the parkway or Skyline Drive, since altitude and latitude play such a great role in the timing of the bloom; the best show in the highest, most northerly elevations will obviously come days or weeks after the lower, southerly flanks have peaked. Far from being a problem for the visiting naturalist, however, this is an advantage, for one can porpoise through the seasons by climbing and descending the mountains.

In mid-April, for instance, the top of Thunder Ridge, more than 3,200 feet above sea level, looks like a page torn from winter, with leafless chestnut oaks trembling in the wind. Start down toward the James River valley to the northeast, and soon shadbush begin appearing along the roadsides, just opening their white flower heads. A little lower, and many more can be seen scattered on the surrounding hills, backlit by the sun and glowing, distant halos in the brown woods. Drop further, toward the "green line" of foliage that creeps a little higher up the mountain slopes each day. Here, the shadbush are joined by the first, tentative redbuds, which within a mile or so becomes a stunning corridor of pink-purple along Battery Creek.

If you can drag your eyes away from the redbuds, you'll notice the small, newly opened bracts of the dog-woods, still tinged with green. Finally, by the time the parkway comes to the James River and crosses to the Otter Creek drainage, the road is lined with snow-white dog-woods and redbuds, counterpoint to the kelly green of new tulip poplar leaves and the fuzzy buckskin of fresh oak foliage. The creeks flow along meadows of lush grass, past stands of mayapples and spring beauties. It is a remarkable transformation—and all within the space of a few miles and a couple thousand feet in elevation.

Wood Ducks

A male wood duck is a self-contained spectacle—a dazzle of blue, purple and green, buff, yellow and red, crested and bejeweled, sparkling iridescently in the spring sun. It has been called the loveliest waterbird in North America, and one would have to have a joyless soul indeed to argue with the judgment.

Thanks to conservation measures, the wood duck is one of the most common species of waterfowl in the forested Northeast, but this was not always the case. Excessive hunting in the nineteenth century, coupled with the frenetic logging that cleared the region of its old-growth timber, struck a deadly double blow to the wood duck. Of the two dangers, the logging may well have been the worst, since wood ducks, unlike most waterfowl, nest in tree cavities— and the scrubby second-growth trees that replaced the virgin forests were far too young to have developed the girth or heart-rot that creates hollows.

Protection against hunting came in the early days of the twentieth century, but the lack of breeding sites was a long-term problem, and while the population of wood ducks grew steadily through World War II, it was only after the placement of artificial nest boxes came into wide practice that wood duck numbers bounced back strongly.

A wood duck box is built along the same lines as a standard bluebird box, but pumped up several sizes larger—about 24 inches high and a foot square, with an oval entrance hole about 3 inches by 4, and a strip of hardware cloth nailed to the inside front to give the chicks something to grip when they climb out.

Whether in a natural cavity or man-made box, the wood duck pair seeks out a nest site in early spring, sometimes returning to the same hole year after year. The gaudy male steals most of the attention, but the hen woodie has a subtle beauty of her own, with a short crest that echoes her mate's and plumage of soft gray-brown, with a hint of violet iridescence. Wood ducks prefer streams, rivers and small lakes with timbered shores, especially if the forest is mature and rather open. Oaks provide acorns, a primary food, while sycamores, with their propensity for developing holes, are favored as nest sites, although a suitable tree a half mile or more from water may be chosen.

The female lays between ten and fifteen eggs, and nests with twice that many have been found, the result of one hen dumping her eggs in another's nest. The chicks hatch after more than a month of incubation and come out of the shell covered in down, eyes open and ready to go—*precocial*, in the jargon of ornithologists, and the opposite of helpless, blind altricial songbird chicks.

With her brood hatched, the hen flies from the nest hole to the ground and starts to call. Excited by their mother's vocalizations, the chicks scramble out of the cavity and launch themselves into the air, feet flailing and stubby, featherless wings spread. For a chick born in a nest box mounted just a few feet above the water, this leap is not a big deal, but wood ducks may nest in cavities 60 or more feet above the ground, and the chicks that innocently jump from this height bounce like rubber balls when they hit. Fortunately, they are never any worse for the wear, and within minutes the family is trailing along single file behind mom, heading for the water.

HOTSPOTS

The single best place in the region to watch wood ducks is **Great Swamp NWR** in north-central New Jersey, which supports one of the largest breeding populations in the mid-Atlantic states. This 7,000-acre expanse of swamps, cattail marshes and woodland cut by slow-moving streams is a paradise for woodies, made even more appealing by the nearly four hundred artificial nest boxes that the refuge staff has erected.

To reach Great Swamp NWR, take I-287 to Exit 26 (Basking Ridge). Coming off the exit ramp you will be on North Maple Avenue; continue straight through the light .5 mile later at Madisonville Road, ignoring the sign to the left for the refuge. Go another 2.1 miles on Maple, then make a left turn onto Lord Stirling Road, which becomes dirt for several hundred yards and then becomes White Bridge Road. Follow Lord Stirling/White Bridge for a total of 2.3 miles. At Pleasant Plains Road you can turn left and go .4 mile to refuge headquarters, which opens at 8 A.M. If the headquarters is not yet open, continue on White Bridge another 1.2 miles, making a left turn onto Long Hill Road. One mile up Long Hill, on the left, is the entrance for the boardwalks and wildlife observation center.

There are two boardwalks and observation blinds. The nearest, on the trail to the right, is .2 mile through fairly open cattail marsh; the other, on the boardwalk to the left, is reached after about a half mile of beautiful swamp, full of blueberries, wild iris, shadbush and trout lilies, and ends at a series of four small impoundments. At each, wood ducks are an all but sure thing, if you are early and quiet.

The blinds are among the most elaborate to be found on a national wildlife refuge, with room for a classroom of children, slanted viewing ports and carpeted floors to muffle sounds. Despite them, however, the waterfowl may be skittish, and the best observations are only possible if visitors speak in whispers and avoid moving too much (the birds can often see silhouettes moving in the slit openings). Even on weekdays bus loads of schoolchildren may begin arriving at midmorning, and when the first tide hits the boardwalk, the shyer birds retreat. So try to arrive as soon after daybreak as possible.

The boardwalks are situated in the western, actively managed half of the refuge, and they are all that most visitors ever see of Great Swamp. This is a shame, because the eastern half of the refuge is a federally designated wilderness area, with three trails and spurs totaling 8 miles that meander through it. Here, it is possible to lose the background noises of civilization completely, surrounded by dense forests that recreate a sense of what primeval New Jersey must have been like.

A further attraction at Great Swamp is the refuge's bluebird population, the largest in the Garden State. Reduced to two or three pairs in the 1970s, the bluebirds now raise more than 120 chicks each year in roughly fifty boxes placed in the refuge's meadows and fields.

Other excellent wood duck areas are *Erie NWR* (see Chapter 17), the central wetlands at *Presque Isle State Park* (Chapter 2) and *Hartstown Swamp* and *Conneaut Marsh* (Chapter 26), all in Pennsylvania, as well as *Huntley Meadows Park* (Chapter 17) in Virginia.

20

Breakout: Amphibian Courtship

It starts, as do most things in nature, quietly. As the sun disappears and twilight takes hold of the marsh on a mild, early spring evening, there is a period of silence, after the last robin's chuckle, after the last red-wing's song—a space of time filled only by the wind in the naked treetops. Then comes a single, reedy voice, a squeaking soprano hidden in the flooded grass. It may sing alone for a time, but always there comes a second, and a third, then a rush of sound as dozens or hundreds more join in, all calling the same, ascending *Pree-e-e-p! Pree-e-e-p!*

Early in the month the chorus may be undiluted, but most nights a humming trill weaves its notes among the higher melody, and a bass line snores and groans and plunks like loose banjo strings. It is the sound of spring, as much as any oriole's song—the sound of sex, amphibian style.

Besides birds, no other group of vertebrates has made song such an integral part of courtship as have the frogs and toads. Each species has its own unique tone and rhythm, enabling the males to call for mates from the concealing cover of darkness. Of course, a raccoon can hear a frog's croak as easily as another frog, so many species breed explosively, gathering in great concentrations and getting the whole business out of the way in a matter of days, thus minimizing the exposure to predators.

Wood frogs, the earliest to breed, are an example of such an explosive species. The first mild days of spring, sometimes in late February and March, are enough to coax these small, brown frogs with black bandit's masks out of hibernation. They seek out woodland wetlands, often gathering in vernal ponds, the ephemeral pools of rainwater and snowmelt that collect in depressions through the forest, and will evaporate by midsummer. Wood frogs do not croak—few frogs do. Rather, they quack very much like ducks, and this unexpected sound makes them easy to overlook.

The sexes are virtually identical, so sound and behavior provide the recognition clues between male and female. The male wood frogs have paired vocal sacs between the jaw and front legs, which they inflate at each call, producing the dry, creaking song. Male frogs and toads will grab any other individual that comes near, attempting to hold the passerby just ahead of the hind legs in the grip known as amplexus. Held so, a female will extrude her eggs, which the male fertilizes externally. If he should grab a male by mistake, however, the offended party gives a special call and indignantly writhes free.

Hundreds of wood frogs may seem to descend on a vernal pool overnight (actually, many will have ascended, having spent the winter in the mud below ground). Unlike many species that wait until darkness to breed, the wood frogs reach a fever pitch at midday, with pairs locked in amplexus floating on the surface of the water. Within a day or so, most of the females have laid their eggs, producing gelatinous masses anchored to sticks and dead reeds. A few days after that, if the weather has stayed mild, the pool will be empty of all but a few holdout males, still quacking to a vanished audience.

The spring peeper takes a much more prolonged approach to procreation. With its huge voice, impossible to miss by anyone within a half mile of the marsh, this minute tree frog is often thought to be the earliest of the spring frogs, but it usually follows the wood frogs by a week or more. Peepers are quite small, about the size of a lima bean, and in spring they can be found in grassy wetlands, damp meadows and cattail marshes, usually near woodlands where they spend the rest of the year.

Finding a peeper marsh is as easy as following your ears. Finding a peeper, on the other hand, can be maddening. Unlike wood frogs, which call from the open, male peepers hide out beneath collapsed mats of marsh grass or deep inside clumps of sedges. Worse, when a human slogs into the marsh with a flashlight and hip boots, the whole chorus may fall silent.

Be patient. Turn off the light and wait quietly, and eventually the frogs will start calling again—more quickly on mild nights, less enthusiastically if the temperature is below 55° F. Once they are again in full voice, turn on the light but do not move; this new intrusion may cause another interruption in the singing, but for a much shorter period. Once the peepers are accustomed to the light, you should be able to move slowly without disturbing them. Force your ears to filter the cacophony of sound and pinpoint a nearby peeper, then gently lift the concealing vegetation until you uncover him. Two searchers, working in tandem, can triangulate a peeper's location more easily than a single person.

Taken by surprise, the little male will let his vocal sac sag to a shapeless mass beneath his chin, but most peepers are more concerned with sex than safety and usually resume calling soon enough. With each series of piercing peeps, the sac fills with air forced up from the body, transforming it into a gray balloon. In addition to attracting females with the standard, single-note call, male peepers also warn away intruding males with a staccato trill if they feel their small territory is being invaded.

Some weeks after the peepers have begun calling, on a night of warm rain, the country roads come alive with American toads heading for the breeding pools. Dumpy and squat, toads have freed themselves of a year-round dependency on standing water, but they must still return to it to reproduce. Far more obvious in their courtship than most frogs, the toads take up positions in the shallows; the males rear back, with a low trill coming from their white vocal sacs. Once in amplexus, the female extrudes coiled ropes of eggs, which on contact with water become encased in protective "jelly"; the rope may be several feet long, containing thousands of eggs, and is usually tangled with the strands from dozens of other females.

Depending on locale and habitat, the breeding pond may also host green frogs, whose *ker-plunk!* call is heard all spring and summer; pickerel and leopard frogs, both of which have a snoring song heard only during the spring breeding season; Fowler's toads along the coastal plain giving their short, bleating call from late spring through summer; and the bullfrog with its famous *jug-o-rum*, a feature of summer ponds. The last in the progression of amphibian singers is the gray tree frog, which does not begin to trill from shrubs and bushes near woodland pools until early summer and continues through autumn.

Many naturalists across North America—indeed, around the world—have noticed a drastic decline in some amphibian populations, with frogs and toads especially hard hit. No one is sure what is causing the drop in numbers or can explain why some populations have vanished while others nearby have remained unharmed. Acid precipitation and increased ultraviolet radiation due to ozone thinning have been suggested for blame, but the reason is still a worrisome mystery.

MAY

May Observations

21

Horseshoe Crabs and Shorebirds

Rarely do the fragile, global dependencies of nature show themselves as clearly, or with such awe-provoking spectacle, as happens each May on the gentle shores of the Delaware Bay. On these sand beaches the springtime invasions of breeding horseshoe crabs and migrating shorebirds converge, uniting continents with two biological tides that create, for a few short weeks, an unforgettable sight.

The onset of spring reaches even the deep waters of the bay, where the horseshoe crabs spend the winter. Not crabs at all, they are members of the genus *Limulus*, a group with an ancient lineage dating back more than 350 million years. Commonly referred to as "living fossils," horseshoe crabs are nothing of the sort, for that term implies obsolescence, and these unusual creatures are perfectly suited to their environment.

There is no mistaking a horseshoe crab for anything else on the beach. The carapace is domed and gray and, as the name suggests, is shaped somewhat like the hoof of a horse, with a round front and two tapered points jutting back. The crab's body is hinged in the middle and ends in a long, spiked tail; two widely spaced eyes sit like bumps on either side of the carapace. The crab's appearance is off-putting to many people, especially if the tide has flipped the animal over, revealing ten waving legs, each tipped with small pincers, and the flapping brown pages of the crab's book gills. But looks aside, the horseshoe crab is utterly harmless; the pincers lack the power of a blue crab's claws, and the tail spike, which looks so daunting, is nothing more than a brace the crab uses for righting itself when upside down.

Although mature horseshoe crabs live most of the year in deep water, they breed in the intertidal zone, so the lengthening days of spring trigger a migration to the shallows. By mid-May there are millions of horseshoe crabs milling about just off the beaches of the Delaware Bay, waiting for the "spring" tide, which in fact has nothing to do with the season. Each month, at the new and full moons, the tide rises to its highest levels. This is the signal the crabs have been waiting for, and they swarm onto the sand in answer to it. At low tide the beach can seem empty, except for the dead and dying crabs left stranded by the last tidal change. But as the water begins to rise, a few gray shells appear in the gentle surf, and as the tide creeps upward, a solid rank of horseshoe crabs marches in with it—more and more crabs until, at high tide, the waves must slosh through layers of *Limulus* to reach the beach.

The females are the larger of the sexes, and most crawl ashore towing one or more males, which grip her shell using special, hooked claspers on the first pair of legs; occasionally a female may drag up to a half dozen males behind her. The crabs move to the high-water mark, where the female digs a nest in the sand and lays several thousand eggs, each greenish and about an eighth of an inch in diameter; the male (or males) fertilize them, and the nest is covered. The sheer fecundity is astonishing—in some places the beach may seem to be more eggs than sand, and the tide may deposit windrows of eggs yards wide and a half foot thick. But this is not biological extravagance, for few of the eggs will survive to the spring tide in June when the highest tides return to trigger hatching.

At the same time that the horseshoe crabs are beginning their landward movements, the changing ratio of daylight and darkness is causing restlessness half a world away, in South America. A large percentage of North America's shorebird population winters in the Southern Hemisphere, and these birds—red knots, ruddy turnstones, semipalmated sandpipers and others—are feeling the urge to head north to their breeding grounds in the Arctic. In May they take off in huge flocks, many leaving land on the northeastern coast of South America and cutting straight across the Caribbean and the Atlantic.

They will not hit land again until they reach the mid-Atlantic coast, a distance of about 2,000 miles. They cannot rest on the ocean without sinking, so the flight must be nonstop, about 80 hours of constantly pumping muscles and laboring lungs. Fat reserves built up through weeks of feeding vanish, and by the time the birds drop in to land, they are emaciated and near death from exhaustion and starvation. They need food in abundance—and the crab eggs are waiting for them. Without the crabs, the shorebirds would suffer devastating losses; without clean water and protected beaches, the crabs would perish. It is a union of time, place and biological circumstance so delicate it takes one's breath away.

It is visually intoxicating as well. Up to a million shorebirds pass through here each spring and, at times, the flocks of birds can literally blanket the beaches, hiding the sand beneath a shifting mat of feathers and beaks as they jockey for position. Each species flocks with its own members—ten thousand red knots forming the core, say, with a similar number of semipalmated sandpipers providing a gray counterpoint to the knots' orange-red breasts, thousands of turnstones skittering around the periphery, and swaths of black and white where several thousand

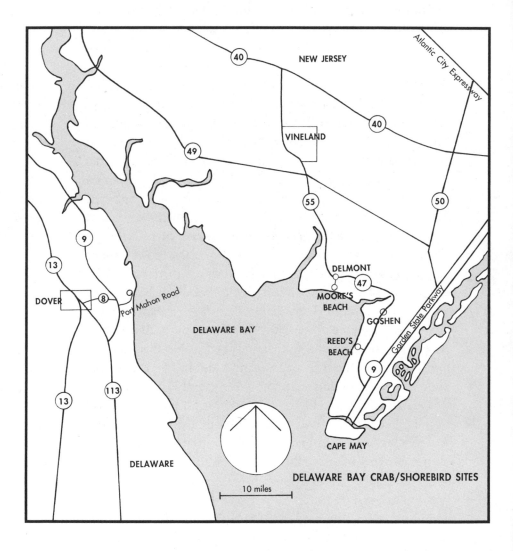

DELAWARE BAY CRAB/SHOREBIRD SITES

laughing gulls have found an especially rich cache of eggs. The noise of screaming birds and rushing wings is beyond description, a symphony without harmony or a score. Periodically the birds are startled—maybe by the sight of a migrating peregrine falcon, maybe a false alarm—and the entire beach takes wing with the sound of gale winds.

A calendar and a tide chart will help you plan a visit to the bay to catch the peak activity, which will fall several days before and after the full or new moon in the second half of May; there will be crabs and birds on the beach through early June, although not in the same numbers. High tide brings out the greatest numbers of crabs and tends to concentrate the shorebirds in dense, spectacular flocks. Binoculars, a spotting scope and good field guide are essential equipment, as is insect repellent, since midges and mosquitoes are also products of the fertile bay ecosystem.

Above all else, bring a healthy dose of respect and circumspection to the beach with you. The shorebirds spend an average of just fourteen days along the bay, feeding constantly to double their weight for the next leg of their journey to the Arctic. They walk a very fine edge of survival, and each time the flocks are disturbed by a thoughtless person walking the beach, or creeping too close for pictures, the birds waste energy and precious moments. Be considerate also of those humans who have their homes along the shore. The decks and patios of beachfront homes may make excellent observation posts, but they are private property and should not be used without specific permission from the owners. In recent years, as word of the spectacle has spread and more and more people have come each spring to witness it, tensions have been rising between visitors and residents who are understandably upset at such rude behavior.

The importance of the Delaware Bay to North America's shorebirds can hardly be overstated; more than 80 percent of the East's red knots pass through it, for example.

Fortunately, the need for protection has been recognized, and critical staging grounds here and in South America, Alaska and Washington are being preserved. State agencies in Delaware and New Jersey have in recent years been acquiring land on both sides of the bay, and much of the New Jersey acreage is being incorporated into the new Cape May NWR; the Delaware Bay was also the first site to be designated under the Western Hemisphere Shorebird Reserve Network. Water quality is less easy to protect, and an oil spill in the heavily traveled bay could be disastrous.

HOTSPOTS

Horseshoe crabs and shorebirds may be found almost anywhere along the bay's shorelines in Delaware and New Jersey, but the easiest access to large concentrations are found at a few spots in each state.

New Jersey has two marvelous locations, **Reed's Beach** on the Cape May peninsula, and **Moore's Beach** to the north, near the town of Delmont. Reed's Beach is a small community off Route 47; northbound 13.7 miles from Cape May, watch for a sign marking a left turn to Reed's Beach. Go 1 mile to the bay, where the cottage-lined road makes a dogleg to the right to parallel the beach. The birds often feed in the town itself. Park on the side of the road away from the beach and stay behind the dunes (better yet, watch from in your car). Another good location is at the far end of the road, about a mile beyond town, where the state has parking areas and interpretive displays including an observation platform and species tally board. The jetty nearby is a good spot to sit and watch the flocks stream overhead, passing between Reed's Beach and the distant sandbars. Do not, however, approach the beach if there are flocks of shorebirds feeding nearby.

Moore's Beach is 15 miles north of Reed's Beach on Route 47 and 1.7 miles south of the state prison complex. Turn at the Moore's Beach sign and go 1.9 miles past homes and through the Heislerville/Dennis Creek WMA, through a vast expanse of tidal marsh. Large flocks of sanderlings, knots and turnstones frequent the beach; the best viewing area is the 100 yards from the end of the road to the cluster of trailers, but it pays to walk west several hundred yards along a trail through the phragmites reeds, where the creek enters the bay. At low tide the tidal guts along the access road are jammed with crabs and excellent numbers of birds, including impressive flocks of least sandpipers, as well as dunlins, long- and short-billed dowitchers, greater and lesser yellowlegs, semipalmated plovers and willets.

In Delaware, ***Port Mahon Road*** offers some of the best viewing; directions are found in Chapter 2. These Delaware Bay hotspots, while the most spectacular, are not the only places where large numbers of shorebirds can be seen. For other suggestions that are worthwhile in May, see the hotspots listed in Chapter 36.

Lost in the shuffle, a laughing gull forages for horseshoe crab eggs among thousands of red knots at Reed's Beach, New Jersey.

22

Landbird Migration

The night sky in spring is alive with movement, cloaked by darkness and altitude, and hidden from the sleeping humans far below. Clues sometimes leak past the mask, however, giving a hint of the grand passage above—the sound of chirps and twitters falling from the twilight, or the flash of small forms across the face of the full moon, just a millisecond's impression of beating wings.

It may seem odd that songbirds that are for most of the year diurnal (that is, active by day) should choose to migrate over a far-flung course by night, but the reasons make sense. As small-plane pilots know, the night air is usually much calmer and less turbulent, making the flight less tiresome and less wasteful of precious energy. Hawks do not hunt at night. Also, the night sky, painted with the patterns of constellations, apparently provides a road map for migrating songbirds, helping them navigate across thousands of miles.

Depending on the species, the spring migration may be short (such as a robin that moves a few miles from a swampy woodland to a backyard) or epic (like the many songbirds that winter in Central and South America but breed in the subarctic). Routes vary as well; many follow the Central American isthmus, which provides dry land and food the whole way, while others take a more direct, overwater path, crossing the Gulf of Mexico or island-hopping across the Caribbean.

Once on the North American land mass, the migrants are liable to spread out in broad fronts, moving at night and dropping out of the sky at daybreak to feed frantically. These waves of songbirds, mostly warblers and vireos, are the seasonal high point for many birders. Their appearance is unpredictable, except in a few places where geography conspires to concentrate the migrants.

Large bodies of water act as both barriers and pathways for migrating songbirds, which will follow the shoreline if possible or wait for ideal conditions to cross if necessary. So it is that the peninsula of Presque Isle, which juts from the south shore of Lake Erie, serves as a staging ground for landbirds preparing for the 40-mile crossing to Long Point on the Ontario side. Likewise, birds that have just flown across the 13 miles of Delaware Bay land, hungry and tired, on Cape May, another of the so-called landbird traps in the region.

The landbird migration has a definite sequence, beginning with the first major push of yellow-rumped, palm and pine warblers in early to mid-April and peaking the first two weeks of May. Obviously, there is a lag as the waves flow north to south, with any given species apt to be seen in southern Virginia as much as one or two weeks before it appears in, say, Presque Isle.

The best times for birding are from first light until about 9 A.M., when the level of activity drops noticeably. Rarely does one encounter flocks of only one species; usually the birds move in mixed batches, and a tree may hold a half dozen or more varieties. Even while feeding, the flocks usually continue to move—and as often as not, their direction is to the north, pulled by the instinctive urge to return to the breeding grounds as quickly as possible.

HOTSPOTS

Lake Erie presents a sizable barrier to songbirds, which understandably look for the easiest way across. For many the jump-off point is **Presque Isle**, a curving peninsula just north of the city of Erie and a birding wonderland any time of the year—especially in spring. For general directions to Presque Isle State Park, see Chapter 2.

At the peak of the migration, and especially during periods of bad weather that trap the birds on Presque Isle, virtually every tree on the peninsula can be full of songbirds, but there are some areas that consistently produce superior results. From the park office go 3.5 miles along the loop road (marked variously as Marina Drive, East Fisher Road, Thompson Drive and Pine Tree Road on the park map) to Misery Bay, an excellent area for mergansers and other diving ducks, while Grave Yard Pond across the road is home to wood ducks, great blue herons and other wetland species. The woodlands in this area also hold large numbers of songbirds.

Just past the turn for the Coast Guard station, park in the paved turnout at Thompson Circle and follow an unmarked path across the road, which passes between two small ponds. This is a good place to look for Virginia rails and other marsh birds, and the shrubby birch, willow and honeysuckle forest is usually full of warblers and vireos. The path ends at Thompson Bay, with the isolated Bird Sanctuary across the water.

Return to the road and walk north along the marsh to the parking lot for Bundy Beach (unmarked); the trees along the road are excellent for songbirds. The entrance to the Bird Sanctuary is at the far right corner of the first parking lot. Another 1.9 miles along the loop road is the north trailhead for the Sidewalk Trail, with a large map of the park's trails. Presque Isle has a surprising number of interesting trails— it also, unfortunately, has one of the worst-marked systems in the region, so be alert at all intersections. Because the park is relatively small it is impossible to get truly lost, but wrong turns are annoyingly easy to make.

Follow the thin pavement of the Sidewalk Trail about 100 yards, then turn right onto the Marsh Trail, which bisects the Cranberry Pond marsh. At the far side, turn left immediately onto the Fox Trail, which follows a sand ridge, eventually becoming Ridge Trail (not shown on current trail maps). In addition to migrants, this area has a healthy population of red-headed woodpeckers, an unusual bird for such a northern site. At the far end of Ridge Pond (on the left), the trail rejoins the Sidewalk Trail. Turn left to return to the north trailhead, a total distance of about 2 miles, or turn right a short distance to Thompson Drive on Misery Bay.

Like Presque Isle, the *Cape May* peninsula is often so awash in songbirds that a naturalist will be happy almost anywhere, but three locations stand out. *Higbee Beach WMA*, at the western edge of the cape near the Intracoastal Waterway, has trails through a mixture of dunes, bayberry thickets, forests, brushy fields, ponds and freshwater marshes—in other words, just the right mix for the greatest variety of birds. For directions to Cape May and Higbee Beach, see Chapter 3; an especially rich trail goes south from the parking area past a hawk-watch platform toward Davey's Lake. On a fine May morning there will be indigo buntings, white-eyed vireos, Carolina wrens, cardinals, yellow-breasted chats, yellow warblers, ruby-throated hummingbirds and dozens of other species, feeding voraciously after a night of migrating.

Along Bayshore Road (Route 607), .6 mile north of Sunset Boulevard and 1.1 miles south of Route 641 (New England Road), an old railroad bed crosses the road. West along the rail path is the "*Beanery*," an almost legendary spot for songbird watching, and traditionally good for rarities and extralimital species. Another excellent area, with a wheelchair-accessible boardwalk, is next to the hawk-watch platform at *Cape May Point State Park*, on Lighthouse Avenue south of Sunset Boulevard; detailed directions to the park are also found in Chapter 3.

At the western anchor of the Chesapeake Bay Bridge near Annapolis, **Sandy Point State Park** juts out into the northern bay from Maryland's Western Shore. Especially on days with strong west winds, the point acts as a landbird trap, concentrating songbirds in the park's old oaks, pines and shrubbier woodlands. Take I-95 to Route 50 East; go 26.5 miles to the last exit before the toll bridge. Turn left at the stop sign at the end of the exit ramp and follow the signs to the park. East Beach and South Beach are linked by a trail that cuts through marsh and has a low observation platform; other trails wind through the wooded sections of the park to the northwest.

23

Spring Wildflower Trails

As April fades into May, the character of the spring bloom of wildflowers changes—sometimes subtly, sometimes dramatically.

In many parts of the region, the white, showy blossoms of the large-flowered trillium (*Trillium grandiflorum*) are a trademark of May's early weeks. One of the most spectacular of North American wild plants, the trillium bears a snow-white flower with three petals—in fact, almost everything about the trillium is in multiples of three, from the flowers to the leaves to the sepals. The plant ranges in height to about 15 inches, with flowers up to 4 inches wide. A clump of three or four growing picturesquely beside a fallen log is enough to make any passing naturalist stop for a second look.

Even more arresting, however, are thousands and thousands of large-flowered trilliums filling the woods like so much snow—an extravagance that can be seen at a number of places, particularly in western Pennsylvania and in Shenandoah National Park. At the weird wilderness in West Virginia known as Dolly Sods, the attraction is several miles of nearly solid wild bleeding heart, growing like ferns beneath a stunted forest.

In other spots, no single species dominates the forest; instead, the visitor finds a diversity of wildflowers, from the uniquely shaped spathes of jack-in-the-pulpits to the pastel blossoms of the showy orchis and pink lady's-slipper, two of the region's wild orchids.

Habitat, elevation and latitude, among other factors, play crucial roles in determining what species of wildflower will be found along any given trail. Generally speaking, the most diverse communities of spring flowers occur in moist, floodplain forests composed of deciduous trees; because the hardwoods do not leaf out fully until the middle of spring, the flowers have full exposure to the sun, without the intervening canopy of leaves. In the wettest places, where the ground is boggy or partly submerged, there will be nonblooming skunk cabbage and false hellebore, as well as northern white violets, blue flag iris and other water-tolerant plants. On higher, better-drained ground grow spring beauty, blue phlox, sessile trillium, foamflower, trout lily, Dutchman's breeches and wood anemone. Large-flowered trillium prefers slopes and uplands, while the driest roadsides may hold dwarf larkspur and vivid fire pinks.

HOTSPOTS

In the fashionable Pittsburgh suburb of Fox Chapel, an especially stunning stand of large-flowered trillium has been pampered and nurtured for years. Known as **Trillium Trail**, it has a slightly manicured appearance that is more than compensated for by the eye-popping expanse of trillium that flows over and down the wooded hillside. *T. grandiflorum* so completely dominates the scene that it is easy to miss other bloomers such as stonecrop, bluebells and cut-leaved toothwort. Watch especially for white-phase red trillium, which have a smaller, slightly nodding flower, compared to the erect, "rippled" petals of the large-flowered trillium.

Trillium Trail is just north of Pittsburgh; take Route 28 to Exit 8 (Fox Chapel). At the stop sign at the end of the exit ramp turn left and go .9 mile, then bear left again onto Squaw Run Road another 1.2 miles. The first of two parking lots for Trillium Trail is on the right, just past the intersection with Squaw Run Road East. Avoid weekend visits if at all possible, although the heaviest crowds do not arrive until midmorning.

Equally remarkable are the expanses of trillium at **Wolf Creek Narrows Natural Area** near Slippery Rock, Pennsylvania. Even better, the setting is much wilder and less controlled than at Trillium Trail, with a steep-sided gorge of hemlock and hardwoods. Even the casual observer can find two or three dozen species of wildflowers, starting with a fine stand of bluebells (including the unusual pink phase), squirrel corn, foamflower, Dutchman's breeches, wild geranium and dwarf ginseng beneath the sycamores at the trailhead. Farther upstream, the sky blue of the bluebells is gradually replaced by the slightly more purple hue of blue phlox, and farther still, large-flowered trillium begins to appear on the hillside until it covers the ground in many areas.

From I-79, take Route 108 East to Slippery Rock. Turn left onto Route 258 North and go less than .1 mile, turning left onto Water Street. Go 1.7 miles to the bridge over Wolf Creek; the small parking area is on the left just beyond the bridge. Park and walk back over the creek and take the trail, which starts on your left and is marked with white blazes. At the fork, about 300 yards upstream, continue straight along the creek. The trail, which forms a 1.5-mile loop, eventually leaves the stream and climbs steeply to the uplands, where for a quarter mile the thickest concentrations of trillium are found. Here, no other flowers compete with the snowy blossoms, which form a discrete layer of white above the green foliage.

In Virginia, the most accessible areas of large-flowered trillium are along the Skyline Drive in **Shenandoah National Park**. By late April the trillium are blooming in lower elevations, like along the scenic South River Falls Trail near milepost 62.8, but the biggest masses on the ridgetop do not come into their glory until the first week of May. The best show is found between South River and Big Meadows, with the heaviest concentrations between South River and Lewis Mountain Campground. Although the trillium will have faded to pink by this time along the South River Falls Trail, this 3.5-mile path has dozens of other species of May wildflowers, including scattered showy orchis, and is good for such hardwood birds as worm-eating warbler, American redstarts and rose-breasted grosbeaks, and phoebes nesting within arm's reach of the 83-foot waterfall.

Getting to the 10,000-acre **Dolly Sods Wilderness**, in northeastern West Virginia, takes some doing, but the trip is worthwhile at any time of the year, and especially so in early May, when the wild bleeding heart comes into bloom. With its feathery foliage this plant can easily be mistaken for a dense fern—until the flower stalks rise up with their dangling, pink-red blossoms hanging down in loose clusters. Each wild bleeding heart flower is composed of two fused spurs that form a tiny heart with outstretched wings, a clear indication of this species' close relationship to Dutchman's breeches and squirrel corn.

Although the Sods (a local name for grassy openings in the forest) look wild and pristine, they are actually a product of human greed. A virgin forest of red spruce and hemlock was clear-cut around the turn of the century and, once the thick humus layer beneath dried out, it and the timber slashings caught fire. In the conflagration that followed, the soil was burned off right down to the sandstone boulders that were once 7 or 8 feet below ground, and the forest was set back to an early stage of succession. Today, Dolly Sods is a mix of open balds, young spruce forests (which look even younger than they are because this mountaintop environment does not encourage rapid growth) and stunted deciduous forests. It is in this last habitat, beneath maples and birch, where the wind brings a gentle snow of falling shadbush petals, that the bleeding hearts grow, forming elfin gardens among the mossy rocks and mats of clubmosses and ferns. In large swaths of woods, the bleeding hearts are the dominant forest floor plant.

To reach the Sods from the east, take Route 28 from Petersburg 10.2 miles. Turn right onto Route 4 North/Jordan Run Road, go 1 mile and turn left onto Route 19. Follow this uphill 6.2 miles to the junction with Road 75, a right, which extends 8.1 miles through the Dolly Sods scenic area, ending at Bear Rocks. Bleeding heart may be found anywhere in the hardwood forest, but the greatest concentrations are a mile or so on either side of the gated pull-off to Bell Knob Tower. To reach Road 75 from the north and west, take Route 32 south from Canaan Valley State Park 1.4 miles, turning left onto East Lanesville Road, a hidden turn at the far end of a road cut. Follow East Lanesville 4.5 miles, bear left at the fork, go another 1.3 miles and cross the bridge into the wilderness area. The intersection with Road 75 is an additional 4 miles uphill.

In central Pennsylvania, the rich, damp woodlands of **Canoe Creek State Park** boasts a stand of more than one thousand yellow lady's-slipper orchids, growing with such other spring wildflowers as long-spurred and yellow violets, fringed polygala, wild columbine and golden Alexanders. To reach the park, take Route 22 East from Altoona 6 miles, turning left into the park entrance. Drive to the last parking area and follow Lime Kiln Trail; past the kilns, watch on the uphill side of the trail for the lady's-slippers, which are spread out along a roughly half mile stretch.

24

Acres of Blossoms

While the preceding chapter dealt with locations where the best displays of spring wildflowers may be seen, there are two floral displays in May that deserve special consideration. Each is a plant near the edge of its range—one overlapping from the west, the other usually more northern—and each produces a magnificent spectacle.

In the extreme southwest corner of Pennsylvania, Enlow Fork, a tributary of Wheeling Creek, has formed a rich floodplain in the surrounding forest. As is so often the case, the creek system serves as a biological conduit, allowing trees, shrubs and herbaceous plants from the south and west to penetrate the wooded hills, with their more northerly plant communities. Pawpaws, redbud and yellow oak are among the fringe species that have threaded their way east and north, but each May the blue-eyed Mary steals the show, as it does another 40 miles to the northeast at Guffy Hollow, a sheltered glen above the Youghiogheny River.

A member of the snapdragon family, blue-eyed Mary (*Collinsia verna*) is a dainty, lovely plant native to the central United States and a few places along the western Appalachians. Thin and airy, the stalks have paired, opposite leaves, while the small flowers are bicolored, the upper two lobes white and the lower a clear shade of blue. Individually, a single plant would be easy to overlook, but blue-eyed Mary grows in masses that can cover acres, flooding the open woodlands with color. The peak comes the first week in May—not because the flowers do not last longer (they do), but because the fast-growing understory of waterleaf and other plants soon crowds out the blue-eyed Mary.

Even though a species may be common elsewhere in its range, it makes sense to preserve peripheral populations like the Enlow Fork tract, since those growing around the fringe of a species' range often exhibit greater genetic diversity than core populations. Because of its limited range in Pennsylvania, blue-eyed Mary is listed as a species of special concern in that state, and the Enlow Fork Natural Area, part of State Game Lands 302, is being managed to preserve it and other unusual plants. Efforts are also underway to gain recognition for Guffy Hollow as an area of unusual natural interest.

Completely across Pennsylvania in the Poconos, May also brings a floral event of a different kind. Here, in a unique dwarf oak barrens, grows the shrub known as rhodora (*Rhododendron canadense*). Common in bogs, along lake edges and on mountain slopes through New England and Canada, this dwarf rhododendron reaches one of the most southerly points of its distribution in the vicinity of Long Pond in Monroe County, where it grows in numbers that rival the best stands farther north.

At the Long Pond Barrens, the rhodora peak usually comes around the beginning of the third week of May, somewhat earlier if the spring has been unusually warm. Unlike mountain laurel or rhododendron, rhodora blossoms do not last very long, and a heavy rain may wash much of the show away. In addition, the intensity of the bloom varies from year to year, but even in poor years it is worth seeing, and a good season is nothing less than magnificent.

HOTSPOTS

To find **Enlow Fork**, take I-70 West from Washington, Pennsylvania, to Exit 2 (Route 231/Claysville). Coming off the exit ramp, turn right at the stop sign and immediately right again at the T-intersection onto Route 40 East. Go .7 mile to Claysville and turn right onto Route 231 South, which is partially hidden by a church on the corner. Follow 231 for 3.7 miles to an intersection by a small store, bearing right and uphill from 231, which goes straight and downhill. Follow this unnamed road for 8.3 miles to the village of West Finley; turn left at the stop sign, go 2.4 miles and cross a concrete bridge. Just on the other side, turn right over an iron, wood-decked bridge onto a dirt road. Follow the dirt road for 1.9 miles, turning right at the sign for state game lands. Go an additional 1.2 miles and stop in the flat parking area across the creek.

While there are patches of blue-eyed Mary along the entrance route, these do not prepare you for the first glimpse of the major stands, which are along Enlow Fork itself. Follow the dirt road past the metal gate and to the left, around the wide floodplain meadow; the road then bends sharply left around the foot of a ridge, crosses the creek on a large bridge and continues on through the woods.

This entire area is carpeted with blue-eyed Mary, growing thickly with a who's who of other spring wildflowers—large-flowered, red and purple-phase sessile trillium; blue phlox, dwarf larkspur, wild geranium, fire pink, smooth yellow and pale violet, swamp buttercup, stonecrop, ragwort and much more. The flowers grow so heavily, in fact, that it is often impossible to step off the road or trails without crushing them underfoot. The white-barked trunks of sycamores rise like Greek columns over the natural garden, lending a cathedral air to the scene.

The trout fishing is excellent, the birding equally good (cerulean warblers, redstarts, northern orioles, rose-breasted grosbeaks) and the wildflowers sublime—Enlow Fork is a place to pass a lazy, early May day, with a picnic lunch and a few friends.

CAUTION: *Enlow Fork is a state game land and is open to spring turkey hunting from the end of April through late May, with heavy hunting on Saturdays. The danger is minimal, but it would be prudent to avoid wearing blue or red (the colors of a gobbler's head) and don't try to sneak up on what sounds like a turkey, since it might be a concealed hunter using a call.*

Blue-eyed Mary is also very much in evidence at **Guffy Hollow**, part of which is included in **Braddock Trail Park**, a township facility. This unique area is known as a Carolinian exposure, a dry, wooded hollow underlaid with limestone, and home for a number of plants near the eastern and northern edges of their range, including blue-eyed Mary and large numbers of snow trillium, which bloom in early March. The trail leading through the hollow follows a creek with a number of small but extremely scenic waterfalls, but the best area for blue-eyed Mary is near the main entrance to the park.

From the Pennsylvania Turnpike, take Exit 7 to Route 30 West, getting into the left lane. At the first traffic light turn left into the Norwin Hills Shopping Center lot and drive all the way through to the far end. Make a right turn uphill onto Barnes Lake Road and drive 2 miles to the intersection with Clay Pike. Turn right and go .7 mile, turning left at the traffic light onto Guffy Road. Follow Guffy for 1.7 miles as the road descends into the hollow, then make the first right onto Mickinin Road. After turning onto Mickinin, make a left at the top of the hill and drive to the parking lot at the Braddock Trail Park entrance.

Walk past the traffic barricade and down the closed section of the road. The main trail cuts across the road

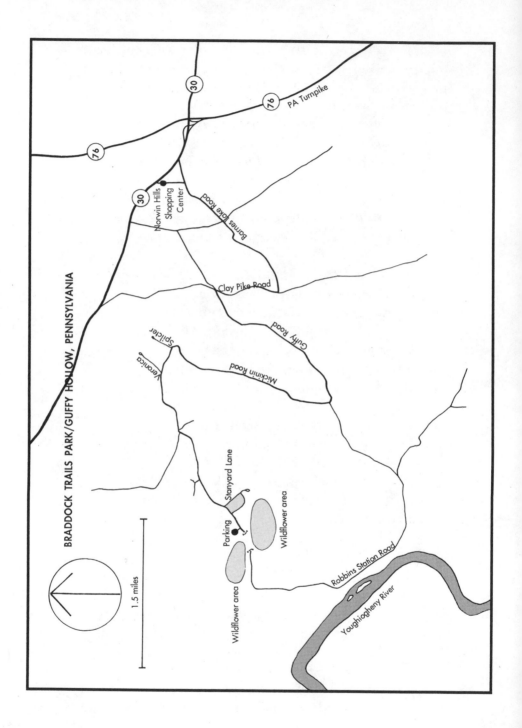

BRADDOCK TRAILS PARK/GUFFY HOLLOW, PENNSYLVANIA

1.5 miles

30
76
76
30
PA Turnpike

Norwin Hills Shopping Center

Barnes Lake Road

Clay Pike Road

Guffy Road

Spitzer

Veronica

Micknin Road

Stanyard Lane

Parking

Wildflower area

Wildflower area

Robbins Station Road

Youghiogheny River

several hundred yards below the parking lot; there is lots of blue-eyed Mary in this area, especially along the branch of the trail to the right, while the area to the left has a variety of flowers.

To see the rhodora bloom at **Long Pond Barrens**, take I-80 to Exit 43, then go south on Route 115 toward the Pocono International Speedway. Approximately 4 miles beyond the speedway, turn left onto Kukenbucher Road (shown as Neval Drive on some maps); go 2 miles, crossing Tunkhannock Creek and turning right on the far side of the bridge onto an unmarked dirt road. Drive another 1.5 miles to an orange gate on the left—park without blocking the gate. The barrens, of scrub oak, pitch pine, blueberry, sheep laurel and rhodora, begin just beyond the gate. Follow the dirt track past the gate along the northwest edge of the barrens, turning right at the first fork; the best stands of rhodora are along this end of the barrens. At the next fork, turn aside to the left to see Grass Lake, an unusual glacial pond popular with fishermen and waterbirds.

The white blossoms of large-flowered trillium carpet the ground at Trillium Trail just outside Pittsburgh, one of several wildflower trails that reach their peak in May.

25

Breakout:
Spring Songbirds

It has often been said that birds are an early warning system of environmental problems. In the 1960s and 1970s, for example, the drastic declines in bird of prey populations, especially eagles and peregrine falcons, raised public awareness about the dangers of agricultural chemicals.

Today, most raptors have recovered well from their DDT-induced slides, but the situation overall has, if anything, worsened. This time the threat is not toxic, however, and the species in danger form a much larger part of North America's avifauna. They are the woodland songbirds, and they are disappearing for reasons at once obvious and subtle.

To understand the danger, it is necessary first to understand something of songbird natural history. Each species has a traditional breeding and wintering range—sometimes overlapping, as with resident species like cardinals and mockingbirds, but more often widely separated. A large majority of eastern North America's woodland songbirds winter in the tropical forests of Central and South America and the Caribbean; in fact, "our" birds actually spend more time on the wintering grounds than in the forests of the Northeast. Rather than being northern birds that fly south to winter, they can more accurately be thought of as tropical birds that fly north to breed.

Unfortunately, those vital tropical forests have been falling at a devastatingly rapid pace, particularly in Central America and the Caribbean. This eliminates wintering habitat for many species and removes resting and feeding habitat for those species that pass through on their way to points farther south. The hope, once voiced by ornithologists, that neotropical migrants might do better in disturbed habitat than resident tropical species is now known to be false; the migrants, it turns out, have extremely specific requirements for habitat, food and range. Complicating matters further, it appears that males and females of the same species may, on occasion, even have different preferences for wintering areas.

The alarm was first sounded nearly thirty years ago, when far-sighted biologists predicted that the greatest threat to North America's songbirds lay south of the U.S. border, but few listened. Eventually, birders began to complain about lower and lower numbers of songbirds each spring, but no one was sure if the decline was real or simply a result of sketchy observation.

More recently, scientific studies have shown a shocking decline in songbird numbers. The North American Breeding Bird Survey, conducted each year at two thousand sites across the continent, shows a decline in most tropical migrants while resident and temperate-zone migrants (those that do not leave North America in winter) were steady or increasing. An examination of weather radar images from the 1960s through the 1980s, on the other hand, provided a chilling measure of the decrease in terms of raw numbers. Because migrating flocks show up on radar, the number of individuals can be estimated, and biologists found that the number of songbirds crossing the Gulf of Mexico each year dropped by nearly 50 percent over the twenty-year period. The radar images obviously do not allow identification by species, but birders have reported the greatest declines among thrushes, vireos and warblers.

Tropical deforestation gets most of the blame for the disappearing songbirds, but scientists think part of the problem may lie closer to home, too. Woodland songbirds evolved for life in large, unbroken forests, and the continuing pace of logging, road building and development has fractured the once vast eastern forest into smaller and smaller fragments.

Like tiny islands, the fragments provide an uncertain refuge for forest birds, which are much more likely to fall victim to crows, blue jays, raccoons and other predators than are those nesting in deep woods. Worse, the brown-headed cowbird, originally native to the Great Plains, has moved east in the last century as the forests fell. A nest parasite, the cowbird female tosses out the eggs of the host species and lays her own in their place. In some hard-hit areas parasitism rates may approach 100 percent, threatening host species like wood thrushes.

Songbirds thus are facing a one-two punch—reproductive stress in the north and declining wintering habitat in the south. Preventing their disappearance will require international cooperation, and may make saving the eagles look easy by contrast.

JUNE

June Observations

Breeding Bird Habitats

June is the peak of the breeding season for songbirds, a time of constant motion and activity. From well before sunrise until the last glimmer of twilight, a mated pair must defend its territory, gather nesting material and, when the chicks hatch, collect vast quantities of insects to stuff into their babies' bottomless gullets.

With so much going on, June is a terrific time to observe the region's songbirds—but what you see will depend on where you look. Most of the region's woodland, for instance, is what biologists call Appalachian oak forest; the common bird species here include wood thrushes, ovenbirds, red-eyed vireos and hooded warblers. But because of their position where North and South, mountains and ocean, meet, the mid-Atlantic states have a tremendous diversity of habitats, which means exciting birding for the naturalist willing to seek out something different. This section looks at four of the more unusual habitats and at the bird specialties that can be found in each.

26

Freshwater Swamps and Marshes

Wetlands are always rewarding places to spend time, since the blending of land and water provides fertile breeding grounds for insects, reptiles, amphibians, fish and other prey species, as well as dense vegetation that offers abundant concealment.

Freshwater wetlands may be natural or man-made, and as long as the finished product has the requisite amount of water, food and cover, birds don't really seem to care which. Even a manicured farm pond with carefully mowed banks will attract a few mallards and Canada geese, with an occasional visit from a green-backed heron, but a lush, untended impoundment, an old beaver dam or a natural cattail marsh will draw far more interesting birds.

Among the more common species at freshwater wetlands in the region are great blue, green-backed and black-crowned night-herons, a number of ducks including black ducks and blue-winged teal, belted kingfishers, tree swallows and red-winged blackbirds. Wooded streams and lakes are most likely to hold wood ducks and common and hooded mergansers, while open marshes are the place to look for king and Virginia rails, soras, common moorhens and marsh wrens; much less common are pied-billed grebes,

American bitterns, least bitterns and sedge wrens. Wooded swamps attract barred owls, red-shouldered hawks and a number of songbirds, such as Acadian flycatchers, prothonotary warblers, Louisiana waterthrushes and swamp sparrows. Cypress swamps, a southern habitat that reaches its northernmost point in the region, and the birds they hold are covered in more detail in Chapter 29.

HOTSPOTS

One of the few areas in the region to have experienced glaciation in the last ice age were the Pocono "mountains" in Pennsylvania, and so this rolling plateau has an abundance of glacially dug lakes, ponds, marshes and bogs, almost all of which are rich in bird life.

The best way to see *Long Pond* in Monroe County is from the seat of a sun-warmed canoe, drifting over the peat-stained water, past willow thickets and stands of emerging pickerelweed where wood ducks, sedge wrens and tree swallows feed. Long Pond doesn't fit the usual conception of a pond—it is really an extremely long, rather wide pool on Tunkhannock Creek, stretching nearly 2 miles through woodland and marsh. Yellowthroats, alder flycatchers, swamp sparrows and kingfishers are very much in evidence along the water; the surrounding woodland is mixed northern hardwoods, with such typical birds as hermit thrushes, veeries, dark-eyed juncos, hairy woodpeckers and black-throated green warblers. To reach Long Pond take I-80 to Exit 43. Take Route 115 South, continuing 1.2 miles past the junction with Route 903. Turn left just before the Pocono Raceway, and go approximately 2 miles around the raceway to the bridge that crosses Tunkhannock Creek.

Hemmed in by a depressing mix of residential, office and highway development, *Troy Meadows* in northern New Jersey seems an anachronism—hundreds of acres of cattail marsh stranded in a near-metropolitan setting. Fortunately, birds are undisturbed by anachronisms, and Troy

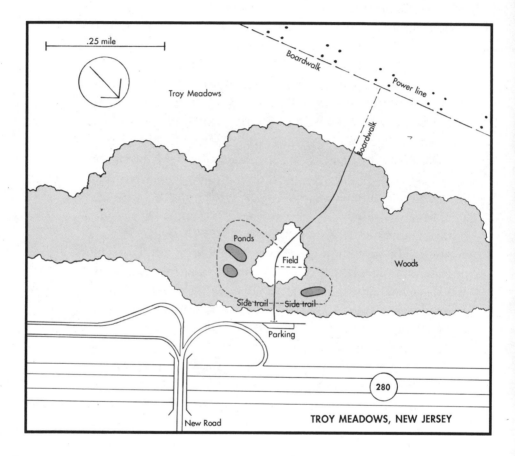

.25 mile

Troy Meadows

Boardwalk

Power line

Boardwalk

Ponds

Field

Woods

Side trail — Side trail

Parking

280

New Road

TROY MEADOWS, NEW JERSEY

Meadows supports breeding populations of such marshland species as least bitterns, Virginia and sora rails, marsh wrens and a very few American bitterns, thanks to the enlightened ownership of Wildlife Preserve Inc., a private group. Because the marsh is so big and access so limited, your ears will be of more use than your eyes, and time spent listening to a recording of marsh bird songs before visiting Troy Meadows will be time well spent.

To reach the Meadows, take I-80 to Exit 47B (Caldwell/Montclair) onto Route 46 East. Go .5 mile, then bear right at the traffic light, following the sign for All Turns. At the stop sign in the jug handle turn right onto New Road. After .8 mile, New Road crosses I-280; immediately upon crossing the bridge, turn right as if entering 280 South, but instead go straight off the entrance ramp and onto a dead-end service road. This is tricky, so be alert. Park along the service road— the trail entrance is on the left, beyond the wooden gate. Follow the trail through the woods to an overgrown field, then bear right, taking the path that shows double tracks from occasional vehicle use. This trail ends at a narrow, slippery boardwalk that leads out to another, somewhat more substantial boardwalk under the high-tension lines; there is a utility company No Trespassing sign at the juncture.

A naturalist could spend a weekend or more exploring the twin wetlands of Conneaut Marsh and Hartstown Swamp in northwestern Pennsylvania, home to such rarities as bald eagles, sedge wrens and king rails, and the only place in the state where the black tern can reasonably be expected to breed. **Hartstown Swamp**, south of Pymatuning Lake (and shown on some maps as Pymatuning Marsh), is easily seen by car and foot, thanks to a dirt road and railbed that cut across it. More confined and wooded than Conneaut Marsh, it harbors a similar, but slightly different bird community than its neighbor to the east.

To reach the swamp, take I-79 to Route 285 West, then go about 6.5 miles to the town of Conneaut Lake. At the traffic light follow 285 left, then at the next block turn left again, this time onto Route 322 West, following a sign for Pymatuning State Park West Side. Go 5.3 miles until the swamp comes in view on the right; as the road climbs the bridge, turn right onto a small dirt road just past a historical marker for the Erie Extension Canal. This dirt road drops to and parallels a railroad for 1.2 miles along the swamp, eventually ending at a metal Game Commission gate. Park here (do not block the gate) and continue north through the swamp.

Conneaut Marsh, just east of Hartstown, is best seen by canoe, and two sections are especially accessible—the central marsh near Geneva and the lower marsh east of I-79. To reach the Geneva Dike area, take Route 285 West 3 miles from I-79. Take the first right in the village of Geneva (a small road just past a drive-in restaurant and just before a green mileage sign for Conneaut Lake). Go 1.2 miles, crossing railroad tracks and a bridge over Outlet Creek. Beyond the bridge, park in the gravel area between the forks of the road. The marsh here is a maze of pathways between the stands of aquatic vegetation, but canoeists should aim for the woodlands to the northwest, where the creek leaves the wooded swamp and enters the open marsh. Paddle upstream (for even though this is a marsh, the current moves at a good clip) for about 2.5 miles to the Brown Hill Road bridge, then turn back to the car. At a leisurely pace, with plenty of time to watch for birds and other marsh inhabitants, the trip will take most of the morning.

A second canoe route covers the lower third of the marsh, from the I-79 crossing to French Creek south of Meadville, and requires two cars. From I-79 turn east on Route 285. Drive 3.9 miles and turn left onto an unmarked road at a large farm equipment dealership; go 1.8 miles and cross two bridges. Just past the second bridge, turn right at the sign for Shaw's Landing Access Point, which is .5 mile down this dirt road. Leave one car here, then take the second car, with canoe, back to Route 285 and turn right. Go .4 mile and turn right on Marsh Road, driving 1 mile. At the fork, turn left onto Towpath Road, go .5 mile and take the left fork onto Shaffer Road. Another 2.4 miles on Shaffer brings you to the Game Commission's Geneva Marsh No. 4 Access Area, between the interstate bridges. Put in here, eventually returning by car to this point after completing the float at Shaw's Landing.

For a shorter trip, go 1.4 miles from I-79 on 285 East, turning left onto an unmarked dirt road that is opposite an intersecting paved road. Go .9 mile across the marsh, leaving the first car at a small Game Commission parking area on the far side of the bridge. Then turn left onto Shaffer Road and go 1.4 miles to the No. 4 access area.

Another excellent freshwater marsh, with such species as king rail and yellow-crowned night-heron, is **Huntley Meadows Park** in Virginia; see Chapter 17 for directions.

Surrounded by marsh and boggy forest, Long Pond, in Pennsylvania's Poconos, is an outstanding example of freshwater wetlands.

27

Salt Marshes and Shore

It takes dedication—and a heavy dose of bug repellent—to enjoy a summer day in the salt marsh, where the air may be thick with mosquitoes, pesky midges and green-headed marsh flies that pack a painful bite. But the salt marsh has a charm all its own, from the pungent smell of the mud, ripe with decaying cordgrass, to the constant sight and sound of birds.

Clapper rails scurry through the cordgrass, heads low, looking more like mammals than birds. Marsh wren songs bubble from the reeds and willets scream their names. Along the tidal creeks, snowy egrets dance on yellow feet, scaring up minnows, while the much larger great egrets, tricolored herons and great blue herons wait more patiently for food. Forster's terns wheel overhead while bulkier gull-billed terns pass by, and seaside sparrows, sharp-tailed sparrows and boat-tailed grackles are very much in evidence. So are other forms of life—fiddler crabs waving their claws on the mudflats, raccoon tracks, river otters and more. The salt marsh is amazingly fertile, producing nearly eight times as much organic matter per acre as the best Midwestern wheat field.

Along the beach itself, birds that may never enter the salt marsh can be found nesting on the open sand—hardly an ideal location, given mankind's summer appropriation of the beach. Two species in particular, the piping plover and least tern, have suffered badly from recreational beach use, and the plover is now listed as a federally threatened species along the coast, with only about seven hundred pairs remaining. Increasingly, parks and refuges are closing off sections of beach to all human use in the breeding season, a strategy that is helping the terns and plovers greatly.

Many of the small, uninhabited barrier islands along New Jersey and the Delmarva Peninsula support large colonies of seabirds, including gulls, terns and black skimmers, as well as American oystercatchers. Most of the islands are closed to the public, but they can be viewed from a discreet distance offshore in small boats, which are easy to rent in most coastal communities. Do not land, and stay far enough offshore that your presence does not have a noticeable effect on the birds. Chasing them away from their nests even momentarily leaves the eggs and chicks vulnerable to the broiling sun and predators like gulls.

HOTSPOTS

The mid-Atlantic region is blessed with an embarrassment of coastal riches—the Chesapeake Bay alone has nearly a half million acres of wetlands on 4,000 miles of crenelated shoreline. With such natural wealth, it is hard to single out a few sites for recognition, but several are exceptional.

Assateague Island, including Assateague Island National Seashore, Assateague State Park and Chincoteague NWR, is the biggest and most famous of the Delmarva barrier islands, and a perfect introduction to the salt marsh–shore ecosystem. The most accessible area is Chincoteague NWR on the southern, Virginia end of the island, where the main road to the Tom's Cove visitors' center passes tidal flats to the south and ends at the beach. If possible, take a canoe (local rentals are available) and explore the marshes that line

Assateague Channel north of the refuge, thus taking you beyond the crowds, which can be crushing in summer, and into the heart of the wetlands. To reach the refuge, take Route 13 to Route 175 East at Nash Corner. Go 10.2 miles on 175 to the town of Chincoteague, turning left at the traffic light onto Main Street and driving another .4 mile north. At Maddux Avenue turn right and drive 1.4 miles to the entrance booth; the refuge headquarters is another .8 mile, and the Tom's Cove center is 2.6 miles from there.

At the northern end of the island in Maryland, Assateague Island State Park offers similar possibilities, with the bonus of a substantial stretch of beach closed to all but foot traffic, making it even more attractive to shore-nesting species like piping and Wilson's plovers and least terns. From Route 50 east of Ocean City, turn onto Route 611 South. The Barrier Island visitors' center for Assateague Island National Seashore is 7.3 miles south of the intersection, with the entrance to the state park 1.1 miles farther, on the other side of the bridge. Park in the day-use lot and walk up the beach as far as your energy and enthusiasm lead you—the Ocean City Inlet is more than 6 miles to the north.

While they lack most of the beach-nesting species, the **Elliott Island** marshes in Dorchester County, Maryland, are a superior place to see marsh birds, and are renowned for the number of rails that can be heard calling at night, including large numbers of Virginia rails and at times as many as four *dozen* usually rare black rails. The black rails, which call most often between 10 P.M. and 2 A.M., will answer a tape recording of their species' *kik-i-doo, kik-i-doo* call, and may be so attracted that they will skitter out of the marsh and between the observer's legs, oblivious to a flashlight beam. Under no circumstances should you enter the marsh itself in pursuit of a rail, for two excellent reasons: Much of the area is posted against trespass, and there is a very real danger of stepping on the rail inadvertently, something that has happened at other black rail sites. Once the rail has been spotted, shut off the tape and lights and leave the bird in peace; overuse of such recorded calls can seriously disrupt breeding. For directions and a map to Elliott Island, see Chapter 2.

In Delaware, two state parks are good bets. ***Delaware Seashore State Park***, separating Rehoboth Bay and the Atlantic, offers easy access, although weekend crowds and oversand vehicles can be onerous for birds and birders alike. To get to the park, follow the directions for Indian River Inlet in Chapter 3; the road on the right just across the inlet leads to productive marshes, as does Savages Ditch Road .8 mile north of the inlet. In addition, Savages Ditch boasts one of the largest osprey colonies away from the Chesapeake. To the north, ***Cape Henlopen State Park*** has common and least terns, piping plovers, oystercatchers and willets, among other shore species. The best area is the north-curving spit of the cape itself; to reach the park take Routes 1/14 to Route 9 East to Lewes; continue on 9 for another mile to the park entrance and proceed to Point Road, a left that leads to a parking area close to the spit.

Other sites with good salt marsh and/or beach birding are the ***Brigantine*** unit of Forsythe NWR (see Chapter 6) and ***Nummy Island***, New Jersey (Chapter 32, under Stone Harbor); ***Bombay Hook NWR***, Delaware (Chapter 11); ***Port Mahon Road*** (Chapter 2), also in Delaware; and ***Back Bay NWR***, Virginia (Chapter 3), which has closed a portion of its beach to protect piping plovers.

28

Northern Forests

There is a biological rule of thumb that 1,000 feet in elevation is roughly equal to 100 miles in latitude—in other words, as you climb higher and higher in the mountains, the plant and animal communities change as if you were traveling north.

This is especially evident in the central Appalachians, where the valleys are verdant with such essentially southern trees as redbud, pawpaw and sweetgum, but the ridgetops, more than 3,500 feet above sea level, have stands of spruce, fir and northern hardwoods that thrive in the cool, wet climate. These forests are leftovers, in a sense, from the last ice age, when most of the region was covered in coniferous forest. Once the climate warmed, the boreal forest retreated to the north—and uphill, eventually becoming isolated on the highest peaks, as well as in relict bogs. In some areas such woods were restricted to a few scattered mountains, while West Virginia's eastern highlands were, until this century, almost solidly covered with red spruce and balsam fir.

As might be expected, the northern forests support a unique community of birds—species that a naturalist might otherwise have to travel to New England or Canada to see. The list is a long one—sharp-shinned hawk, northern goshawk, northern saw-whet owl, yellow-bellied sapsucker, olive-sided flycatcher, alder flycatcher, common raven, brown creeper, red-breasted nuthatch, winter wren, golden-crowned kinglet, Swainson's and hermit thrushes, solitary vireo; a number of warblers including Nashville, black-throated blue, blackburnian, magnolia, black-throated green, mourning, Canada and northern waterthrush; dark-eyed junco, purple finch and, rarely, red crossbill.

The species are not spread uniformly through the northern forests. Some, like kinglets, are found only in the alpine red spruce forest; others, like blackburnian warblers, occur in both conifers and hardwoods. Bogs, with their black spruce and balsam fir, attract olive-sided flycatchers and hermit thrushes, among others. Each habitat variation has its own rewards for the curious naturalist.

HOTSPOTS

Northern forests are the norm in many parts of Pennsylvania's upper tier, particularly hardwood communities in the Poconos, but they become increasingly restricted the farther south one goes. A good example of this biological isolation can be found in the **Mount Rogers National Recreation Area** of southwestern Virginia, just a few miles above the North Carolina and Tennessee borders. The Iron Mountains, which pass through this area, are high and rugged (Mount Rogers is 5,726 feet, for instance), with peaks covered by red spruce and treeless, naturally occurring heath "balds," a far cry from the oak-hickory communities in the valleys below.

To reach the Mount Rogers area from the east, take I-77 to Route 58 West. From its junction with Route 16 North, continue to follow 58 over an extremely scenic road, crossing ridges and dipping past small hill farms. After 15.5 miles, watch for Route 600, a right turn with a sign for Mount Rogers National Recreation Area. Go uphill 1.7 miles until you reach a dirt road on the left with a directional sign for Whitetop Mountain, a further 3-mile drive. The road climbs from oak forest to northern hardwoods to red spruce, with occasional views of Mount Rogers to the northeast, its summit completely capped by coniferous forest.

After 2 miles the road leaves the forest and crosses a wide "bald"; do not be so taken with the stunning view that you neglect to watch for protruding rocks. Near the top of the bald the road forks; take the right fork, which leads to a flat parking area at the edge of the spruce forest.

Retrace your path down the dirt road to Route 600, then turn left and go 1.3 miles to Elk Garden, a wide bald that separates the flanks of Whitetop and Mount Rogers; the parking area is on the left. The gate on the other side of Route 600 is the jump-off for the trail to Mount Rogers roughly 4.5 miles away, most of it along the Appalachian Trail, which bears left of the trail register shelter.

> CAUTION: *As the signs at the trailhead strongly warn, the high country in this area can be fatal to unprepared hikers, with sudden weather changes and rapid drops in temperature at all seasons. All hikers—including birders—should carry a detailed map, know their route, take clothes for a variety of weather conditions (despite sunny forecasts) and inform someone of their route and expected time of return.*

From Elk Garden, continue north on Route 600 another 5.4 miles to Route 603, a right turn. Cross the small bridge and turn right immediately to stay on 603. Go about 11 miles to a T-intersection, turning left onto Route 16 North and traveling another 16 miles to I-81 at Marion.

West Virginia Red Spruce Belt

At one time, much of the West Virginia highlands were cloaked in solid stands of red spruce, a forest community that fell almost completely to the lumberman's saw in the late 1800s and early 1900s. In the highest peaks the spruces have come back, albeit in far more restricted patches of second growth—but enough remains to attract a large number of boreal forest birds.

A tour of the West Virginia spruce belt is a fine way to spend a June weekend, looking for such northern species as Canada warblers and hermit thrushes, and enjoying some of the prettiest scenery the region has to offer. The tour starts at Cranesville Bog, which straddles the Maryland line; then winds south to the balsam swamps and montane spruce forests of Canaan Valley State Park; crosses the Cheat Mountain range, one of the wildest areas in a wild state; and ends at the beautiful Cranberry Glades bogs, the southernmost point for several species of northern birds.

Cranesville Bog, at 2,500 feet of elevation, preserves a piece of Ice Age history on the border of West Virginia and Maryland. Actually two long bogs running north-to-south and connected by Cranesville Creek, the bog boasts the most southerly natural stand of American tamarack, as well as red spruce and such characteristic northern hardwoods as yellow birch, black cherry and red maple. Because the bog forest is surrounded by farm fields, the visiting naturalist finds odd juxtapositions—indigo buntings and brown thrashers singing from shrubs on one side of the road, and northern waterthrushes and black-throated green warblers calling from the spruces on the other side.

From Oakland, Maryland, take Route 219 North approximately 7 miles to Mayhew Inn Road, a left marked with signs for Swallow Falls State Park. Go 4.4 miles to a stop sign, turn left .4 mile and turn right onto Swallow Falls Road. Drive 2.7 miles to Cranesville Road, a right, and go another 4.1 miles. To go to the smaller, southern arm of the bog turn left onto Muddy Creek Road; to see the larger, northern tract, take the next left beyond Muddy Creek and go .5 mile to a clearing. The West Virginia chapter of the Nature Conservancy has purchased 300 acres of the bog's two sections, including the southwestern quarter of the northern bog, where a trail and boardwalk lead into the wetland from this clearing. Much of the bog is still privately owned, however, so obey No Trespassing signs.

Return to Route 219 South. About 29 miles south of Oakland in the village of Thomas, go straight onto Route 32 South to Davis, another 2 miles. Past the bridge in Davis the road begins to climb into the Monongohela National Forest, a parcel of 850,000 acres that covers most of the eastern highlands of the state. Several miles later the road tops out and begins to drop into the **Canaan Valley** (locally pronounced ka-NANE, instead of the Biblical KANE-in). In this huge bowl between the mountains, red spruce was the predominant tree until a forty-year orgy of clear-cutting, ending in the 1920s, stripped the forest and turned the valley into a mix of fields and bogs. There is lots of second-growth spruce around the rim of the valley, however, and the bogs below are thick with balsam fir.

About 6.5 miles from the crest of the mountain, turn right into the entrance of Canaan Valley State Park, which incongruously features ski slopes, tennis courts, resort lodges and a sprawling golf course along with its more natural attractions. Park by the nature center and walk north to the woods, where Deer Trail and its boardwalks lead into the middle of a balsam swamp, in which golden-crowned kinglets, hermit thrushes, solitary vireos and a number of boreal warblers nest. For the more adventuresome, pull on old pants and a pair of (laced) high-topped boots, and slog into the huge swamp between Route 32 and the entrance road, or the smaller one below the Balsam Swamp Overlook.

Next, head for the high red spruce forest by crossing Route 32 to the ski area; park in the lower lot and walk across the road and up a gravel drive to an auxiliary parking area, to the start of Bald Knob Trail. This path leads steeply up through hardwood forests to a thick, pure stand of red spruce, but the hike is hard and those visiting on a weekend may want to pay a few dollars and take the ski lift to the top of the ridge, since the trail's other end is next to the upper lift platform. From there, it is a 2.5-mile hike back down, with a stupendous view from the knob.

From Canaan Valley head south once again on Route 32 about 10 miles to Harman, then west 21 miles on Routes 33/55 to Elkins. Here, turn south on Routes 219/250 and go another 18 miles to Huttonsville, where the routes split; continue straight on 250 South, which 5 miles later begins to climb **Cheat Mountain**. A total of 9.3 miles from Huttonsville, turn left on Forest Service Road 92, which passes through a mix of hardwoods and spruce for the next 4.4 miles. At the intersection with Road 47 (Whitmeadow Run Road) turn right. This road descends through a superb example of red spruce forest, where the ground is carpeted by young spruces and blackburnian warblers are abundant, along with black-throated blue, magnolia and Canada warblers, brown creepers, kinglets and dark-eyed juncos. The road dead-ends after 2.3 miles at Shavers Fork, where the hardwoods hold rose-breasted grosbeaks, veeries and hooded warblers. Sphagnum bogs midway down the road offer further birding possibilities.

Return to 250 South and turn left. For the next several miles the highway crosses the high plateau formed by Cheat and Shavers mountains, with a number of well-marked roads branching off to either side that beckon exploration. Make sure, however, that you turn left after 5.8 miles onto Road 209, which leads to the Gaudineer Knob picnic grounds and overlook, a distance of 2.4 miles. The area near the overlook is solid red spruce, full of golden-crowned kinglets, solitary vireos and—on occasion—red crossbills. Just .8 mile from the fork for the picnic ground is the Gaudineer Knob Scenic Area, a 140-acre stand of virgin spruce and an excellent place to find Canada warblers.

Back out on Route 250 turn left once more and drop

out of the Cheat range. The final stop is *Cranberry Glades Botanical Area* near Marlinton, an outstanding example of an Appalachian relict bog and the most southerly point for several species of spruce forest birds, including hermit and Swainson's thrushes, mourning warbler and purple finch. Just past Bartow turn south 25 miles on Routes 92/28 to Huntersville, then west 6 miles to Marlinton; directions to Cranberry Glades from here can be found in Chapter 31.

Other northern forests worth visiting for boreal birds can be found: *Bear Meadows Natural Area* and *Bruce Lake Natural Area*, Pennsylvania (Chapter 34); *Dolly Sods Wilderness*, West Virginia (Chapter 23); and *Spruce Flats Bog*, Pennsylvania. To reach the latter, a state Forest Service property, take Route 30 East from Ligonier to Route 381 South to the village of Rector, then follow signs to Linn Run State Park. Drive through the park and into Forbes State Forest, a total of 7.5 miles from Rector. At the top of the ridge turn onto one of two gravel lanes that enter from the left, drive to where they meet and park. The trail, leading about a third of a mile to the bog, starts here. There is no boardwalk, so wear old clothes and waterproof footwear.

One of the finest expanses of mixed northern forest in the region, as well as Pennsylvania's last stand of virgin spruce, can be found at *Hickory Run State Park* in the Poconos, with good birding on the Boulder Field Trail and on the Mud Run and Hawk Falls trails (an unnamed, orange-blazed path links these two). From I-80 take Exit 41 onto Route 534 South; go 1.7 miles to a stop sign, turn left and drive another 3.2 miles to the park office for a trail map.

29

Cypress Swamps and Southern Woodlands

The mid-Atlantic region is a unique biological blend, with the boreal Appalachians protruding deep into otherwise southern regions, and a number of southern habitats extending far to the north. One of the most fascinating is the cypress swamp, emblematic of the Deep South, but found as far north as Maryland and Delaware—and with a variety of "southern" birds nesting in and near it.

Baldcypress is an oddity, a deciduous conifer which, like the tamarack of northern bogs, drops its needles each autumn. The cypress originally grew to great size in the swamps of the Atlantic coastal plain but it produces valuable timber, and virtually all of the virgin stands are gone, leaving much smaller second-growth trees in their wake. Even small cypress have an air of mystery about them, growing as they do in standing water, with flaring trunk bases and surrounded by strange "knees," knobs of wood that rise above the water's surface for reasons that remain unclear.

The birds of the cypress swamp include prothonotary, Swainson's, black-and-white, parula and yellow-throated warblers; barred owls, red-shouldered hawks, wood ducks, blue-gray gnatcatchers and pileated woodpeckers. Where the water table drops away and the ground becomes drier, the canopy changes to loblolly and pond pine, mixed with southern hardwoods; here, watch for brown-headed nuthatches, summer tanagers, whip-poor-wills, chuck-will's-widows and orchard orioles.

HOTSPOTS

The most northerly cypress swamp in the East is *Pocomoke Swamp*, which sits on the Maryland/Delaware border (and which is often known as the Selbyville Swamp or Great Cypress Swamp on the Delaware side of the line), then continues south along the Pocomoke River through Maryland to the Chesapeake. *Trap Pond State Park* in Delaware also protects a portion of the swamp; take Route 13 South to Route 24, then follow county Road 449 1 mile to the park entrance. A canoe (your own or a park rental) allows you to explore the 90-acre pond, which features a canoe "trail" at the southeast end among the cypress. By road, the swamp can be enjoyed by leaving the park and driving east on Route 24 to Route 26 South; go 4 miles and turn east onto Route 54 toward Selbyville. The road passes through an extensive, privately owned stand of cypress.

Farther south, *Pocomoke River State Park*, between Snow Hill and Pocomoke City, Maryland, has nature trails through cypress forest, as well as many opportunities for canoeing from Milburn and Shad Landings.

In southeastern Virginia, *Dismal Swamp NWR* preserves a large portion of what was once a vast swamp of cypress, water tupelo, red maple and oak, with access by dike trails and boardwalk. Take Routes 460/13 to 460 Business just north of Suffolk, where the road joins Routes 10/32 South. Follow Routes 13/32 South to the intersection with Washington Street (Route 337) at the Bank of Suffolk; turn left onto East Washington Street. Go .7 mile to the light at the intersection of White Marsh Road, turn right and go .9 mile to Jericho Ditch Road, a dirt lane on the left under a high-tension line. In .9 mile there is a gate; if it's open, continue another 1.2 miles to the parking area and interpretive display along Jericho Ditch. Paths follow several intersecting ditches through a seasonally flooded forest.

Return to White Marsh Road and turn left, going 4.8 miles to an unmarked gravel road on the left with a sign for Dismal Swamp NWR. Turn onto it and go .8 mile to the parking area at the beginning of the boardwalk.

Just to the northeast of Dismal Swamp, on Cape Henry, is **Seashore State Park**, preserved despite the rampant resort development of Virginia Beach just next door. For directions to the park see Chapter 3; turn right at the entrance instead of left and park at the visitors' center. A number of trails run through the park, with the 1.5-mile Bald Cypress Trail, blazed in red, taking the visitor through a classic cypress swamp, with trees draped in lacy strands of Spanish moss.

30

Breakout:
The Melting Pot

Experienced naturalists know that one of the best places to look for wildlife is where two habitats meet—field and forest, pond and marsh, hardwoods and conifers. In such an edge, or ecotone, habitat, the possibilities are multiplied by having several different communities of plants and animals nearby.

The same principle holds on a vastly larger scale, too, and is one reason that the mid-Atlantic region is so fascinating from a natural perspective. Here, several of the great life zone regions of North America meet, each bringing its own unique blend of life.

Even though scientists draw lines on maps to show where, say, the Carolinian life zone ends and the Alleghenian begins, the distinctions are by no means clear-cut in the field. There are endless transitions, and the demarcations do not follow the dictates of cartography, but the realities of biology; for this reason, you can find spruce and balsam bogs that clearly belong to the Canadian life zone on mountains far *south* of hardwood forests that are typical of a milder Carolinian zone. In fact, many ecologists no longer talk about life zones at all, but refer instead to forest zones, each with its distinct blend of trees, smaller plants and animals—the mixed mesophytic forest typical of the southeast, with its white oak, beech, tulip poplar, red oak and basswood, or the Appalachian oak forest common through the ridge-and-valley areas. Generally speaking, the animals follow the plants; thus, the zebra swallowtail butterfly is found along the Susquehanna basin but is scarce to the east of the river, where the climate is wrong for its only food tree, the pawpaw.

In the melting pot that is the mid-Atlantic region, North and South meet (and to a lesser degree, so do East and West)—northern species following the mountains and southern varieties the river valleys. The distinctions may not always be clear. The rabbit that nibbles off the young pepper plants in a Pennsylvania garden is probably an eastern cottontail (*Sylvilagus floridanus*), a species that thrives in dense brush, second-growth woods and suburban landscapes. Take a walk through dense woodland on a nearby mountain, however, and the rabbit that races through the bracken fern may be entirely different, even though it looks identical. From Maine south through the Appalachians, the New England cottontail (*S. transitionalis*) replaces its more common cousin in large, mature tracts of forest. The two are virtually the same in appearance, although the "woods rabbit" is somewhat bigger, and the shape of the skull is consistently different.

There can be little confusion on the highest, spruce-clad mountains of the region, where both cottontails are replaced by the snowshoe hare, famous for its white winter coat and its enormous hind feet, which buoy the animal in the deep snows common here. The three species of lagomorphs—eastern cottontail, New England cottontail and snowshoe hare—may well be found on the same mountain, separated by altitude and forest type.

Birds, being highly visible, are among the most intensely studied of wild animals, and here again they provide evidence of the melting pot in action. Dozens of species reach the northern or southern limits of their range within the region, although the boundaries are flexible, and many are steadily pushing into new territory. This trend is especially evident among southern birds like cardinals, mockingbirds, yellow-throated warblers and blue gros-beaks; the first two have pushed as far north as southern Canada. The northern boundary of the Carolina wren's range expands in years with mild winters, only to shrink back (sometimes drastically) when deep cold kills those adventuresome individuals that have pushed too far north. In many parts of the mid-Atlantic region, the blue-winged warbler is moving into areas traditionally occupied by its very close relative, the golden-winged warbler. Where the two meet, the blue-wingeds almost invariably force the golden-wingeds out, raising fears for the latter's future.

The reasons seem plain—by turning what was once unbroken forest into a patchwork of fields and towns, mankind has made the mid-Atlantic states more suitable for "southern" animals than for those species that require boreal habitats. Red fox and opossums were unknown in the Pennsylvania mountains until the solid forest cover was stripped, but both have now adapted to the climate and the woods.

Human intervention, albeit unintentional, continues to churn the mix in the melting pot. Spruce and pine plantations, like those in watersheds and on Christmas tree farms, have provided pathways for prairie warblers heading north and golden-crowned kinglets expanding south. In nature, nothing ever stays the same for very long.

Other June Attractions

There is obviously more to June than breeding birds, and it would be shameful to neglect the bloom of mountain laurel and rhododendron which is the month's floral highlight.

Both mountain laurel and great, or rosebay, rhododendron (*Rhododendron maximum*) are common mountain plants in much of the region, the laurel more tolerant of open, dry conditions and the rhododendron preferring a moist, cool habitat, such as a north slope beneath hemlocks. In addition, in the Blue Ridge and southern Appalachians there occur catawba (or purple) rhododendron (*R. catawbiensis*) and flame azalea, a May bloomer. Several other members of the heath family, including the early azaleas and the tiny sheep and pale laurels, also grow in the region.

The **Blue Ridge Parkway** and **Shenandoah National Park** (Chapter 18) are famous for their heath blooms, which may cover the balds and line the roadways with color. The rolling balds of **Dolly Sods Wilderness** (Chapter 23), especially in the northern scenic area, can literally become white with mountain laurel blossoms, while in Pennsylvania, **Mount Davis Natural Area** in Somerset County and **Bruce Lake Natural Area** in Pike County both have

Impressive stands of mountain laurel can be found in June at Mt. Davis and Bruce Lake in Pennsylvania, Dolly Sods in West Virginia and parts of the Blue Ridge Mountains in Virginia.

exceptional laurel displays. To reach Mount Davis, take Route 219 to Meyersdale, then turn west onto SR 2004, following signs for Mount Davis High Point, a total of 9.8 miles from town. From the picnic ground, take the High Point Trail to the summit. The best laurel areas at Bruce Lake are found on the East Branch Bruce Lake, Rock Oak Ridge and Brown trails, a circuit of more than 8 miles. This is also a good area for northern songbirds, and a day spent admiring the laurel and watching the birds here is time well spent. Directions are given in Chapter 34.

As always, blooming times anywhere in the region depend on latitude and elevation; the rhododendron around the Peaks of Otter, on the Blue Ridge Parkway, are usually at their best the first week of June, while in high elevations of northern Pennsylvania they may last through the beginning of July. Mountain laurel generally blooms earlier, with the first two weeks of June the rough peak.

JULY

July Observations

31

Orchids, Mallows and More

Spring is usually considered the season of the wildflower, but there is lots of color splashed across the land through the hottest days of summer as well. Some of the displays are extravagant, while other species are smaller and more difficult to find but unusual enough to warrant the effort. And as an added incentive, July is the peak of the blueberry season across northern Pennsylvania, where the moist, acidic soil of bogs produces the finest crops at the same time that rare wild orchids are in bloom. (For more on blueberries, see Chapter 34.)

Mallows

The summer coastal marshes can take a toll on a human visitor. On a muggy day the sun beats mercilessly, and shade is nowhere to be be found. Even worse, this is the peak of the mosquito and marsh fly season, and if the breeze deserts you, the bugs will descend in hordes.

But there are rewards aplenty, and one of the finest is the mallows, which explode into bloom in late July and last through the remainder of the summer, coloring the marshes with splashes of white and vivid pink.

The mallows are members of the hibiscus family,

native to the wetlands of the East Coast. There are several species (including a number of introduced, roadside varieties), but the showiest of the lot is the swamp rose-mallow (*Hibiscus palustris*)—6 or 7 feet tall, bearing clusters of flowers that may be as large as 8 inches across. Most of the rose-mallows bear white flowers with maroon centers, but scattered through the stands will be many individuals bearing pink blossoms—not a different species, but a separate variety. (Once, the white form was considered a distinct species, the crimson-eyed rose-mallow, but botanists now lump the two together.)

Growing among the rose-mallows, somewhat overshadowed by their larger cousins, will be seashore mallows, which reach a height of about 3 feet and bear smaller, pink flowers. Unlike the rose-mallow, which does well with brackish or fresh water around its roots, the seashore mallow is found only in tidal marshes.

HOTSPOTS

You can find mallows growing almost anywhere along the region's coast during late summer, but a few areas have veritable fields of mallows, including **Prime Hook NWR** in Delaware. This refuge, with limited road access, is best seen by canoe, with Slaughter Creek and Petersfield Ditch being popular canoeing routes. For directions to Prime Hook, see Chapter 54. Another regional refuge with mallows is **Eastern Neck NWR** (Chapter 12) on Maryland's Eastern Shore; a boardwalk leading to the observation tower at Calfpasture Cove, about a half mile south of the bridge, runs through a nice stand. Other spots for mallows are **Chincoteague NWR** (Chapter 27) and **Back Bay NWR** (Chapter 3), both in Virginia, and **Bombay Hook NWR**, Delaware (Chapter 11).

Unusual Bog Flowers

Midsummer is the time when many of the plants that grow in the harsh conditions of the bog bloom, among them a number of carnivorous plants and wild orchids.

Carnivorous plants have nothing in common with the old Grade-B movie image of man-eating vines. Most are quite small; the round-leafed sundew, one of the most common, is easily overlooked against the background of sphagnum moss and dwarf cranberries. It is an innocuous-looking plant with tiny, paddle-shaped leaves covered with glistening hairs. Each hair, in turn, is tipped with a glob of a sweet, sticky liquid that insects find attractive. If they make the mistake of touching the goo, however, they find themselves trapped, as the leaf ever so slowly curls up around them. Enzymes released by the leaf dissolve most of the bug, a process that takes days.

The pitcher-plant takes a different approach. Its leaves form upright tubes that fill with water, drowning any insect that tumbles in, while short, down-pointing hairs prevent escape. Both the pitcher-plant and the sundew have taken to meat eating as a way to supplement their meager diet, for the bog's acid soil is notoriously poor in nutrients.

Both carnivorous species are visible all spring and summer, but they come into bloom in June and July in most areas—the sundew raising a curved stalk with tiny pinkish or white flowers, the pitcher-plant producing a much more impressive, reddish-brown flower that hangs down like a bell from a stalk a foot or more tall. The bogs also host a number of beautiful orchids, including the rose pogonia, calopogon (or grass-pink) and arethusa.

HOTSPOTS

By far the best place for summer bog specialities is ***Cranberry Glades Botanical Area*** in West Virginia, where the U.S. Forest Service has constructed a self-guiding board-walk through the glades, as bogs are locally known. The

The spectacular blooms of the swamp rose-mallow brighten many coastal wetlands in late summer, like this stand lining Shearness Pool at Bombay Hook NWR in Delaware.

largest bog system in West Virginia and one of the finest in the East, Cranberry Glades encompasses four bogs, of which two are closed to the general public. This is no hardship since, in a good year, hundreds of orchids can be seen from the half mile–long boardwalk, while sundew and pitcherplant (the latter an introduced species here) are also present.

To get to Cranberry Glades from the south, take I-64 West to Route 219 North, then go 32 miles to the intersection with Routes 39/55 West at Mill Point. Coming from the north, follow Routes 219/55 South to Marlinton, then go another 8 miles to Mill Point. From either direction, at Mill Point turn onto Routes 39/55 West and go 6.5 miles to the Cranberry

Glades visitors' center, which has maps and interpretive displays. The entrance to the glades is .6 mile beyond, on the right, with the start of the boardwalk an additional .6 mile from the highway.

The New Jersey **Pine Barrens** are also world famous for their unique plant communities, including the rare curly-grass fern, a variety of carnivorous plants and such orchids as rose pogonia and arethusa.

In the northern Pine Barrens, **Whitesbog Conservation and Environmental Studies Center** near Browns Mills, part of Lebanon State Forest, features typical Pine Barrens habitat, including bogs, streams and oak-pine forest, as well as commercial cranberry bogs; a naturalist can spend hours here, exploring the varied plant communities. From Route 70, turn onto Route 530 West and follow the signs 1.1 miles to the center; ask at headquarters for recommendations of good areas for exploration.

One of the most accessible Pine Barrens areas, with a boardwalk for close views of the bog ecosystem, is **Webb's Mills**, a state-owned tract south of Whiting; visitors can see sundews, pitcher-plants, curly-grass fern, arethusa and rose pogonia orchids, as well as golden-crest. From Route 206, drive east 8 miles on Route 70, then east 13.9 miles on Route 72; turn left onto Route 539 North for 6.2 miles, watching for a sign for Greenwood Forest WMA. At the bridge, park along the road and look for the trailhead on the right just south of the creek. The boardwalk is back through the woods along the trail.

Canoeists may want to consider spending a day lazily botanizing from their boats, since the Wading, Mullica, Oswego branch and Batso rivers in the Pine Barrens all offer wild conditions and interesting plants. Canoe rentals are available in many areas, but expect heavy crowds on weekends, especially on Wading River. In addition, many of the blueberries sites listed in Chapter 34 are also good for summer bog flowers.

32

Heronries

The word *heronry* is not a familiar one to most people—a pity, for it means they have never experienced the sights, sounds (and smells) of a heron breeding colony.

Long-legged and gangly, herons are adapted to a life shin-deep in water, but each summer they take to the trees to nest, usually returning to traditional colonies along the coast or near major rivers and wetlands systems. Some of the colonies can be quite large, with dozens, even hundreds, of pairs jockeying for the best nest sites.

Colonies may be composed of a single species or they may be an amalgam of several varieties of herons and egrets. Inland, the most common species is the great blue heron, an inhabitant of marshes, river edges and beaver ponds—not to mention municipal parks, golf course water hazards and farm ponds. About 4 feet tall, with a wingspan of more than 6 feet, the great blue heron is all but unmistakable in its pale gray plumage and black eye stripe.

Coastal heronries, on the other hand, may host a half dozen or more species of herons and egrets, including black- and yellow-crowned night-herons, tricolored (formerly Louisiana) herons, snowy and great egrets, and little blue herons. Green-backed herons, which are not as habitually colonial as the others, sometimes join the heronry as well, taking advantage of safety in numbers.

Heron nests are all rather similar—shallow, flattened bowls of sticks and twigs, to which a lining of finer material may or may not be added; in fact, the nests and eggs of several species are indistinguishable from one another. The colony usually chooses a thicket of low, shrubby trees on an island, where humans and mammalian predators cannot reach them easily. Great blue heron colonies, on the other hand, are often found in swamps where beaver flooding has killed the trees, and the nests may be as high as 50 or 60 feet off the ground.

The chicks, usually numbering three or four, hatch in staggered sequence in many species, because the female begins incubation as soon as the first egg is laid. Known as asynchronous hatching, this is an insurance policy; if prey is abundant, the whole family will thrive, but in lean times, the oldest (and hence the biggest and strongest) chick will monopolize the food at the expense of its siblings, which may very well starve to death. It seems cruel, but from the species' view it is better that one chick survive than for the entire brood to starve.

The colony is a noisy, bustling place at midsummer, when the chicks near fledging and the parents are kept busy shuttling back and forth between the marshes and the heronry, regurgitating each load of food before heading out again for more. Nor is the smell easy to forget, since heron guano has a thick, penetrating quality. The droppings have another effect, killing the trees on which the colony survives. If the woodland is big enough the birds simply shift the colony a short distance, but if all the trees are killed and eventually become too fragile, the colony may have to be abandoned completely. At other times, thriving colonies are abandoned for no clear reason. This happened to Rookery Island, a well-known heronry on the lower Susquehanna that supported hundreds of pairs of cattle egrets, great egrets, snowies, black-crowned night-herons and glossy ibis—until the birds failed to appear in 1989. Whether they will ever return is an open question.

HOTSPOTS

Because disturbance is dangerous during the breeding season, most heronries are closed to human visitors. Fortunately, the famous **Stone Harbor Heronry** is easy to observe, since it is set, incongruously, in the middle of town. A community bird sanctuary, the heronry was established by the far-sighted citizens of this Jersey shore town in 1947. A 21-acre thicket of marsh, trees and shrubs was set aside to protect one of the largest nesting colonies of wading birds in the region.

Stone Harbor itself is part of the string of heavily commercialized barrier islands along the New Jersey coast, a swath of condos, motels and T-shirt shops that stretches from Wildwood to Seaside Heights. But smack in the middle of the ticky-tacky monotony stands the heronry, a tangle of green alive with birds, surrounded on all sides by residential development and carefully tended streets. It is an odd, but welcome, sight.

Dusk is the best time for a visit, although a stop is rewarding at any hour. The colony's biggest attraction is its black- and yellow-crowned night-herons, which are most active in the evening as they head out to the salt marshes to feed, croaking morosely as they fly. In addition, the heronry supports breeding pairs of great, cattle and snowy egrets, as well as green-backed, little blue and tricolored herons and glossy ibis. Black ducks and a variety of songbirds are also found within the heronry.

To reach Stone Harbor, take Exit 10 off the Garden State Expressway, traveling east on Route 657. In town, turn right at the first traffic light onto Third street; the heronry occupies roughly a block between Third and Second streets. On the left off Third is a small parking lot and observation area that overlooks a phragmites marsh and gives the best view of passing herons. The nests may be hidden in the trees and are not always visible. The heronry itself is closed to all public access to prevent disturbance to the birds.

While visiting the heronry, take time for two more stops in Stone Harbor. On Route 657 just before town is the Wetlands Institute, a nonprofit research and education facility dedicated to the study of the salt marsh ecosystem. With an observation tower and marsh boardwalk, newly expanded interpretive displays and guided walks, the institute is worth the small admission fee.

And after leaving the heronry, continue south on Third Street, which makes a sharp right curve and crosses a bridge to Nummy Island, a beautiful salt marsh that is excellent for shorebirds throughout the spring, summer and fall.

One of the largest regional heronries is **Pea Patch Island** in the Delaware River southeast of Wilmington. In recent years as many as ten thousand herons and egrets nested here, including the only lowland colony of great blue herons north of Virginia—a fact even more surprising when one considers that the island is part of Fort Delaware State Park, and that great blues are usually even shyer about human disturbance in the breeding season than their relatives. Although park visitors are kept at a discreet distance from the nesting area, an observation deck permits visitors to see the comings and goings of the wading birds.

To reach Pea Patch Island, take Route 13 South from Wilmington approximately 12 miles to Route 72 East; this becomes Route 9 and leads to Delaware City. At Clinton Street turn left and drive .6 mile to the gray park office building, where the ferry takes visitors across to the island; through Labor Day, the boat operates Wednesday through Sunday and holidays, beginning at 11 A.M. Adults and children are charged a ferry fee. Once on the island, walk north of the fort to Wading Bird Trail, which leads to the observation area.

Marsh Wren
Song Flights

Under most circumstances, marsh wrens can be maddeningly difficult to find. They call boisterously from the reeds, but the songs are disembodied—standing in the bed of a pickup truck for a better vantage point, with a wren singing just a few yards away, you can spend half an hour looking hard and never see it.

Fortunately, the male wrens use visual displays to reinforce their claims to territory. Launching himself from the vegetation, the male makes a low, circling flight over the reeds, his wings buzzing like a hummingbird's, calling excitedly all the while; then he coasts gently back into the reeds, only to repeat the performance a few minutes later. In a good wren marsh, males are constantly popping up momentarily, like winged jack-in-the-boxes. When they land, the males often choose a more exposed perch, and they can be seen, tails cocked high in challenge, still bubbling away with their twitters and chirps.

When you locate a marsh wren territory, look carefully from the road for a globular mass in the reeds—again, a high vantage point like a van roof or the back of a pickup truck helps. These are dummy nests, the size of canteloupes and woven by the males of reeds and leaves; each male may build as many as two dozen of them, although the female usually winds up building a real, better concealed nest of her own for breeding. The purpose of the dummy nests is unknown, although they may serve to confuse predators or simply be a courtship activity. During cold winter weather, the dummy nests may be used by the wrens for roosting.

Marsh wrens are a polygynous species, in which males may mate with more than one female. The key to mate selection seems to be the quality of the territory—those males holding parcels that contain a high percentage of lush, emergent plant growth like phragmites or cordgrass tend to mate more often than those holding poorer territories. It may also be that the females can discern a difference in the quality of the courtship flights as well, but to a human every male in the marsh seems to be giving it his all.

HOTSPOTS

Many of the salt marsh sites previously listed are good for marsh wrens, including *Fishing Bay WMA* and *Elliott Island* in Maryland and *Port Mahon Road* in Delaware (Chapter 2); *Little Creek WMA*, Delaware (Chapter 47); the salt marshes of *Assateague Island* in Virginia and Maryland (Chapter 27); and *Heislerville/Dennis Creek Wildlife Management Area* (Chapter 21, under Moore's Beach) and *Brigantine* (Chapter 6) in New Jersey. In addition, marsh wrens are particularly common and easy to see at *Bombay Hook NWR* (Chapter 11) and *Prime Hook NWR* (Chapter 54) in Delaware, as well as the marshes of *Back Bay NWR* in southeast Virginia (Chapter 3).

Away from the coast, marsh wrens are harder to find, but they occur in good numbers in Pennsylvania in the reedy wetlands of *Presque Isle State Park* (Chapter 2), *Hartstown Swamp* and *Conneaut Marsh* (Chapter 26) and *Erie NWR* (Chapter 17), as well as *Troy Meadows* (Chapter 26) in northern New Jersey.

34

Wild Blueberries

Few people can resist the lure of a blueberry bush, hanging full with glossy, indigo berries. Members of a large and confusing group, the native blueberries range from low species barely knee-high and bearing small, dry berries, to the highbush blueberries found commonly in wetlands and damp meadows across northern Pennsylvania. The highbush blueberry is the monarch of the clan, often more than 8 feet tall and producing magnificently large, flavorful berries that ripen in July. It is enough to make anyone forget about the mosquitoes.

Humans are not the only ones who like blueberries, of course. Watch the ground around an especially productive stand of bushes, and you are likely to see the large, humanlike droppings of black bears, scat which at this time of year is full of blueberry seeds. This graphically demonstrates the survival strategy followed by most fruiting plants, which produce large, nutritious fruits as a bribe for birds and mammals. The small seeds within the fruit are passed, unharmed, through the animal's digestive system and are spread far and wide as the animal travels. (There is a chance that you may even come across the bear itself among the bushes. Black bears are not usually aggressive, but they are potentially dangerous and should always be treated with a great deal of respect. The bear will probably flee at the first sight of you, but if not give it a wide berth and leave it in peace. This is especially true if it is a female with cubs.)

Wherever you pick berries, exercise restraint in your collecting. Taking a hatful for the morning pancakes makes more sense than stripping every bush in the neighborhood, since it leaves berries for the wildlife that depend upon them, not to mention other human visitors. Pick individual berries, rather than than stripping twigs indiscriminately of ripe and unripe ones, and never break branches to get to berries that are too high.

HOTSPOTS

One of the largest wetlands in central Pennsylvania is found at **Bear Meadows Natural Area** near State College. Part open marsh, part spruce and balsam swamp, Bear Meadows is rimmed with blueberry bushes. From State College, take Business Route 322 East to its merger with Route 322 East. From the merger go .7 mile and watch on the right for Bear Meadows Road, poorly marked except for a sign for Tussey Mountain Ski Area. Follow it for 4.6 miles. Just past the intersection with North Meadow Road, take the right fork and go .1 mile to the parking area. The trail, which circles the huge bog and its surrounding forest, begins on the left at the gate, with the rickety observation tower about 200 yards from the road. Especially in a wet summer, this trail requires waterproof boots, and since the 3.3-mile path itself stays in the woods, out of sight of the bog, the only way into Bear Meadows proper is by slogging down a tributary creek. It is messy, but it's the only way to experience the bog itself or to reach the berries.

If you stay on the trail for the whole circuit, don't be misled by a blue-blazed trail that joins the loop path for several hundred yards, then forks left at a spring—take the right fork, which leads to an open glade in the woods. Again, hug the right edge of the glade and turn onto the trail that reappears there. Eventually, the trail joins North Meadow Road; turn right for .5 mile, then right again on the Jean Aron Path, which leads back to the parking area.

Three large bogs full of highbush blueberries, not to mention carnivorous plants and wild orchids, make **Bruce Lake Natural Area**, part of Delaware State Forest in the Poconos, a good place for a berry-sampling hike. Take I-84 to Exit 7, turning south on Route 390; within .1 mile of the exit ramp, turn left into a small parking area. Follow the gated trail (Egypt Meadow Road) to a fork, then go right on Panther Swamp Trail. At the next fork, Panther Swamp is in view to the right; this is a good area for blueberries (and, like Bear Meadows, for mosquitoes). The round trip to Panther Swamp is about 1.5 miles.

For a longer hike, turn left at the fork by Panther Swamp, following Bruce Lake Road, which passes Egypt Meadow Lake and comes to Bruce Lake a total of 2.3 miles from the parking area on Route 390. One of the finest remaining glacial lakes in Pennsylvania, Bruce Lake has a wide area of bog and marsh at its southern end; take the East Branch Trail south, then either loop back north again on the West Branch Trail or continue southeast to the intersection with Rock Oak Ridge Trail. Follow Rock Oak Ridge to Brown Trail which leads at length to Bruce Lake Road at Panther Swamp. The entire circuit is more than 8 miles, and although Rock Oak Ridge and Brown trails are rocky and narrow, the whole loop is fairly level. Brown Trail passes near, but not in sight of, Balsam Swamp; if you head off the trail and into the swamp itself, use a compass to take a bearing for your return.

Hickory Run State Park (Chapter 28) has excellent berry picking in meadows along the entrance road, a mile or so before the park office. Just down the road from Bruce Lake is **Promised Land State Park**, which like most Poconos parks has good stands of highbush and lowbush blueberries; check with the park office, about 4 miles south of I-84 on Route 390, for suggestions.

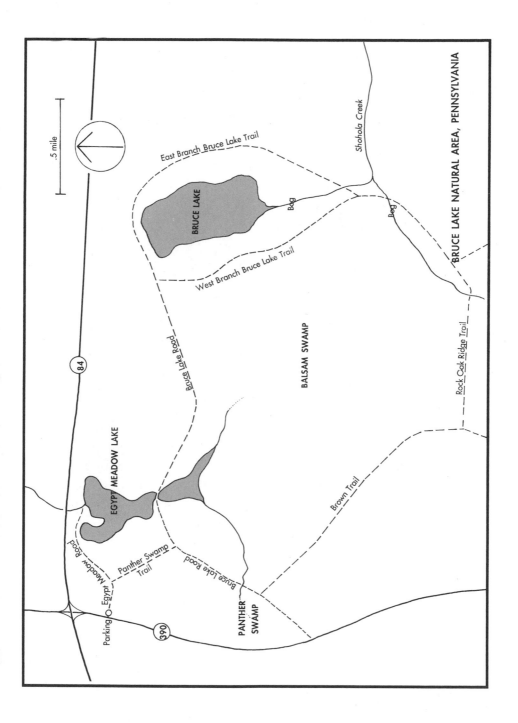

BRUCE LAKE NATURAL AREA, PENNSYLVANIA

.5 mile

East Branch Bruce Lake Trail

BRUCE LAKE

Bog

Shohola Creek

Bog

West Branch Bruce Lake Trail

BALSAM SWAMP

Bruce Lake Road

Rock Oak Ridge Trail

84

EGYPT MEADOW LAKE

Brown Trail

Meadow Road

Panther Swamp Trail

Bruce Lake Road

Parking Egypt

PANTHER SWAMP

390

35

Breakout: Vanishing Wildflowers

When most people mention endangered species, they are thinking of animals, not plants. Yet human development and destruction have taken as great a toll among native shrubs, wildflowers and trees as among birds or mammals.

Wildflowers in particular have been hard-hit. Many require specialized habitats, while others, like the native orchids, have suffered from collecting for the plant trade. The numbers are startling; in Pennsylvania alone, nearly 450 species of native plants are considered endangered, threatened, vulnerable or of undetermined status, while another 100 have been lost completely. That represents more than 10 percent of the state's original native species—and the same sad story is repeated in the region's other states as well.

Habitat destruction has inflicted the worst damage. Many of the threatened plants are wetlands species, found only in bogs, marshes and swamps—exactly the kinds of habitats that humans have assiduously destroyed for so long. Others are found only in such restricted niches as shale barrens, where dry, rocky growing conditions support unique plant communities; the endangered Kate's mountain clover, found only in a narrow band from Virginia to south-central Pennsylvania, is one such shale barren specialist. Destruction of tidal areas, too, has driven many plants to the brink.

The loss of habitat is often due to anonymous destruction, but the collection of rare plants cannot be excused by ignorance. Many naturalists keep the location of unusual wildflowers, especially orchids, a closely guarded secret, for fear that someone will dig them up for their own gardens or for sale to the wild plant trade. (Even many of the wildflower hotspots listed in this book, protected from most threats by public ownership, are not completely safe from thieves with shovels.)

Overcollecting for the plant trade threatens a number of native orchids, including the yellow lady's-slipper shown here, while other species have been endangered by habitat destruction.

Ironically, the recent interest in gardening with native species has put many wildflowers under even more stress. Many of the most popular woodland varieties, like wild orchids and trilliums, are taken from the wild, either legally or illegally. A few retailers purchase nursery-propagated plants, but the supply is limited—it may take years for a trillium to reach marketable size, for instance. In the case of native orchids there is currently no domesticated source at all, since the plants cannot be captively propagated like hothouse orchids. What is worse, wild orchids like lady's-slippers require symbiotic microbes in the soil, and very few survive in their new surroundings.

As a rule, shun all wild orchids, and do not buy any native wildflowers unless you can be certain that they have been nursery-*propagated*, and not just nursery-reared, since some unscrupulous plant merchants sometimes apply that label to wild-collected specimens that have been kept for a short while in the greenhouse.

An alternative is to try your hand at home propagation, by collecting a small quantity of seed from wild stands; experts recommend taking no more than 10 or 20 percent of the seed crop, to allow an adequate level of natural reproduction. A few conservation organizations, like the Brandywine Conservancy in Chadds Ford, Pennsylvania, propagate unusual wildflowers in limited quantities for sale to the public; see the Appendix for the conservancy's address, or check with your local natural history museum, nature society or garden club for information on other wild plant sales.

While it may be easier to work up enthusiasm for bald eagles and otters than for awl-shaped mudwort or Kalm's lobelia, we are coming to understand that every member of the natural community has an intrinsic value, no matter how seemingly insignificant. We would do well to remember the words of the great ecologist Aldo Leopold, who wrote: "To keep every cog and wheel is the first precaution of intelligent tinkering."

AUGUST

August Observations

36

Autumn Shorebirds

By August, the "autumn" migration of shorebirds is already more than a month old, having started for some species by the end of June and for many others in July; indeed, shorebirds of one sort or another (or of one age or another) are moving through the region in virtually every month of the year.

Fall migration in the middle of summer? The idea seems absurd to humans, who take the traditional spring/ autumn dichotomy for granted, but shorebirds follow their own calendars. Straggling red knots and semipalmated sandpipers are still passing north through the region in mid-June, bound for the islands of Arctic Canada, while female Wilson's phalaropes, which nest much farther south (and which leave incubation and chick rearing to the males), are already heading the other way again in small numbers, with western South America their ultimate destination.

This is an extreme example, but the point is that a significant flow of shorebird migrants are going south weeks or months before people think to look for the first hint of fall (the same applies to songbirds, covered in Chapter 38). By July, small numbers of lesser golden-plovers, yellowlegs and least sandpipers, as well as other species, are filtering south.

These early migrants are usually adults, and after they pass through the area, shorebird numbers drop again—but only for a time. With the coming of August, the pace quickens as the tidal flats, beaches and mud bars come alive with newly arrived flocks, a peak that continues through early September.

There is one crucial difference between the northward and southbound migrations—plumage. In the spring, shorebirds are generally sporting their breeding finest (technically referred to as full alternate plumage), freshly molted, crisp and colorful; many have distinctive patterns, like the dunlin's black belly patch, or the red knot's rusty underparts. That all changes on the return trip south. The adults are threadbare and worn, their plumage faded by exposure to the sun and rain, feather edges tattered. Many will have begun molting into their drab winter, or basic, plumage, resulting in some odd-looking combinations.

Even worse, they are joined by the juveniles, most of which are a confusingly similar shade of what might be called shorebird gray, in patterns close but not identical to those of the winter adults. Identification often hinges not on bold field marks like wing bars, as in songbirds, but on extraordinarily subtle clues, like the marginally curved tip of a western sandpiper's bill, compared with the somewhat straighter tip of the semipalmated sandpiper's. Squinting through a spotting scope, trying to see through the heat waves while marsh flies are dive-bombing your head, it is enough to discourage even the most ardent beginning shorebird-watcher.

Persevere. Fall shorebirds are a challenge that can be mastered with patience and practice. Learn the common species first, and don't be afraid to ignore those you can't identify. Neither should you be afraid to ask for help; the hotspots listed below are frequented by some of the most experienced birders in the country, and most are delighted to help a novice with troublesome identifications. Ten minutes' instruction in the field can be more valuable than a shelf full of field guides.

HOTSPOTS

With the Atlantic coast and the Delaware and Chesapeake bays lying within its boundaries, the mid-Atlantic region is rich in good places for shorebirds. In addition to the hotspots listed here, make a habit of checking possible sites in your own area. Away from the coast, sewage treatment ponds are consistently productive, as are reservoirs which (through planned drawdowns or drought) have large stretches of exposed shoreline. Mud flats are especially attractive to shorebirds, as are flooded fields and meadows.

Even at a known hotspot, water levels can be a shorebird fanatic's best friend or worst enemy. Many national wildlife refuges, for example, are managed almost exclusively for waterfowl, so impoundments are kept brimming—great for ducks, but lousy for shorebirds. In a drought year, however, even the wildlife managers may not be able to keep the pools full, and the resulting flats can attract thousands of shorebirds. By the same token, areas that normally have shallow water in late summer may be arid as a result of an unusually dry season. Take local conditions into account, and learn to think like a shorebird.

One of the best shorebird stops in New Jersey is the **Brigantine** unit of Forsythe NWR, just north of Atlantic City. Semipalmated and black-bellied plover, ruddy turnstone, yellowlegs of both species, dunlin, short-billed dowitcher, sanderlings and semipalmated, least and western sandpipers are all common at this time of year, and nearly three dozen species have been recorded during the fall migration. The tidal area to the right (south) of the loop road just beyond the entrance, and the vast, vegetation-pocked East Pool, are the prime shorebird areas here. For general directions to Brigantine, see Chapter 6.

Cape May, about 45 miles south of Brigantine, is

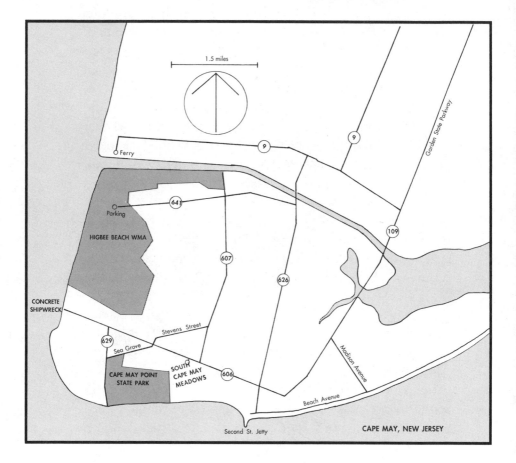

1.5 miles

Garden State Parkway

9

9

○ Ferry

641

○ Parking

HIGBEE BEACH WMA

607

626

109

CONCRETE
SHIPWRECK

Stevens Street

629

Sea Grove

SOUTH
CAPE MAY
MEADOWS

606

Madison Avenue

CAPE MAY POINT
STATE PARK

Beach Avenue

Second St. Jetty

CAPE MAY, NEW JERSEY

another stellar site on the fall shorebird circuit, particularly the 200-acre assemblage of pools and brush known as the South Cape May Meadows, which can produce fabulous birding. For general directions to Cape May, see Chapter 3; at the intersection of Broadway (626) and Sunset Boulevard (606) turn right onto Sunset, heading west. Go .6 mile and pull into the small parking area on the left for the Nature Conservancy's Cape May Migratory Bird Refuge, as the meadows are more properly known. Take the trail that begins on the right and heads straight across the flats to the dune line; once at the beach turn left, walk several hundred yards and follow the path back across the dunes and toward the road once more.

While at Cape May, also check the ponds at Cape May Point State Park (Chapter 3) and along the trail south of the parking lot at Higbee Beach WMA (Chapter 3). To the northeast of the peninsula is **Nummy Island** (see Chapter 32, under Stone Harbor), site of a huge gull colony and one of the best places in southern New Jersey for shorebirds.

Delaware's outstanding shorebird site is **Bombay Hook NWR** near Smyrna, which routinely produces such tantalizing rarities as ruffs, curlew sandpipers and, consistently, Hudsonian godwits, as well as huge concentrations of the more typical autumn shorebirds. The refuge is also well known for black-necked stilts, which breed here on occasion, and for the region's biggest gathering of American avocets; the avocets usually peak later in the fall, however, and are covered in detail in Chapter 47. For directions to Bombay Hook, see Chapter 11; for shorebirds, the best bets are the tidal flats east of the auto tour road and (depending on water levels) Raymond and Shearness pools. Nearby and well worth a side trip is **Port Mahon Road**, with directions given in Chapter 2, and **Little Creek WMA** (Chapter 47).

Still further south, **Assateague Island** is considered by many birders one of the best shorebird locations in the region, with sanderlings, knots and plovers along the beach and dowitchers, semipalmated sandpipers, western sand-pipers and many other species on the mud flats of the tidal areas and impoundments. Directions for both the northern (Maryland) end of Assateague and Chincoteague NWR at the Virginia end are found in Chapter 27.

Back Bay NWR in Virginia, as well as *False Cape State Park* just to its south, are both exceptionally good for sanderlings in most years; see Chapter 3 for directions to Back Bay; False Cape is accessible by foot from the refuge trail system.

Generally speaking, the Chesapeake Bay is not as good for shorebirds as the Atlantic coast or lower Delaware Bay, but in recent years an exceptional hotspot has come to light at the northern end of the bay, just a few miles east of Baltimore. Maryland's *Hart-Miller Island State Park*, a cluster of low islands just off the mouth of Back River, is accessible only by boat, but for the birder willing to make the trip, the rewards can include more than thirty species of shorebirds, with large numbers of yellowlegs, semipal-mated, least, western and pectoral sandpipers, and the potential for rarities including Baird's and buff-breasted sandpipers.

For those with their own boats, a ramp is available at Rocky Point Park; from I-695, go east on Route 150 (Eastern Avenue). Approximately 1.5 miles after crossing the river, turn south on Marlyn Avenue, which leads to Back River Neck Road and the park. Boat rentals are also available at the park, as well on the south side of the river, reached as follows: Take 695 to Exit 42 (Sparrows Point/151 South). Then follow signs for Route 20, Edgemere and Fort Howard, a right exit. At the T-intersection, turn right onto Route 20 South. Go 1.7 miles through the village, and turn left onto Miller Island Road, which dead-ends 2.1 miles farther. There are two boat rentals with ramps, but no public launch.

Without a doubt, the region's best shorebird spot west of the Appalachians is *Presque Isle State Park* (general directions in Chapter 2). With its abundance of shoreline and wetlands, varying from small woodland marshes favored by solitary sandpipers to wide beaches of the sort sanderlings love, the peninsula draws thousands of migrating shorebirds. An area that merits special mention is Gull Point and the Bird Sanctuary at the eastern end, although some of the best areas are being steadily swallowed by growing vegetation.

37

A Blaze of
Blazing Star

Several times in earlier chapters, reference has been made to the last period of glacial advance in the region, about fourteen thousand years ago, which resulted in a cold, wet climate suited to boreal plants and animals. This was not the only climatic change, however; about seven thousand years ago the pendulum swung the other way, and the climate became somewhat warmer and drier than it is now.

Such seemingly insignificant changes in temperature and rainfall can have profound effects on living things, and paleobotanists believe that the prairies of the Midwest began expanding east, replacing what had been mixed hardwood forests. One "tongue" of prairie apparently made it as far as the Pittsburgh Plateau in western Pennsylvania, bringing with it a Plains community of animals and plants.

The conditions that suited the prairie ecosystem lasted for about three thousand years, until the climate made another of its unpredictable twitches, this time toward the wetter, cooler end. Prairies do best in fairly dry conditions, when fires can control the encroachment of trees, and the Pennsylvania prairie slowly retreated as the forest reasserted itself.

It retreated everywhere, that is, but for a few tiny patches where local conditions continued to favor prairie plants (especially those tolerant of wet meadows) over trees. One of these relict prairies is protected at Jennings Environmental Education Center, a Pennsylvania Bureau of Parks facility just south of Slippery Rock—and the highlight of its natural calendar is the bloom of the dense blazing star the first week of August.

Blazing star (*Liatris spicata*), a member of the diverse composite family that includes sunflowers and asters, is relatively inconspicuous for the first half of the summer, but by late July it raises a single, tall flower stalk that may reach as high as 5 feet. When the flowers open a week or so later, the stalk becomes a spire of purple, intermingled with the yellows of the goldenrod and coreopsis. At Jennings, the blazing star blooms in such profusion that the spectacle is breathtaking, even though the prairie fragment is only a portion of the 300-acre preserve.

A wide variety of late summer wildflowers bloom along with the blazing star, among them boneset, Joe-Pye-weed, bowman's-root with its shadbushlike petals, blue vervain and meadowsweet. Late summer is also the time to look for purple fringed orchis, which blooms in damp areas along the creek.

Signs alert visitors that the blazing star is not the only prairie species at Jennings. The eastern massasauga rattle-snake, a small, inoffensive—and endangered—species, is also found on the preserve, one of only six places where it can still be found in Pennsylvania. Usually less than 2 feet long, the "swamp rattler," as it is sometimes called, is dusky gray, with a series of large, blackish blotches running down the back and a matching series of smaller spots along the sides. Eastern massasaugas are found in wet prairies from western Pennsylvania to Wisconsin and eastern Missouri, preferring to hibernate below the waterline in crayfish burrows, which a visitor to Jennings quickly finds are common here. Shy and very rarely seen, the massasauga is no cause for concern, although if you are lucky enough to find one, do not disturb it. Because it is listed as an endangered species by the state of Pennsylvania, the massasauga is fully protected by law.

HOTSPOTS

To see the relict prairie at *Jennings Environmental Education Center*, take Route 173 South from the town of Slippery Rock. Go 4.9 miles to the junction with Route 8 South, turn right and make an immediate right again onto Route 528 South, following the sign for Jennings. Three-tenths of a mile down 528 are two parking areas; the one on the left is for the nature center, while the lot on the right has access to the prairie fragment. Follow the Blazing Star Trail to the Prairie Relict Trail, which forms a short loop.

To the casual eye, the fragment looks like fingers of field penetrating into the forest, when in fact the reverse is true, as the young white oaks and maples dotting the prairie attest. Scientists speculate that the Jennings prairie was spared forest encroachment because it is underlaid by fine glacial silt, laid down several thousand years before the prairie ecosystem arrived. The damp silt apparently discourages trees, and periodic fires—which actually benefit prairie plants like blazing star—further reduced competition. To maintain the prairie, portions are burned off in early spring each year; after the fire the dead, blackened stalks of last year's plants stand forlorn, while already the new, green growth of the coming summer is appearing at ground level.

38

Fall Landbird Traps

The same combinations of geography and weather that funnel the spring landbird migration into a few narrow corridors work, as well, in autumn—in fact, some sites are even better in August and September than they are in April and May.

The ideal situation (from a naturalist's perspective, if not a bird's) is strong west winds, which force the migrants to the edge of the ocean, and a south-pointing peninsula, which focuses the flight into a small area; all the better if the birds must face a long water crossing, so that they linger for several days on the peninsula before trying to leave. That is a perfect description of Cape May, Cape Charles and several other seasonal hotspots.

Songbird-watching in the fall is a more complex, frustrating undertaking than in the spring. In May, the birds are in their fresh breeding plumage and the males are singing almost continuously, drawing attention to themselves. By autumn—which for songbirds begins in August—the situation has changed. With the breeding season over the males have fallen silent, except for the flight calls and chips that serve as flock communication, and which are much harder to learn than the territorial songs.

Adding to the difficulty, some species will have molted into drabber plumage patterns for the winter—male scarlet tanagers change from brilliant crimson to greenish-yellow, while male bay-breasted warblers lose all but a hint of their distinctive rusty coloration. Even among those species that do not change patterns, the easily identifiable adult males will be greatly outnumbered by females and juveniles of both sexes, all of which are much harder for the beginner to separate confidently. The ratio of juveniles to adults rises even more in September, when most of the adults have already passed through the region.

The situation is far from impossible, however. The young birds may have a drabber set of feathers, but most bear at least passing resemblance to their parents' pattern, and the general body shape, habitat and habits provide other vital clues. And remember—as nice as it is to identify everything that passes your binoculars, there is nothing wrong with just sitting back and enjoying the parade without fussing over who's who.

HOTSPOTS

Anyone with an interest in birds owes himself or herself a trip to **Cape May** in autumn to catch the landbird migration. In effect, the entire state of New Jersey acts as a funnel, feeding migrants down through the Pine Barrens and depositing them on this incredibly rich peninsula separating Delaware Bay and the Atlantic. See Chapter 3 and Chapter 22 for directions to Higbee Beach WMA and the Beanery, two of the best places for small birds. The bayberry and poison ivy thickets that surround the red-blazed boardwalk trail at Cape May Point State Park (Chapter 3) are also very good; the yellow and blue trails at the park lead through woods, fields and marshland, with several observation platforms. Nearby, and worth checking, are the South Cape May Meadows (Chapter 36). The woodlands immediately around Lily Lake and the Cape May Bird Observatory

(CMBO) office can be productive; from Cape May Point State Park walk north along Lighthouse Avenue .5 mile, then left on Lake Drive to the CMBO office, where a list of recent area sightings is maintained.

Starting in August, but reaching a peak in September, tree swallows congregate at Cape May, sometimes by the tens of thousands; the passage of a big flock, covering the sky in a living sheet, is spectacular, but even more remarkable is the sight of thousands of swallows forming a huge funnel cloud over their evening roost trees, spiraling down like a tornado collapsing upon itself. The flocks may be anywhere, but the hawk-watch platform at Cape May Point State Park is a good place to scan for the evening roost concentrations.

Also in New Jersey, **Sandy Hook**, within sight of New York City and part of Gateway National Recreation Area, can be good for fall songbirds, even though this peninsula juts north instead of south. For general directions see Chapter 2; the woodland north of Parking Lot F is especially productive.

Far less well known among birders than Cape May, **Cape Charles**, at the southern end of the Delmarva Peninsula, can be every bit as rewarding as its more famous New Jersey counterpart. Bird banders have long recognized its potential, with a major songbird banding project in operation since the 1960s, and the establishment of Eastern Shore of Virginia NWR is bringing new interest to this unsung hotspot. Unfortunately, the Kiptopeke banding site on the west side of the cape is being developed into a major campground, but the new refuge should provide a focus for naturalists. For directions to the cape, see Chapter 46; an early morning walk along the wooded, half-mile trail is most productive the last two weeks of August and in early September.

The **Chesapeake Bay Bridge-Tunnel**, just south of Cape Charles, would seem to offer little to attract songbirds, with nothing but barren, rocky islands connected by ribbons of highway. But since the bridge crosses the wide mouth of the Chesapeake Bay, it provides a resting spot for weary migrants, which forage on the treeless islands, completely exposed to birders. As detailed in Chapter 3, access to all but one of the four islands is by permit only, but the permits are issued free to birders who apply in advance of a trip and are good for the calendar year. In addition to the normal regional migrants, the CBBT islands have a deserved reputation for producing completely unexpected rarities, including—once—a rock wren, a species not usually found east of Texas. Clay-colored sparrows, rare migrants elsewhere in the region, usually stage several appearances on the bridge-tunnel each fall.

Also good for fall migrants, especially warblers, is **Sandy Point State Park** in Maryland; see Chapter 22 for directions and suggestions.

Barren of any greenery, the rocky islands of the Chesapeake Bay Bridge-Tunnel are nevertheless an excellent place in autumn for songbirds, which rest here while crossing the bay.

39

Blue Crabs and Crabbing

Like collecting a hatful of blueberries and tasting the bog in their tartness, there is something deeply satisfying about finding your food along the ocean—perhaps a chord that echoes far back in our species' history, when we lived off the provender of the land and sea. Although most of us are far removed from that kind of life today, its flavor is easily recaptured. All you need is a piece of fresh fish tied to a length of string, a long-handled net and a tidal creek. The crabs will do the rest.

Blue crabs, to be exact, the gourmet's delight and one of the most important species along the Atlantic coast and Delaware and Chesapeake bays. The focus of a multimillion-dollar commercial fishery, the crabs provide untold hours of fun (and uncounted meals) for weekend crabbers as well.

Most of the activities described in this book are "nonconsumptive"—matters of watching and appreciating from a distance, rather than using the plants or animals directly. To some, the idea of consumptive use is a natural outgrowth of their interest in natural history; to others, it is a repugnant intrusion on nature. Certainly, from a biological standpoint, recreational crabbing poses no threat to the vast stocks of blue crabs in the region's coastal waters.

Crabbing is a decidedly low-tech undertaking and can be as minimalistic as the crabber chooses. Commercial crabbers often use large wire traps, while weekend crabbers tend toward folding wire traps, bought for a few dollars in shore-town hardware stores. The trap consists of a heavy wire framework with a mesh top and bottom and four hinged sides, each with a string tied to the top. The four strings are, in turn, knotted to a single cord, and the trap is baited and lowered from a boat or dock. On the bottom, the sides open flat, allowing the crabs to enter for the bait, but when the trap is hoisted the sides snap upright, trapping (one hopes) a crab or two within.

Such is the temperament of an Atlantic blue crab, however, that a trap isn't really necessary. When a hungry crab finds a piece of food it is loathe to release it, so a piece of bait tied to a string and tossed into shallow water can— once it begins twitching and moving, evidence that a crab is on the other end—be ever so slowly retrieved, with the crab tenaciously tugging at the bait. The trick is to ease the crab over the opening of a long-handled net, then neatly scoop up the crustacean. Commercial trotline crabbers exploit the same weakness on a larger scale, but an adept novice can fill a bushel basket with a little practice. Expect to lose a few, and expect also get nipped by a couple of crabs, which are amazingly agile and exceedingly accurate with their claws. A pinch *hurts*.

Another method of catching crabs is to stalk them on foot with a dip net. Take a bushel basket with a lid and tie it securely into the middle of an inflated inner tube, so that half the basket is submerged. Rope the tube to your belt, don shorts and sneakers, and head into waist-deep water with a long-handled crab net. Poke slowly through aquatic vegetation, and when a crab makes a break from cover, dip it up quickly. Polarized sunglasses help tremendously.

The object of all this effort is one of the tastiest crustaceans, with a trim beauty to boot. The carapace, or shell, of an adult blue crab ranges from 5 to 7 inches, measured across the back from point to point. The carapace is olive, shading to white underneath; the claws and legs are tinged with cobalt blue, and in the females, the tips of the claws are bright red. Sex is more accurately determined by looking at the crab's apron, the triangular abdominal segment between the legs on the underside. In an immature female the apron is straight-sided, forming an equilateral triangle, while an adult female, known as a sook, has a wider, more rounded apron. A jimmy, or male, has an apron that is extremely long and narrow. Sexing the crabs is important, since regulations in some states differ for males and females.

There is no calculating the number of chicken necks that are dunked as crab bait each year in the mid-Atlantic region, even though poultry makes rather poor bait. A much better choice is fresh fish, replaced frequently as it becomes tattered and pasty, since crabs are epicures in their own right and scorn old or rotten food, popular opinion to the contrary.

Bushel baskets with wooden lids are the traditional repository for captured crabs, but any dry, ventilated container with a lid will work, provided the crabs are kept cool and out of the sun. The crabs must be kept alive until the moment of cooking, and any dead crabs should be discarded immediately—spoiled seafood is dangerous, and crabs no less so.

Cook the crabs by steaming them for about 30 minutes (boiling for about 10 minutes also works, but is frowned upon by many crab connoisseurs), with a dash of salt and vinegar in the water and seafood seasoning to taste. Allow the cooked crabs to cool for several minutes. To peel, or pick, a crab, pull back the apron and lift off the carapace, cutting off the legs from the inside of the shell. Crack the shell down the middle along the seam of the apron, and pick out the nuggets of meat on either side; use a nutcracker and nutpick to extract the sweet meat from the claws and legs. It is messy, delicious work.

There is scarcely a tidal cove or fishing pier in the region that won't produce blue crabs, a testament to this species' incredible abundance. Still, there are some places where crabbing is better (or easier) than others.

Most coastal states allow recreational crabbing without a license and with minimal restrictions; crabbers are usually required to observe a minimum 5-inch shell size, but details vary. For example, Virginia traditionally has no closed season and no size limit on females, while imposing a 5-inch limit on males; Maryland closes the crab season from January to the end of March and dictates that all crabs must be at least 5 inches long. Size limits also vary for softshell crabs and peelers in molt. Check with the state conservation department or with a local tackle store for current regulations.

Assateague Island in Maryland and Virginia has always been popular with weekend crabbers, especially Swan Cove at Chincoteague NWR at the Virginia end. Salt water containing the tiny larval, or megalops, stage of the blue crab is pumped each year from Tom's Cove on one side of the causeway into brackish Swan Cove; because crabs grow in proportion to the salinity of the water, the crabs in Swan Cove get bigger, faster, than those on the salt side of the barrier. On a summer weekend dozens of families line the road separating the coves, patiently pulling in handlines; because no boats are allowed in the cove, lines and nets work better than traps.

At the north end of the island in Maryland, saltwater crabbing is available at Old Ferry Landing and, just across Sinepuxent Bay, at the boat launch near the visitors' center and at South Point boat launch. A rising tide is best. For directions to Assateague, see Chapter 27.

Also in Maryland, the waters around **Eastern Neck NWR** are good for crabbing, and the Ingleside Recreation Area has a boat launch and picnic grounds ideal for crabbing; local boat rentals are available at the entrance to the island beside Eastern Neck Narrows. For directions to the refuge, see Chapter 12. To reach Ingleside, take the main refuge road 1.6 miles and turn right at the sign onto a gravel road, which leads another 1.2 miles to a short bluff above the water. The picnic tables are nearby in a grove of locust trees, with toilet facilities. The recreation area is open from dawn to dusk, May 1 through September 30. Car-topped boats can be launched at Ingleside, but trailered craft must be put in across the island, at Bogle's Wharf Landing, where a current Kent County boat license is required for launching.

More detailed information on specific sites for crabbing is available from the coastal state conservation departments. In addition, hundreds of crabbing spots are listed in the excellent *Chesapeake Bay and Susquehanna River Public Access Guide*, published jointly by Virginia, Maryland, Pennsylvania and the District of Columbia; for information on obtaining the 72-page guide, contact the state fish and game departments in those states (addresses are listed in the Appendix).

Fresh from the steamer and ready to eat, a pot of blue crabs speaks of the natural wealth of the region's coastal waters.

40

Breakout:
Hidden Signs of Autumn

Nature study is often a matter of knowing where to look, recognizing that which would otherwise go unnoticed. The change in the seasons is a good example; four times a year, the mid-Atlantic region undergoes a pronounced shift in climate, so dramatic that even the most insulated urbanite, the most dedicated non-naturalist, is forced to sit up and take notice. Of course, they only realize the seasons have changed when the signs become impossible to ignore. For a naturalist, the clues can be vastly more subtle, signaling the passage of one season into another long before the rest of the world knows what's happening.

Take autumn, the season of colorful leaves and cold winds. The first hints come long before October, if you know where to look. In July, the barn swallows, having raised their chicks to fledging, begin to mass in great flocks, weaving through the bug-filled air; starlings, robins and mourning doves are doing the same thing by August, as the hormonal animosities of the breeding season dissipate. Territoriality vanishes, and the birds gather in anticipation of the fall migration. Along the coast, thousands of tree swallows decorate the roadside telephone lines, and shorebirds pass south along the mud flats like a ripple of gray.

In August, the landscape reaches a turning point of color. Through May and June the mountains and fields shone with a fresh, glossy green that became tempered in the muggy days of July. Now, as the corn goes to tassel and the pasture grasses set seed, the farmlands take on a patina of yellow-brown, like the warm polish on hand-worn wood. Even the mountain trees have lost their kelly green luster, and the oaks and hickories have settled into a duller tone, as though they absorbed too much blue from the hazy summer sky.

Here and there in the forest and field edges, though, the first hints of true autumn color are showing. Some species are more precocious than others, and within these varieties are individuals that push the opening bell even further. By August's end, a few black gums will have flared into crimson and maroon, standing out starkly against the backdrop of green; a few sweet birch, usually those growing on the driest hillsides their species can stand, will have changed to gold, especially in the northern reaches of the region. On the staghorn sumac growing thickly along roadsides and fencerows, a scattering of leaves on otherwise green plants will jump the gun by turning blood red a full month before their neighbors change.

When the East is baking under the heat-pump effect of a humid Bermuda High weather system, laying like a wet washcloth across the region, a cold front may seem like nothing more than weather relief. But on the ridges from Pennsylvania south, the first cool, northwest winds of August signal the start of the autumn hawk flight. It is a tentative start, to be sure; only two or three kestrels in a morning, perhaps, or an osprey and an early broad-winged hawk sharing the thermals. As August closes, however, a strong cold front may bring the first significant movement of migrating bald eagles—birds native to Florida, which apparently wander north for the summer and return in August and September.

The songbird and shorebird flights dominate the month's migration, but August skies carry the first of many travelers: the first monarch butterflies on their way to Florida or Mexico, the initial waves of dragonflies heading south, the first ruby-throated hummingbirds to forsake their breeding grounds. Even while these migrants are floating south, others are traveling aimlessly in the other direction—egrets and herons that were reared early in the year in the Deep South and wander north as far as New England for several weeks in late summer and early fall before turning around and heading back again. It is a strange movement and no one is quite sure why they do it at all, but it adds another layer of interest and spice to an already fascinating time of year.

SEPTEMBER

September Observations

41

September Hawk Flights

The earliest days of September seem to hold little of autumn within their hazy, humid hours, but a cold front can change all that overnight, replacing summer's dregs with the first taste of true autumn weather. That same blast of cool air also brings the first major push of migrating hawks, starting a grand passage of raptors that will last until early December.

The autumn hawk flight is the mid-Atlantic region's greatest wildlife spectacle, touching sites as widely spaced as the New Jersey shore and the West Virginia mountains. The migration is as dynamic in composition and timing as it is to watch, and because the flavor of the flight changes drastically from week to week, each distinct phase will be treated separately in three monthly sections, September through November, with information on identification in Chapter 46, and tips on equipment and ways to make your first hawk-watching trip a success in Chapter 51.

A first-time visitor to a hawk lookout will have wandered unknowingly into a world with a language all its own, where initiates talk about buteos and kettles, flying TVs and bird time. Understanding the basics of birds of prey and the mechanics of their migration helps enormously.

As summer fades to autumn, hawks, eagles and

falcons (known collectively as raptors) begin moving south to their wintering grounds, which may be as close as the mid-Atlantic states for a red-tailed hawk, or as distant as Peru in the case of a broad-winged hawk. They do not wander south aimlessly, however, but rather follow traditional pathways determined by geography and weather. Known as leading lines, these geographic features may be mountain ridges, lakeshores or coastlines, and where the migratory path is especially concentrated, the best hawk-watching sites are usually found.

Many of the lookouts are in the mountains, where the specialized structure of the northern Appalachians is particularly helpful. In the ridge-and-valley province of Pennsylvania, for instance, the ridges form neatly parallel lines, pacing each other diagonally across the state and providing a perfect route for migrating birds. When the wind is out of the northwest, as is usually the case following a frontal passage, it strikes the ridges at a 90-degree angle and deflects upward, creating lift. Thus, a migrating hawk can ride the wind along the ridges with a minimum of effort.

If the wind speed or direction is wrong, the hawks may leave the ridges and strike out instead across the valleys, relying on thermals—those bubbles of hot air that are generated by sunlight on fields, roads or rock slides. Inside a thermal, a soaring hawk is lifted rapidly without flapping a wing, a technique shared by sailplane pilots. When the thermal's lift begins to peter out at the top, the hawk simply glides to the next bubble on its flight path (although exactly how they find thermals is an unresolved question), repeating the sequence over and over again through the day. A group of hawks circling tightly in a thermal looks, at a distance, like a cloud of gnats, or a pot of something boiling—perhaps the origin of the word *kettle* to describe a thermaling flock.

To be a successful hawk-watcher means paying attention to the weather, which is the make-or-break factor in all hawk flights. At most lookouts, both along the inland ridges and on the coast, the best flights follow, by a day or so, the passage of a low-pressure system through New England and the arrival of a cold front through the lookout area. Ideally, the winds should be blowing steadily from the north or west at 10 or 15 miles per hour, the humidity and temperature should be falling, and the barometric pressure rising. Generally speaking, a rainy or windless day is a poor bet.

The September hawk flights are dominated by broad-winged hawks, chunky forest raptors that breed north throughout New England and southern Canada. Broad-wings are buteos, the group of soaring hawks that also includes the red-tailed and red-shouldered hawks and which possess wide, rounded wings and fan-shaped tails suited for milking the most lift from a thermal.

Broad-wings are also the only eastern hawk to habitually migrate in flocks, sometimes forming kettles of several hundred. When the broad-wing flight peaks during the second week of the month, it is not unusual for five thousand or more to pass a single spot in the course of a day, and the totals can go much higher. On one September day in 1978, stunned observers at Hawk Mountain Sanctuary in Pennsylvania counted more than twenty-one thousand broad-wings—more than the site's usual tally for the entire season. Broad-wings also seem less dependent on "correct" flight conditions, and good movements may occur on sparse winds or winds from the east or south.

Sharing the September skies with the broad-wings are several other species of raptors. Bald eagles, the highlight to anyone's day, are especially likely on the most blustery winds. More common are ospreys, American kestrels (North America's smallest falcon) and lesser numbers of northern harriers and red-tailed, sharp-shinned and Cooper's hawks.

When the weather looks promising, die-hard hawk-watchers like to get to the lookouts as early as possible so as not to miss a single bird; as a further incentive, the morning air has little in the way of thermal activity, and the first hawks to pass are usually low and close, affording spectacular views in the morning sun. The heaviest migration does not usually start until about 8:30 A.M. standard time (or bird time, as it is known), and the bulk of the broad-winged flight ends about two hours before dark. Other species fly much later, however, particularly ospreys, which can be seen passing in the gloom of twilight.

By the third week of September the broad-winged hawk migration will have noticeably peaked, even as totals for accipiters—the small, agile forest hunters like the sharp-shinned hawk—are growing steadily, setting the stage for the next phase of the flight, in October.

HOTSPOTS

Hawk-watching as a science and a hobby was born in the mid-Atlantic region, and the number of hawk-watching sites here is large and growing each year, as new locations are discovered and publicized. Most are good throughout the fall, but some are better for, say, broad-wings in September or falcons in October. This chapter covers some of the major lookouts in the Pennsylvania and New Jersey mountains; Chapter 46 lists the major coastal sites, while Chapter 51 has suggestions for inland locations south of the Mason-Dixon line.

Hawk Mountain Sanctuary, balanced on a spur of the Kittatinny Ridge, is the granddaddy of hawk lookouts, but it suffers from its own fame, drawing extremely heavy crowds on nice autumn weekends. If you have a choice, visit on a weekday; on a weekend, Saturday is usually less chaotic than Sunday, when the biggest crowds hit from late morning on.

There are two lookouts—South, about 200 yards from the blacktop road and good on days when the wind is from the southeast, and North, the main lookout, a small boulder field perched dramatically a thousand feet above the valley. The trail to North is about three-quarters of a mile long, occasionally steep and quite rocky, so wear sturdy shoes.

Hawk Mountain first came to prominence in the 1920s as a place to shoot hawks rather than watch them. The killing ended in 1934 with the establishment of the sanctuary, and things are more peaceful now. Despite weekend crowds, Hawk Mountain remains one of the best places for a beginner to start. Daily between Labor Day and Thanksgiving there are trained staff naturalists on the lookouts to answer questions, identify hawks and take the daily migration count. On fall weekends outdoor talks cover the natural history of the sanctuary and birds of prey and, if the hawks are not flying well, some hiking trails are open to the public, although much of the 2,000-acre sanctuary is kept closed to human disturbance. The sanctuary visitors' center has museum displays of mounted raptors and interpretive exhibits, a bookstore, an elaborate bird-feeding station and restrooms (latrines are found near North). Bring a lunch, since no food is sold on the sanctuary.

To reach Hawk Mountain, take I-78 to Exit 9 near Hamburg, then follow Route 61 North for 4 miles to Route 895 East. Go approximately 3 miles on 895 to Drehersville, turn right at the sign for the craft village, cross the Little Schuylkill River and follow the road to the top of the mountain. A trail fee is charged, but admission to the visitors' center is free.

Like Hawk Mountain and many of the other lookouts, *Bake Oven Knob*, north of Allentown, Pennsylvania, had a blood-soaked history. Located on the same ridge as Hawk Mountain, it bore the brunt of the hawk shooting after the sanctuary was established. The shoots didn't completely end in Pennsylvania until the early 1970s, when the state belatedly granted full protection to all hawks.

While Bake Oven Knob (named for its similarity to the shape of an old beehive oven) is not a formal sanctuary, it is protected from development by its owner, the Pennsylvania Game Commission, which manages it and the surrounding land for wildlife. In most respects the flights are the same in content and timing as Hawk Mountain's, and there are two lookouts—South, for days of southerly winds, and North, for when the wind is from the northwest. To reach the knob, take I-78 West from Allentown to Route 309 North for 14 miles. Exactly 2 miles beyond the intersection with state Route 143, turn right onto a paved road for 2 miles, then left onto an unmarked dirt road. The parking lots are at the top of the mountain. Bake Oven Knob is along the Appalachian Trail to the northeast, while **Baer Rocks** (known variously as Bear or Bears Rocks), another good lookout with fewer people, is about a mile down the trail in the opposite direction.

What **Waggoner's Gap** and the **Route 183 Lookout**, both in Pennsylvania, lack in wilderness feeling, they make up for in numbers of hawks. Both are close to main roads, one next to huge radio towers, the other near a ruined building—hardly the best esthetics. Waggoner's Gap is on the Kittatinny Ridge northwest of Carlisle; take Route 74 North from Carlisle for 8.5 miles to the communications towers at the mountaintop. Either park on the left without blocking access to that tower, or carefully drive up the rutted dirt road on the right to a flat parking area. The hawk-watch is a boulder field to the east of here, behind a set of smaller towers.

To reach the Route 183 Lookout in Schuylkill County, take I-78 to Route 183 at the Strausstown exit, then follow 183 to the top of the Blue Mountain. Turn right and park at the sign for state game lands, then walk up the highway to the crest and watch from the open area on the west side. With northwest winds, stay near the northern edge of the clearing and watch to the east and north. There are no panoramic views of incoming birds here—they appear suddenly above the trees and may move across the ridge in a wide front.

Tuscarora Summit, just east of McConnellsburg in south-central Pennsylvania, is another excellent ridge overlook for northwest winds. From the Pennsylvania Turnpike take the Fort Littleton exit onto Route 522 South 8 miles to Route 30 East; drive approximately 2 miles to the top of Tuscarora Mountain and park. The lookout, a boulder field known locally as the Pulpit, is nearby.

Montclair Hawk Lookout Sanctuary, a former quarry, leads the list of inland hotspots in New Jersey, especially for broad-winged and sharp-shinned hawks. Owned by the New Jersey Audubon Society, this spot on First Watchung Mountain has been the site of organized watches since the late 1950s. To get there, take the Garden State Expressway to Bloomfield, getting off at Exit 151 (Watchung Avenue). Go west on Watchung 2.1 miles to Upper Mountain Avenue, turn right and go .6 mile to Bradford Avenue; make a left onto Bradford, go .1 mile and make a right onto Edgecliff Road. Follow Edgecliff to Mill's

The autumn migration of hawks, eagles and falcons is the mid-Atlantic region's greatest wildlife spectacle, luring naturalists to such lookouts as Hawk Mountain Sanctuary in eastern Pennsylvania, shown here.

Reservation, park and backtrack on foot down the road to the trail and stairs on the right, which lead to the lookout.

Raccoon Ridge, in Warren County, New Jersey, sits on the Kittatinny Ridge. Hawk flights are excellent, although a long hike from the road discourages many would-be visitors. From I-80, take Route 521 north 5 miles, then go west on Route 94 through Blairstown to Walnut Valley. Turn north on Walnut Valley Road and drive to the end, parking at the Yard's Creek Pumped Storage Station. From the picnic grounds, follow the road (on foot) 1 mile to Yard's Creek Reservoir, then around the reservoir another 1.2 miles to a trail that bears off to the northwest. Follow the trail a quarter mile to its junction with the Appalachian Trail. Turn right and take the AT a short distance to Big Raccoon Lookout, the best spot for northwest winds. If winds are from the east or south, go another quarter mile on the AT to Little Raccoon Lookout.

In the northwestern corner of New Jersey, the **Sunrise Mountain** overlook offers both excellent flights and easy access, with only a short uphill trail from the parking lot to the summit. It is also one of the few all-weather hawkwatches in the region, with a large, stone pavilion perched right at the top, a perfect shelter on a blustery, showery day. All this combines to make it one of the most popular hawkwatching points in the state, and it can be very crowded on a good weekend. To reach the overlook, take I-80 to Route 15 or 206 North, which join at Ross Corner, about 20 miles north of the interstate. Follow 206/15 north another 6.4 miles to Route 636, a right turn marked by a sign for Upper North Shore and Sunrise Mountain. Go .2 mile and turn left onto Sunrise Mountain Road, which is one-way to the summit; after 4.2 miles bear right at the fork (be alert here for two-way traffic) and go another .8 mile to the parking lot. The path to the summit is on the right. To leave, return to the fork and turn right, go 3.2 miles to a stop sign, turn left and travel another 4.7 miles to Route 206. There is no directional sign, but north is to the right and south to the left.

42

Bugling Elk

Once, the forests of the mid-Atlantic region rang each fall with the grunting squeal of bull elk, bugling to call females and challenge rival males. Before colonization, these massive deer were common across the East, but unrestricted market hunting and the felling of the virgin forests doomed them.

The last Pennsylvania elk was killed in 1867, along a stream called Bennett's Branch in what would, ironically, become Elk County. The entire eastern subspecies became extinct not long after that, eliminated across its range along with timber wolves, mountain lions and several other wilderness animals.

But that was not quite the end of elk in Pennsylvania. Between 1913 and 1926, the state Game Commission released 177 Rocky Mountain elk in scattered locations across nine counties. At first the animals did well enough to support annual hunting seasons, but after stocking ceased the species began a second decline. The 1931 hunting season was the last, and shortly afterwards elk again disappeared from the Blue Mountain and the Poconos. Today, elk survive in only one small area of Pennsylvania— a rugged corner of Cameron and Elk counties in the state's remote north-central region. The herd's number fluctuates each year, but normally about 180 elk can be found here, their movements centered around the 14,000 acres of State Game Lands 14. It is the only wild elk herd east of the Mississippi.

Although elk are sometimes mistaken for deer, the differences are dramatic. White-tailed deer average about 120 pounds and have forward-sweeping antlers and a conspicuous tail. Elk weigh anywhere from 500 to 1,000 pounds and have huge antlers that sweep back from the head and a stubby tail surrounded by a large, pale rump patch. Unlike deer, which can tolerate areas as heavily developed as the fringes of Philadelphia, elk are wilderness animals. Elk and Cameron counties, with their steep mountains and relatively unbroken forests, are considered the one ideal place in the state for elk. Game Commission biologists consider it unlikely that elk would thrive anywhere else in the state, so no further introductions are planned.

The elk can be seen here year-round but are most visible in summer and fall, when they graze in farm fields scattered among the forests. In September, however, the bulls begin to gather their harems of cow elk, bugling to the frosty air and affording the observer an unmatched opportunity to see them—and hear them.

Those who have never heard an elk bugle are usually surprised that such a big animal can make such a high-pitched sound. The bugle starts as a series of deep grunts, then breaks into a rising squeal that carries across long distances, and serves as both a trespassing notice to interloping males and a challenge to a fight. During the rut, bulls will battle each other for dominance, lowering their heads and crashing their majestic racks together, each straining with all the strength in its powerful legs and neck to rout the other. Constantly on edge through the rut, bull elk take offense easily, and unlucky ponies and cattle have been gored to death when they crossed paths with an irritable elk. Human observers would do well to remember this lesson and keep a distance from the elk.

Though such attacks on livestock are obviously rare, the elk have caused major problems for farmers in their range. A bull that weighs half a ton can pack away plenty of food in a night's grazing. If that food happens to be wheat or corn—and if it is a herd of elk instead of just one, and if they come back night after night—one quickly appreciates the damage they are capable of inflicting on crops. The elk have always been a problem, but farmers feel especially beleaguered in recent years by a herd that has more than doubled in size since the early 1970s. In 1981 the Pennsylvania Game Commission proposed a very restricted hunting season to thin the herd, but strong public opposition convinced the agency to scrap the plan.

Unwittingly, the Game Commission and the state Bureau of Forestry may have caused the miniexplosion in elk numbers. In the early 1970s, crews bulldozed openings and clear-cut blocks of forest on state game lands, which were then seeded with grasses and crops. The idea was to lure the elk away from the farmlands, and it worked to a degree—but it also gave the herd a new food supply and an impetus for growth. The increase leveled off in the early 1980s, and despite slight changes the herd has numbered between 150 and 180 ever since. Biologists feel that illegal shooting, legal culling by farmers for crop damage and a parasite called brainworm are just balancing out the calf crop.

Each January, the Game Commission conducts a two- or three-day survey of the herd, which has usually broken into scattered, small bands for the winter. Biologists on snowshoes and in helicopters fan out, trying to count all the elk to determine the herd's sex and age structure and health. The count is conducted in the traditional elk range, however, and local residents have, in recent years, reported elk much farther afield, suggesting that the herd may actually be bigger than the surveys would indicate.

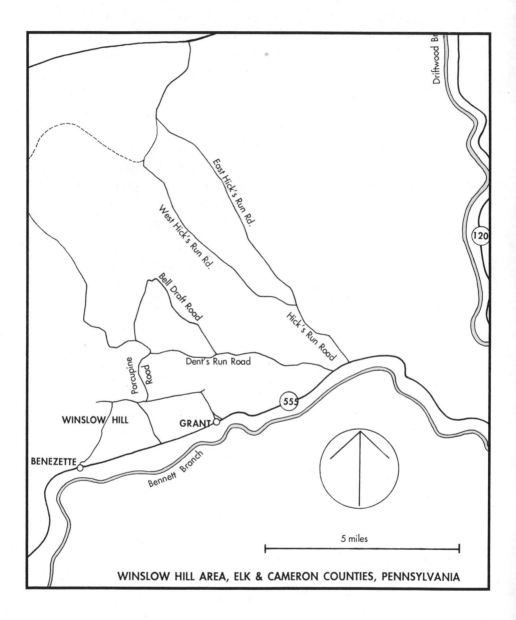

5 miles

WINSLOW HILL AREA, ELK & CAMERON COUNTIES, PENNSYLVANIA

HOTSPOTS

Because the elk are wild, unfenced animals, it is impossible to predict their exact whereabouts on a day-to-day basis. There are a few places within their range, however, where they can be counted on to make regular appearances, and local residents (who are coming to realize the tourism value of the herd) are usually happy to direct visitors to the current hotspot.

The rut is the ideal time to look for elk. The mating activity begins in late August, reaches a peak during the second and third weeks of September, and dwindles in the early days of October. During the rut, bull elk in particular are careless about exposing themselves to view and less concerned about the presence of humans. As with deer, dawn and dusk are the best times to look.

The elk usually stay within a roughly rectangular, largely roadless area bounded by the towns of St. Mary's and Weedville in Elk County, and Emporium and Driftwood in Cameron County. For car viewing, the best bet is **Winslow Hill** near Benezette, an area of reclaimed strip mines that now supports grass, attracting the elk regularly. Because much of Winslow Hill is open rather than forested, it provides an excellent opportunity to watch, listen to and possibly photograph the elk. Remember that a car acts as a very effective blind, and animals that ignore vehicles may panic when a person steps out. If no elk are visible, get to a high elevation and listen for bugling. Those who know how to use an elk call may be able to lure a bugling bull in for pictures during the rut, but this takes considerable skill.

Finding elk on foot is a much chancier affair. Even though they are not hunted, the elk are extremely wary, and the steep mountains and thick woods make for difficult walking. Nevertheless they can be stalked, if the stalker uses care and perseverance, and the **Dent's Run** area and west branch of **Hick's Run** are both excellent. While looking for elk on foot, move slowly and, if possible, into the wind, stopping frequently to look for movement. The elk tend to congregate in stream bottoms, especially where there are dense stands of pines or hemlocks.

While hiking, watch for elk sign, including piles of scat; the droppings are similar in shape to a deer's, but each is about three-quarters of an inch long and usually pointed at one end. Look, too, for elk rubs, the ravaged trees where bulls have stripped the velvet from their antlers. In some places, whole groves of young pines have been smashed— testament to the power of these magnificent creatures.

Take I-80 northwest of the town of Clearfield, then take the exit for Route 153 North. Go 7.9 miles, turning right at the light onto Route 255 North, then another 2.5 miles to the juncture with Route 555 East toward Driftwood. Follow 555 for 13.9 miles to Benezette; just after crossing a small bridge at the west edge of town, turn left and go .1 mile, following the road sign right and uphill for 2.3 miles to the top of Winslow Hill. The road becomes dirt and passes through old farms, brushy fields and reclaimed mine lands. At the fork in the road go left (a dead end) 100 yards and scan the distant hills for elk, then return to the fork and go right for .7 mile.

At the next fork, go right, a steep descent on Township Road 424 through thick woods which, after 1.4 miles, returns you to Route 555. Turn left and go 2 miles to the village of Grant. Watch carefully on the left for Grant Hill Road, a hidden dirt road with two outlets a short distance from each other. Take this rather rough road for 1.2 miles to a fork, then go left for another 1.5 miles. Turn right onto Porcupine Road, a badly rutted road that may be dicey in wet weather. Follow Porcupine for 1.7 miles, turning left at the fork partway through. Cross a small bridge to Dent's Run Road (unmarked), and turn right.

Dent's Run is an orange, mine-acid drainage creek, but it flows through beautiful woodland at the heart of elk country. Take it for a total of 5.2 miles, turning right midway through at the junction with Bell Draft Road. Dent's Run Road ends at Route 555.

Turn left again on 555. Go .6 mile, watching for the sign marking the Cameron County border. Just past it is a small bridge, and on the far side of the bridge is Hick's Run Road, another hidden left. For the next 12.1 miles, the road follows Hick's Run, a jewel of a trout stream set in a steep-sided valley—and a traditional hotspot for elk. When the road forks take the left turn along the west branch (the right has a washed-out bridge). At its north end Hick's Run Road joins a paved road; bear left .9 mile to Route 120. The town of St. Mary's is about 11.5 miles to the left.

43

Butterfly Migrations

The idea of butterflies—fragile, delicate butterflies—actually migrating any distance at all seems ludicrous. It is, however, true; some species of butterflies travel farther in their lives than many humans.

The long-distance champ is the monarch, not coincidentally also the most famous of butterfly migrants, so much so that it overshadows other migratory species like the buckeye and painted lady. Monarchs are found in summer as far north as central Canada, even though the family to which they belong is essentially tropical. The larvae feed on milkweed, taking the digitalis-like toxins from the plant and storing them in their own tissues—a chemical defense that the caterpillar advertises with its bright yellow and black markings and which carries over into the adult form's bright warning coloration.

There are several major differences between what we might consider the "normal" migration of birds and that of butterflies. The biggest disparity is that birds are individual migrants, while monarchs are generational; that is, the same individual bird is born, flies south for the winter and then comes back north again in the spring to breed. Not so with monarchs. One generation hatches in late summer and migrates south; those from the East and Great Lakes winter in the Gulf states and Mexico. Come spring, these butterflies begin to fly north, but they do not return to their natal area. Instead, most stop well short of it, lay eggs and die. The next generation, upon maturing, finishes the northward migration and lays another set of eggs to begin the cycle once more. The round-trip distance is between 2,000 and 3,500 miles, but the longest any one monarch will fly is probably half that.

Migrating monarchs are easy to observe in September and, thanks to their bright orange-and-black pattern, they are easy for even beginners to identify. When the wind is blowing from the south or southwest, the butterflies use the landscape to their advantage, hedgehopping from one bush to the next, keeping low to avoid the worst of the wind. When the winds are northerly, however, the monarchs stay high and travel almost due south, enjoying a substantial energy savings from the tail wind. They can also make excellent time; one tagged individual traveled more than 1,000 miles in just eighteen days, an average of about 60 miles a day.

Monarchs migrate on a broad front, and almost any high point or field is a good place to watch them pass. The same leading lines that concentrate bird migration help focus the butterfly flight as well, however, and so it is not surprising that most of the hawk-watches are also good places to see monarchs; some days, when the winds are light and the hawks aren't flying, counting monarchs is the only way to stave off boredom. The butterfly exodus begins in late August and reaches its peak in September, but there are often a few hardy monarchs still braving the gales well past Halloween. Along the way they may form nightly gatherings of hundreds or thousands, dripping from a tree branch in the same dense mass that they form on the wintering grounds.

Many people are aware that monarchs migrate, but fewer realize that other butterflies are also migratory. Along the coast, millions of buckeye and painted lady butterflies annually drift south in September and October, concentrating (sometimes spectacularly) on peninsulas like Cape May and Cape Charles. The painted lady is found across the Northern Hemisphere, a smallish, rust-and-brown beauty that belongs to the group known as brush-footed butterflies; this species is famous as well for mass emigrations, like the flight of 3 billion butterflies seen passing through part of California in 1924. The buckeye, a close relative, is recognizable by the large, dark "eye spots" on the brown hindwings.

HOTSPOTS

As mentioned earlier, any of the ridge hawk-watches are also good places to see migrating monarchs in September, as well as migrant dragonflies and ruby-throated hummingbirds. Some hawk-watches have even gone so far as to maintain annual monarch counts in an effort to learn more about their migration. See chapters 41, 46 and 51 for more details.

A butterfly crossing a ridge can always stop for a rest, but those crossing Lake Erie do not have that luxury, making the monarch migration at **Presque Isle State Park** in Pennsylvania all the more remarkable to watch; the largest numbers cross with north or northwest breezes. See Chapter 2 for directions.

Cape May (Chapter 3) is one of the best places along the coast to see migrant monarchs, painted ladies and buckeyes; at times, the goldenrod fields positively flicker with butterflies, especially at Cape May Point State Park and the South Cape May Meadows. Other good coastal locations are **Cape Charles** (Chapter 46), **Eastern Neck NWR** (Chapter 12) and the south end of Assateague Island at **Chincoteague NWR** (Chapter 27).

44

Whales and Pelagic Birds

The way a whale appears from the empty sea, suddenly filling it with smooth skin and rushing breath, is at once humbling and uplifting. One moment the water is featureless; the next, a flat-topped jaw breaks through the surface and the blow rises with a whoosh, then the head arcs down and the long, wet back curves above the waves behind it, a moving island. It may simply sink again without fuss, or the whale may start a deep dive, raising its tail flukes high as it plunges—one of the most dramatic sights a naturalist can experience.

Whale-watching as a pastime has become increasingly popular, particularly in New England and on the West Coast. Fewer people realize that whales—sometimes in large numbers—can be seen off the shores of the mid-Atlantic states.

In fact, long before Nantucket and other New England ports became famous for their globe-circling, nineteenth-century whaling fleets, Cape May County in New Jersey boasted the nation's most productive coastal whaling station, hunting those that migrated close to shore. After nearly three centuries of intensive exploitation, the North Atlantic's whale stocks are far below what they once were, and while most species seem stable, few whales pass within sight of land.

Whales comprise two major groups—the baleen whales, which feed by straining animal matter from the water with curtainlike filter plates in the mouth, and toothed whales, which include the sperm whale, bottlenose dolphin and harbor porpoise. Toothed whales feed on a variety of foods, including fish, squid and (in the case of killer whales) other marine mammals.

The most common large whale off the mid-Atlantic coast is the finback, the second largest mammal in the world after the closely related blue whale. The record length is 79 feet, but most adults are between 60 and 70 feet long (about as long as many of the boats that set out to watch them). A finback is graceful and streamlined, with a narrow pointed head, small flippers and a prominent dorsal fin set far back toward the tail. The spout, or blow, is distinctively high and strong, but the most unique characteristic is the finback's asymmetrical coloration, with a large swath of white on only the right side of the baleen, lips and head of the whale; there is also a pale V running back from the blowhole.

Finbacks are fish eaters in the main, taking small species like sand launce as well as planktonic crustaceans. It has always amazed mankind that such a minute diet can support so large an animal, for even a newborn finback is 19 or 20 feet long.

Smaller and much less common in the region is the minke (pronounced *minky*) whale, a baleen species shaped like a finback, but with a maximum size of about 30 feet. Humpback whales, the mainstay of New England whale-watches, are rarely seen in the mid-Atlantic region, although trips in autumn may intercept some migrating south from their northern feeding grounds. Smaller cetaceans, like pilot whales and bottlenose, Risso's, striped and common dolphins, are more frequently spotted. There is always a chance at a real rarity, like a sperm whale, northern right whale, killer whale or one of the odd beaked whales that pass like ghosts through area waters.

While whales get most of the attention on any offshore run, the same waters that supply the giant mammals with food also support large numbers of unusual seabirds. Known collectively as tubenoses, they include the shearwaters, petrels and storm-petrels, birds that spend most of their life on the wing, far beyond the sight of land.

A late summer or early fall pelagic, or open ocean, trip off the mid-Atlantic coast will likely produce numbers of Cory's and greater shearwaters, Wilson's storm-petrels and perhaps the much rarer Audubon's shearwater and black-capped petrel. Other seabird possibilities include red-necked and red phalaropes; sooty and Manx shearwaters; Leach's storm-petrels; parasitic, pomarine and long-tailed jaegers; and the season's first black-legged kittiwakes, northern gannets and alcids, all of which become more common as fall slides into winter.

HOTSPOTS

The most difficult thing about watching whales and pelagic birds is getting out to them. At this writing only one whale-watching boat (running out of **Cape May**) is operating in the region, although there are several other people who organize pelagic trips to see both seabirds and marine mammals through the year; their addresses and telephone numbers are given in the Appendix. If whale-watching continues to grow in popularity, there may be more boats in the future from other ports, and it would be a good idea to check with the local chamber of commerce or state tourism board for recent additions.

The other option is to sign up for one of the many fishing boats that operate in New Jersey, Delaware, coastal Maryland and Virginia; make it clear that you are not going to fish—some boats will not carry birders or whale-watchers, while others offer handsome discounts to nonfishermen. Choose a party boat that will be going at least 20 or 30 miles offshore, the farther the better, since under normal circumstances neither whales nor pelagic birds are going to be seen close to shore. In northern New Jersey, for instance, the deep water of the Hudson Canyon holds birds and whales, but the trip is almost 100 miles each way and the outing lasts for nearly 24 hours.

Keep abreast of the rare bird alerts on birding hotlines listed in the Appendix as well, since special pelagic trips are often advertised on these tapes.

45

Breakout:
Birds of Prey and People

Few groups of animals have had such a long, uneven relationship with human beings as the birds of prey. On the one hand, hawks, eagles and falcons have been used for falconry for more than four thousand years, partners in the hunt with people. On the other hand, they have been condemned as wanton killers and slaughtered at every turn.

The conflict was especially bloody in the mid-Atlantic region, where untold thousands of hawks were killed along the ridges and at coastal points like Cape May. The phenomenon of hawk migration was first noticed in southeastern Pennsylvania on the Kittatinny Ridge, known locally as the Blue Mountain. As early as the end of the nineteenth century, locals knew that the spur in the mountain near Drehersville, north of Reading, was a good place to shoot hawks in the fall, especially if you hoisted a flapping pigeon up a pole to lure them in.

The farmers of the area tried to keep it to themselves, but by the 1920s the hawk shoots were attracting large numbers of gunners—so much so that a local businessman peddled shotgun shells near the old inclined railroad bed that served as a shooting platform, and others turned a small profit collecting the spent shells for their brass bases. Word eventually reached an audience with different attitudes toward hawks. In 1932 Richard Pough, then a photographer and later a respected leader of the conservation movement, visited the Kittatinny with his brother. His photographs of dead and maimed hawks galvanized a New Yorker named Rosalie Edge, who vowed to do something to stop the slaughter.

When her pleas for action by the Audubon Society led nowhere, Mrs. Edge and her small group, the Emergency Conservation Committee, put up a $500 down payment for the mountain in 1934 and bought it outright later. They named it Hawk Mountain Sanctuary, and it became the world's first refuge specifically for birds of prey. At the time, no one knew that a local gunning club was also debating whether to spend the $3,000 necessary to buy the ridgetop; if they had acted faster, the history of raptor conservation would have been radically different.

The Hawk Mountain concept was revolutionary—in those days, even many ornithologists hated raptors. And while creation of the sanctuary stopped the slaughter on Hawk Mountain, the gunners simply moved to other ridge overlooks, like Bake Oven Knob to the east, and continued to shoot hawks with the state and federal government's blessing. Only a few "beneficial" species, like the kestrel and bald eagle, were protected then; full protection for all hawks and owls did not come until 1972, as public opinion finally shifted in favor of the birds.

Today, far more people climb the mountains and visit the coast to watch hawks than ever came in the past to kill them. Organized hawk-watches occur at hundreds of sites across the world, with the densest concentration in the northern Appalachians. At places like Hawk Mountain and Cape May, hawk-watching is big business, a major part of local tourism in the fall. Even more importantly, thanks to decades of public education, most people realize that birds of prey have a valuable role to play in the proper functioning of natural systems and as indicators of ecological health.

OCTOBER

October Observations

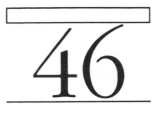

October
Hawk Flights

A northwest wind in October, blowing in cold and crisp from Canada, ushers in some of the best of the three-month-long fall hawk migration—best in terms of variety and often in sheer numbers.

Earlier in the fall, during late August and September, the flights were made up largely of broad-winged hawks, bald eagles and ospreys. The broad-wings in particular rely on thermal updrafts during migration, so good flights can occur on days of little wind. In October, however, accipiters and falcons take center stage—birds that require a stiff wind as an incentive to move.

Just as northwest winds provide the motive force for migrating raptors along the inland ridges, winds also make things happen at the coastal sites like Cape May, New Jersey. Here, northwest winds push the birds right to the ocean's edge, concentrating them along the beaches. On days of little wind, the birds may spread out inland over a wide front, or not move at all.

Wind dynamics aside, one thing that coast and ridge overlooks share in October are sharp-shinned hawks—thousands and thousands of them. The smallest of the accipiters, or forest hawks, sharpies are only a bit larger than blue jays. Predators of small birds and mammals, they are found in woodlands across North America, although those migrating in the East come mostly from New England and southeastern Canada.

On a day of strong winds, the sharp-shins will hug the ridges, skimming just over the treetops. This is perhaps the most exciting kind of hawk-watching; many times the birds will pass within a stone's toss of observers, especially if someone has stuck a plastic owl decoy on a tall pole above the lookout. All hawks have an aversion to great horned owls, but sharp-shins act out their animosity with a passion, repeatedly dive-bombing the decoy, oblivious to the crowd a few feet away.

In the days of organized hawk shoots, before the establishment of refuges and protective laws, sharpies took the greatest losses because of their low-flying habits and apparent recklessness. At Cape May and in the Pennsylvania mountains, tens of thousands were killed, along with lesser numbers of other species.

The sharp-shinned hawk migration generally peaks the first two weeks of October, with the exact date varying each year with weather conditions. At Hawk Mountain or Bake Oven Knob, a flight of more than one thousand in a single day is considered excellent, and usually only happens once or twice a year. Sharpie counts are considerably higher at Cape May, although radio telemetry studies suggest that individual hawks may spend several days on the peninsula, which may lead to multiple countings.

But it is the variety of species, rather than raw numbers, that many hawk-watchers find most exciting about October. As many as fourteen species of raptors may be seen on a good day. With the sharpies come the similar Cooper's hawks; red-shouldered hawks, uncommon migrants throughout the region; northern harriers; and the first significant movement of northern goshawks. Ospreys and bald eagles are still passing through, and the last of the broad-wings trickle by in the first half of the month. The red-tailed hawk migration, which will crest in November, picks up momentum, as do flights of golden eagles and rough-legged hawks. Kestrels, merlins and peregrine falcons also move during the month in excellent numbers, especially along the coast, where peregrine tallies may defy belief.

Of course, the first trick is to know what you are watching, and hawk identification can be terribly confusing to beginners. Experts rely less on formal field marks than on behavior, or the way the incoming hawk carries itself—what Europeans refer to as the bird's jizz, or essence. That takes experience, but there are some clues to keep in mind for the most common October species.

A sharp-shinned hawk is small, with fast wingbeats, a small head that shows no neck and usually a squared-off tail. The sharpie's larger cousin, the Cooper's hawk, has somewhat slower wingbeats, a protruding head and a rounded tail. (Complicating any discussion of size is the fact that, in most raptors, the females are substantially bigger than the males. Thus, a female sharp-shin may be nearly as big as a male Cooper's.) At a distance, a sharpie or Cooper's will usually give itself away with a distinctive flight pattern— several quick wingbeats followed by a short glide.

Red-tailed hawks generally soar rather than flap, with their wings held flat or with a slight upward tilt. At closer range, look for the red-tail's white belly crossed by a dark band of streaks (absent in some birds), but don't expect to see the orange-red tail unless the hawk banks—the color is only visible from above, and then only on adults. Northern harriers, formerly called marsh hawks, carry their wings in a shallow V and have a prominent white patch above their tails; males are pale gray, while immatures and females are brown.

Eagles, the icing on any day, are a possibility throughout the month. Inland, bald eagles are more common in early October and goldens in the second half. Both are enormous and can be distinguished from the ubiquitous turkey vultures by the eagles' flat wings, as opposed to the shallow V of the vulture. Because a bald eagle does not develop the trademark white head and tail until its fourth or fifth year, there is a chance of confusing an immature bald with the all-brown golden eagle. Experts look for the more massive head of the bald, which appears to protrude almost as far forward as the tail does behind. Both species tend to stay high or far out from the lookouts, apparently cautious of the crowds, but occasionally one will soar past at close range—an unforgettable sight.

While rare inland, falcons grab the limelight at the coastal lookouts. The endangered peregrine falcon can be downright common at Cape May—more than 140 were sighted on an exceptional day in 1986—and merlins are a mainstay. The reason for their coastal preference is probably linked to food, since the small birds upon which they feed are coastal migrants themselves.

In the years following World War II, peregrine falcon numbers crashed due to pesticide poisoning. Thanks to a ban on the most potent chemicals, and an aggressive captive breeding and reintroduction program, peregrines are rebounding from their near brush with extinction. The reestablishment of breeding pairs in a number of eastern locations, and gradually increasing migration counts, give good reason for optimism. At Hawk Mountain, for instance, peregrine totals have jumped from ten or twelve a year in the 1970s to around fifty in recent autumns.

Because October is also the month of peak foliage color, the ridge overlooks can be completely overrun on a nice weekend, and the jostling crowds at any of the popular sites can be onerous. If possible, visit on a weekday, but if you must come on a weekend, remember that Saturdays are usually somewhat less crowded than Sundays, and arrive as early as possible.

HOTSPOTS

To someone accustomed to watching hawks on a remote mountainside, a visit to **Cape May** can be disconcertingly suburban—at times, it is possible to watch passing raptors from the windows of waterfront motels in the town itself. But the hawk-watch platform at Cape May Point State Park, the Higbee Beach area and the South Cape May Meadows are the best seats for the remarkable parade of migrants that funnel through this peninsula in Delaware Bay.

The numbers of hawks at Cape May can be staggering; most years the total exceeds seventy-five thousand, with daily osprey counts in the hundreds and annual kestrel tallies in the thousands. What most people come for, though, are the peregrine falcons, because an observer at Cape May can see more in a single day than in a decade at an inland site. The peregrines may come in fairly low, and people on the wooden hawk-watch platform, which overlooks a beautiful marsh, may find themselves looking down on the passing falcons. Merlins pass through in high numbers as well, with total fall counts of five hundred or more being the rule rather than the exception.

Cape May is also the focus for intensive raptor banding, a cooperative project that has been going for years, and which has greatly increased science's knowledge of hawk life histories and migration. Banding stations can be observed from a distance at the South Cape May Meadows and other sites; to avoid scaring the hawks do not approach the station. On weekends throughout the fall, the volunteer banders use freshly captured hawks to illustrate talks on raptors and banding at Cape May Point State Park, usually at the picnic pavilion near the hawk-watch platform; check at the park office for details.

For directions to Cape May, see Chapter 3. A strong west wind will usually concentrate the hawks along the eastern edge of the peninsula, but Higbee Beach WMA on the Delaware Bay side can be very good, and hawks can be

seen at almost any time, almost anywhere; the shoulders of
Sunset Boulevard (Route 606) can, for instance, be extremely productive. Early in the morning, walk quietly along
the boardwalk nature trail at Cape May Point State Park,
where the dense shrubbery attracts migrating songbirds—
and the songbirds attract sharp-shinned hawks, which can
often be surprised while dining. Accipiters pluck their meals
before eating, and the discovery of "feather puddles" along
the trails is a common occurrence.

All 37 miles of **Assateague Island** are good for
migrating hawks, especially falcons, which peak during the
first two weeks of October. There is no formal hawk-watch
here, and birders simply take up positions along the barrier
island dunes. Peregrines follow the beach, but the merlins
tend to stay behind the dune line over the thickets.

At the Chincoteague end of the island, try Wash Flats,
a strenuous, 5-mile hike north of the Tom's Cove Visitors'
Center; an alternative is reserving space on the commercial
wildlife tour that passes this area. Less productive overall,
but easier to reach, is the area immediately north of Snow
Goose Pool off the Wildlife Drive and the west edge of Swan
Cove, viewed from the road leading to the Tom's Cove
Visitors' Center. Hawk-watchers looking for the best site at
Assateague's north end also face a long hike—about 6 miles
from the state park parking area to the spoil heaps near
Ocean City Inlet that provide a vantage point. For those
willing to settle for a less perfect spot, there are many places
along the beach that offer solitude, the cries of gulls and the
swift flight of peregrines. For directions to either end of
Assateague, see Chapter 27.

Hawk banders have long appreciated the excellent
flights that funnel through **Cape Charles** at the southern
terminus of the Delmarva Peninsula, but only recently has
this area become known among those who merely watch
raptors. Part of the problem was the lack of a formal hawk-
watch, but plans call for a regularly manned station at

Eastern Shore of Virginia NWR, a small refuge founded on what was until 1980 an air force base. One of the huge World War II–era bunkers that dot the refuge has been fitted with wooden stairs and a platform on its overgrown summit, providing excellent views of tidal marshes and Fisherman's Inlet to the southeast, and Kiptopeke to the northwest. With the loss to development of the traditional banding area at Kiptopeke, the refuge's hawk-watch is likely to become even more important.

To visit the refuge, take Route 13 South from Pocomoke City, Maryland, roughly 68 miles. Turn left onto Route 600, a small two-lane road, go .4 mile to a T-intersection and turn right into the refuge. The office and interim visitors' center is another .3 mile, on the left. To reach the hawk-watch, do not turn into the visitors' center but continue straight another .3 mile, past a bunker to the small parking area where the road makes a sharp left bend. Follow the trail to the south end of a second bunker and climb the wooden stairs.

Birders line the hawk-watch platform at Cape May Point State Park, New Jersey, one of the best sites in the world for raptor migration.

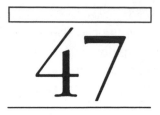

47

Avocet Concentrations

The bill of an avocet is unique among North American shorebirds—needle-thin and long, it curves gracefully *up* at the tip, a trait especially evident in females. This unexpected twist lends the avocet an odd air, but the reasons have nothing to do with esthetics and everything to do with food gathering.

Avocets feed in shallow water, striding along belly-deep while swinging their bills from side to side just beneath the surface. With the head lowered, the upturned tip of the beak becomes parallel to the water and perfect for capturing tiny insects, crustaceans and worms, which the avocet detects by feel.

Avocets are daintily constructed birds, long in the neck and even longer in the legs. Their plumage varies with the season—white and black on the back and wings, with cinnamon on the head and neck in the breeding season, changing to cool gray in winter. Sitting at rest with its head folded back between its wings and one leg tucked under its belly feathers, an avocet looks like a perfectly proportioned sculpture.

A rare breeding species in the East, American avocets attract attention anytime they are seen, but they make the biggest splash in autumn, when large numbers gather at

Bombay Hook NWR in Delaware, a spectacle that cannot be seen with certainty anywhere else in the region.

The avocets actually start congregating much earlier, with sizable numbers appearing in late July and August. In this, they keep company with another speciality of the Delaware shore, black-necked stilts—a closely related shorebird with the longest legs, proportionately, of any bird in the world. Early in the season, many of the avocets will still be in their rusty breeding plumage, while others will have made the transition to the monochromatic gray and white of winter. The flock continues to build through the fall migration, reaching its peak in October, when there may be as many as several hundred avocets decorating the pools.

HOTSPOTS

At Bombay Hook, **Raymond Pool** and, especially, **Shearness Pool** are the two likeliest places to find avocets, although excessive rainfall may flood the shallows where they like to feed, forcing them elsewhere. Lesser numbers of avocets may also usually be found at **Little Creek WMA** just to the south; follow Route 9 South from Bombay Hook to Port Mahon Road, then continue straight on Route 9 another 1.4 miles to the entrance road on the left; follow this another 1.4 miles to the parking area by the impoundments. The south impoundment is also accessible from Pickering Beach Road, which can be reached by returning to Route 9 South for 1 mile, then turning left. Go 1.5 miles to the small access road on the left, which leads to the southern edge of the lake. Avocets are also regularly seen at **Chincoteague NWR** in Virginia (Chapter 27), although rarely in large numbers, and usually earlier in the fall.

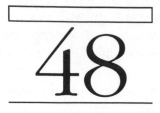

48

Lake Erie Salmon and Migrating Owls

Two of the region's most unusual wildlife spectacles occur in October, so seemingly unlike that linking them in a single chapter strikes a strange note. The unifying feature is that each is an extremely local phenomenon—the spawning run of salmon in several Lake Erie tributaries and the chance to see migrating owls in the beam of the Cape May Lighthouse.

Spawning Salmon

Salmon are not native to the Great Lakes; they were first introduced in the 1960s, with the idea of producing a sport fishery. The idea succeeded beyond anyone's dreams, and today Lake Erie supports chinook and coho salmon that attain weights in excess of 20 pounds.

On their native Pacific coast, salmon spawn in fresh water and then migrate to the ocean for several years, fattening on the abundant small fish and invertebrates of the open sea before returning to spawn and die. In the Great Lakes, the salmon follow much the same routine, passing the years before maturity in the deep waters of the lakes, then homing in (by smell) on the waters of their natal creeks. Natural reproduction is poor or nonexistent, however, so salmon stocks are carefully managed to keep the supply of fish constant. It does not always work; in recent years, Lake Erie's coho numbers have dropped, due in part to heavy predation by gulls and diving ducks on the newly stocked smolts.

In Lake Erie, the mature salmon begin congregating offshore in late summer and early autumn; charter boats troll closer and closer to land as the weather cools and the salmon begin to focus on the tributary streams, where even more fishermen wait. By the first weeks of October the spawning run is in full swing, with salmon surging up Elk Creek, Walnut Creek, Trout Run and other streams to mate and die.

At the Pennsylvania Fish Commission's Fairview Fish Culture Station on Trout Run, west of the city of Erie, the salmon are directed to holding tanks, then carefully removed and stripped of their eggs and milt. The fertilized eggs are hatched and the fingerlings eventually released in the tributary streams to form the next year class of salmon. The spent adults, which die immediately after spawning anyway, are donated to the needy.

Watching fish is obviously harder than watching birds or mammals, but patience—and polarized sunglasses to cut the surface glare—will pay off.

HOTSPOTS

Although you can see salmon (and salmon fishermen) on most of the tributaries to Lake Erie, *Trout Run* is the easiest and most productive spot to visit.

To reach Trout Run, take I-90 to Route 98 North just below Fairview; at Route 5 continue straight onto Avonia Road, which parallels the creek to Lake Erie, or turn left onto Route 5 and drive .2 mile and turn left again to the Fairview Fish Culture Station. Here, the coho salmon (and lesser numbers of steelhead) migrate to the hatchery's holding tanks and are netted for artificial propagation. The hatchery is open Monday through Friday from 7:30 A.M. to 4 P.M. and can provide visiting naturalists with suggestions on current hotspots; in addition, visitors may be lucky enough to chance on biologists netting the salmon, an operation carried out most often on Wednesdays from early October through mid-November, weather permitting.

One of the heaviest salmon runs occurs just east of Avonia on *Walnut Creek*, a very popular spot with salmon fishermen. From Avonia Road go east 2 miles on Route 5, then turn north on Manchester Road for about half a mile to the Fish Commission's Walnut Creek Access Area, a 25-acre site.

Migrating Owls

Even longtime birders are often surprised to find out that owls migrate. Hidden by darkness, their seasonal movements have long been overlooked and are only now coming to light.

One of the few places in the mid-Atlantic region—or anywhere, for that matter—where owl migration has been studied is Cape May, where banders have been trapping and ringing owls for a number of years. In the process, they have learned that saw-whet, barn and long-eared owls commonly follow the coastline south, with the heaviest flights coming in October and November.

While the banding operation is closed to the public, there is a unique way to glimpse the migrants as they head south—by joining one of the organized owl watches at Cape May Point State Park and watching for owls impaled by the beam of the lighthouse.

The outings, run by naturalists with the Cape May Bird Observatory, are usually scheduled for Saturdays from early October through the middle of November. Because the park closes at sunset, joining one of the CMBO sessions is the only way to enjoy the show.

As dusk falls, mallards and wood ducks drop into the marshes near the lighthouse in twos and threes, even as black-crowned night-herons are flying out to feed for the evening. Great blue herons lift off, necks tucked and legs trailing, heading out across the Delaware Bay on the next leg of their migration. Back in the thickets of wax myrtle and oak, the owls, too, are gearing up for their flight, perhaps doing a little hunting from a concealed perch.

With the coming of full dark, the lighthouse beam stands out sharply against the black sky as it slowly revolves. Anything that crosses the beam is starkly illuminated, just for a half second, but the afterimage is usually so clear that your eye registers the shape and position exactly, like a photograph. What's more, the owls sometimes seem attracted to the light, like moths to a flame, and may circle the lighthouse repeatedly.

Barn owls, with their ghostly faces and ghastly screams, are the bread and butter of the owl-watch, for even though they are not the most common species to pass through Cape May, they are large and easily seen. Or heard; it is not unusual to be startled by their rasping, screeching *kii-i-i-i-i-schh!* coming from overhead in the darkness, a moment before the owl is illuminated by the powerful lighthouse beacon.

Barn owls begin migrating early, the first passing through by the middle of September and continuing until the first weeks of November. Saw-whet owls, the East's tiniest species, are the most common migrant at Cape May, judging from banding captures, but they are rarely seen at the lighthouse; their migration begins in mid-October and lasts until around Thanksgiving. Through roughly the same period, long-eared owls appear at Cape May, adding more spice to an owl-watcher's evening.

HOTSPOTS

For directions to **Cape May Point State Park**, see Chapter 3; the group usually meets in the small parking lot near the entrance of the park. Call the Cape May Bird Observatory at (609) 884-2736 to confirm dates and times; a fee is charged for the session.

49

Spectacular Fall Foliage

For many naturalists, the year has two pinnacles—the rush of new plant and animal life in May, and the explosion of color in October. In both cases, much of the excitement comes from the rapidly changing, ephemeral nature of the season. Each day is different, and the passage of a week alters the landscape dramatically.

Across much of the mid-Atlantic region, September ends with only the first hints of color—the purple-reds of the black gum, a few precocious maples or sumacs. With startling speed that changes, and at times it almost seems possible to see the mountains' color deepen before your eyes.

Just as the green line of spring leaves started in the valleys and worked its way uphill, the color of autumn starts high and begins to drop steadily down the mountains. On a larger scale, the color creeps north to south as well, with the peak coming in the first days of the month in the northern Pennsylvania mountains, but not until the end of the month in the southern Blue Ridge and lowland areas.

Even in a single area, there is a predictable progression. On the Pennsylvania ridges, where the forest is dominated by late-turning oaks, the first color comes from the red maples, hickories and sweet birch; since maples and hickories are common in valley fencerows and woodlots, there may at first be more color down below than on the mountainsides. By the second week of the month, however, the oaks have caught up, changing from green to yellow-orange or bronze. The intensity of the color depends on many factors, which are discussed in more detail in the next chapter; some years the hills are a vivid orange, while in others a drab yellow-brown. Often there is no predicting which it will be.

Within the fabric of the oak forest, many other species of trees weave their own colors. Flowering dogwoods become crimson, sassafras bright orange, and aspens, striped maple and the various birches contribute yellow to the picture. Sugar maple, with its intense reds, yellows and oranges, is one of the highlights of the northern hardwood community in autumn. American beech takes on a luminescent gold that is unlike any other tree in the woods, while the rocky outcroppings along the mountaintops are orange with the leaves and berries of American mountain ash.

Not even those who grow up in the mountains get tired of the scene. Still, the pleasure is bittersweet, for of course this is nature's last hurrah before winter sets in, the long days of snow and cold. Yet it may be that this knowledge only makes the enjoyment sharper, as the eye fills with a horizon of color and tries to store it up against the season to come.

A night of windy rain will strip away most of the weakened oak leaves, revealing the gray skeleton of the forest for the first time in five or six months. The color is again reduced to pockets—a witch-hazel with its pale lemon leaves, or the majestic yellow crowns of tulip poplars clustered along hidden springs and stream courses. A week more, and they are gone, too, leaving the hills bare until next year.

HOTSPOTS

The mid-Atlantic region boasts some of the finest displays of fall color in North America, as evidenced by the

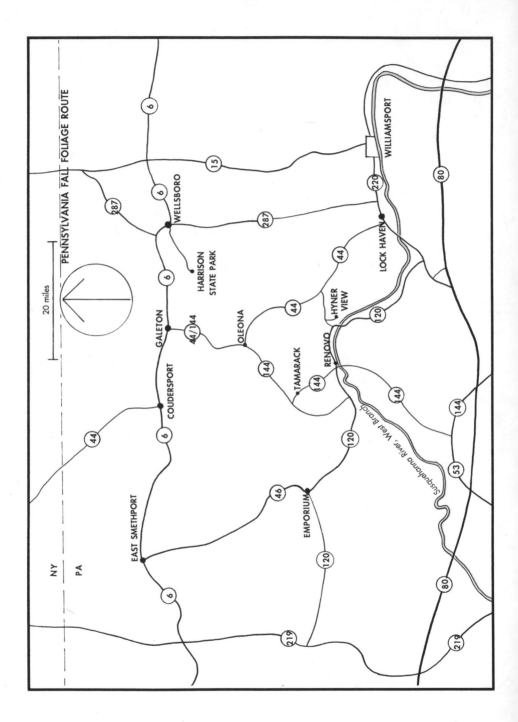

many "flaming foliage" festivals throughout the region. Generally speaking, the most intense color will be found in areas with northern hardwood forests, across northern Pennsylvania and down the highest spine of the Appalachians through western Maryland, West Virginia and Virginia. The oak forests of the lower ridges can be fantastic in a good year, but generally lack the vivid colors provided by red and sugar maples.

For a two-day excursion (during the week, if possible), consider a 265-mile loop through *Pennsylvania's northern tier*, some of the most remote, rugged and spectacular scenery in the Keystone State, and usually at peak color the first week of October.

From Williamsport drive west on Route 220 to Route 287 North, which leads 40 miles through the Little Pine and Pine Creek drainages to Wellsboro. In Wellsboro follow signs for Route 660 to Leonard Harrison State Park, which has marvelous views of the Pine Creek Gorge but can be overwhelmed by weekend crowds. Route 660 is a dead end, so backtrack to Wellsboro and drive west on Route 6 (Grand Army of the Republic Highway). For the next 74 miles, the road winds and twists through the mountains of the Allegheny High Plateau, through forests of oak and northern hardwoods; maples in particular lend brilliant splashes of red and orange to the scene. At East Smethport turn south onto Route 46 and go 27 miles to Emporium, then follow Route 120 East another 46 miles along the looping course of the Driftwood Branch of Sinnemahoning Creek.

The Sinnemahoning eventually joins the west branch of the Susquehanna River, a waterway sorely abused by acid runoff from coal mines upriver. Just before reaching the town of Renovo, turn left onto Route 144 North, a small two-lane that leads back into the hills of Sproul State Forest again, passing Tamarack Swamp Natural Area, where the gold of tamarack needles and the more vibrant fall colors create a beautiful combination. Beyond the town of Tamarack the road drops and crosses Kettle Creek; at the far side of the bridge turn right at the T-intersection and continue on 144, past the village of Cross Fork to Oleona. Turn south onto Route 44 and go 21 miles to Hyner Mountain Road, a right that leads to Hyner Run State Park; follow the signs to Hyner View, one of the most remarkable overlooks in Pennsylvania. From the view, return to Hyner Run Road and drop down to the Susquehanna, rejoining Route 120 East. Take 120 another 22 miles to Lock Haven to pick up Route 220 East, go 17 miles and return to the beginning of the loop.

> NOTE: *Much of this loop goes through sparsely inhabited country, so don't pass up an open service station if your gas tank is getting dry. Hotel accommodations are equally scarce, but there are a number of state parks on or near the route that offer camping, including Ole Bull, Colton Point, Sinnemahoning, Hyner Run, Kettle Creek, Leonard Harrison, Patterson and Sizerville. For more information, contact the Pennsylvania Bureau of Parks at (800) 63-PARKS.*

There is no doubt that **Shenandoah National Park** and the **Skyline Drive** in Virginia's Blue Ridge Mountains are spectacular in autumn—but so, unfortunately, are the traffic jams that form on October weekends. One solution is to get out of the car and hike some of the more than 500 miles of trails that meander through Shenandoah. Good possibilities are the South Falls, Jones Run and Whiteoak Canyon trails, but check with a ranger or at the Dickey Ridge or Byrd visitors' centers for more suggestions and trail maps. Depending on temperature, rainfall and latitude, the fall color in the Blue Ridge hits its peak between October 10 and 27.

Scenery and foliage combine splendidly in southwestern Virginia in the area of **Grayson Highlands State**

Park and *Mount Rogers National Recreation Area*; see Chapter 28 for directions.

To the north, mountains of color lie on both sides of the Virginia–West Virginia border, hill country largely contained within *Monongahela* and *George Washington* national forests. The following route covers a roughly 300-mile loop through the two states, crossing some breathtakingly beautiful country.

Start at the Harrisonburg, Virginia, exit of I-81, and take Route 33 West through Harrisonburg and into the mountains, following the road's torturously serpentine course across Shenandoah Mountain, the boundary between the two states. On the West Virginia side, 33 passes through the towns of Brandywine, Oak Flat and Franklin; 14 miles west of Franklin it joins Route 28 North. Follow 33/28 to Mouth of Seneca; the Seneca Rocks Visitors' Center is just a mile up Route 28 North and well worth a stop. Then continue west on Route 33/55 to Elkins, a distance of 32 miles. At the traffic light turn left and follow Route 219/250 South; the next 58 miles are a delightful blend of farms and mountains.

About 6 miles north of Marlinton, turn right onto Route 150, the Highland Scenic Highway, which loops 14.5 miles to the Cranberry Mountain Visitors' Center at the junction with Route 39/55. The area stretching almost 25 miles to the west is the Cranberry Wilderness and Cranberry Back Country, some of West Virginia's most scenic forestland, and a region laced with excellent hiking trails; there are also many trails in the Tea Creek Area north of the highway. Trail maps are available at the visitors' center (which is open on weekends in October) or by contacting the Monongahela National Forest, the address for which is listed in the Appendix.

From the visitors' center, take 39/55 East 6.5 miles to Mill Point, then go north 8 miles on Route 219/55 to Marlinton. Turn east on Route 39, a 67-mile series of hairpin turns, mountain passes and picturesque creeks that culminates with the passage of the Maury River between Hogback Mountain and Little North Mountain. Just north of Buena Vista, Virginia, Route 39 joins Route 11; follow 11 north 3.9 miles to I-81 North, which returns you to Harrisonburg, 59 miles to the north.

50

Breakout:
Fall Foliage Mysteries

It never ceases to amaze: A leaf that for month after month has been plain green changes almost overnight to the most vivid red, or orange, or yellow imaginable. No wonder our ancestors credited Jack Frost—no other explanation could have made as much sense to them as a supernatural painter.

There is an explanation, of course, but not even cold science can rob the mystery entirely from the coming of the fall colors. Nor do we have all the answers; although we know why leaves change, we cannot yet accurately predict whether the impending autumn display will be eye-popping or unusually dull.

A leaf is a food factory, one of thousands on the average hardwood tree. Seen in cross section, each leaf has a waxy surface layer, the epidermis, that prevents it from drying out, while allowing the transfer of gases through tiny pores called stomata. Beneath the epidermis lie rows of specialized cells known as chloroplasts, which contain chlorophyll—the vital chemical that gives green plants their color and allows them to use the energy of sunlight to convert carbon dioxide and water into sugars.

The leaves already contain many of the pigments that will make the hills glow in October, but the abundant chlorophyll masks them. As the days shorten through September, however, the trees begin to shut down their food production, withdrawing some of the precious chlorophyll into the twigs and trunk, and revealing the "true" colors of the leaves for the first time as the rest of the chlorophyll breaks down. These carotenoid pigments account for many of the oranges and yellows that are seen each autumn.

It is not the impending cold that spurs the hardwoods to drop their leaves; after all, conifers keep their needles through the entire year and can tolerate much colder conditions than most deciduous trees. The real threat in winter is desiccation. With the ground frozen and the tree unable to draw more water through its roots, it would quickly (and fatally) dry out in the low humidity of winter if it kept its lightly protected leaves. (Conifers, on the other hand, have needles with extremely thick, waxy epidermal layers to prevent excessive water loss.)

The leaves do not shut down immediately, but continue to produce sugars almost as long as they cling to the trees. For this reason, the best conditions for fall foliage are warm, sunny days followed by cool (but not freezing) nights. The daytime warmth spurs the leaves to produce sugars, but the low nighttime temperatures prevent the tree from withdrawing the food. Trapped in the leaves, the sugars produce fiery reds, while other chemical combinations and breakdown products result in the bronzes, purples, oranges and crimsons that make the fall so appealing.

The intensity of the autumn foliage varies a great deal from tree to tree, place to place and year to year. Within a clump of sugar maples, one or two may, for whatever reason, consistently wear much brighter colors than the rest, while a tree of identical species just a short distance away simply goes brown. A drought can greatly reduce the tree's sugar production, resulting in a dull foliage season; likewise, gypsy moth defoliation, which forces the trees to grow a second set of leaves in July, also dampens the sugar production and color. An unusually warm October (especially when combined with lots of rain) likewise spells disaster, since the trees are able to remove almost all the sugar from their leaves each night. In 1990, much of Pennsylvania suffered through a major gypsy moth infestation; then one of the warmest Octobers in recent record hit the region. It was no surprise, therefore, when the foliage display was one of the poorest in memory in many areas.

The tree's final step in shutting down for the winter is to weaken the bond between the leaf and the twig; the minute vessels that carried sap all summer are sealed off, and the leaf falls, torn by the wind or simply giving in to gravity and its own weight. The dominant chemical reaction within the leaf now is decomposition, and the flaming hues of autumn quickly fade to brown on the forest floor.

NOVEMBER

November Observations

51

November Hawk Flights

By November, the balmy days of the broad-winged hawk flight in September are a memory. Gone are the T-shirts and shorts and tubes of sunscreen—instead, hawk-watchers bundle up in layer upon layer of wool and down, trying to block out the harsh Arctic winds that rip across the ridgetops and beaches.

Yet if the cold is miserable, the rewards are great, for November brings the big birds in a fitting finale for the season—red-tailed hawks, goshawks, golden eagles and rough-legs, with the tantalizing possibility of a rare Arctic gyrfalcon to insulate you from the wind.

Red-tailed hawks are the bread-and-butter species of the month, moving in large numbers from the end of October through Thanksgiving. They are not nearly as numerous as their buteonine relatives, the broad-wings; where a big day in September might mean more than ten thousand broad-wings, the season's biggest red-tail total is usually between five hundred and one thousand at most ridge sites, and even lower on the coast. You hear few complaints from the watchers, however, because the big, bulky red-tails tend to hang much closer to the ridges, passing at or below eye level as they jockey on the mischievous winds.

The red-tail migration is a fairly reliable spectacle, varying little in timing or intensity each year. Not so with the goshawks, the biggest and rarest of the accipiters. Native to the boreal forests to the region's north, goshawks are for the most part nonmigratory, although a few wander down the flyway each autumn. At erratic intervals, however, something happens on the northern breeding grounds that sends large numbers of goshawks flying south, to the delight of hawk-watchers. An examination of migration statistics at Hawk Mountain, dating back to the 1930s, shows a spike in the count every three or four years, when the total may jump by 100 percent or more. Some years only twenty or thirty pass the lookouts, while even more rarely, the goshawks stage a major invasion. The autumn of 1972 was such a year, when more than four hundred of these big, ghostly predators were counted at the sanctuary.

In a way, the migration of golden eagles in the East is even more enigmatic than the goshawk flight. Before formal hawk counts were started in the 1930s, ornithologists believed golden eagles did not exist in the East, and reports of forty or fifty each fall at Hawk Mountain were greeted with what may politely be called skepticism. The experts were wrong, though, for a relict population of goldens, presumed to breed in remote corners of New England and eastern Canada, still exists, and passes through the mid-Atlantic region each fall, with the flight peaking in mid-November.

Just as their breeding grounds are something of a mystery, the golden eagles' wintering sites are also unclear. A handful pass the cold months in association with bald eagles at such communal roosts as Conowingo Dam and Blackwater NWR, others in farming valleys throughout the region and most (based on band returns) in the southern Appalachians and coastal plain. This lack of fundamental knowledge about where the eagles come from and where they go has many biologists worried, especially when coupled with the slow, steady decline in golden eagle totals at many lookouts.

Regardless of the season or the species being watched, there are some basic items of equipment that a hawk-watcher needs. Most important are quality binoculars; 7x35 glasses (the most common for general birding) are fine, although experienced observers often prefer binoculars with higher magnification and a wider field of view—8x40 or even 10x50. Size and weight are important consider-ations, but most compact binoculars are a poor choice, since their field of view is so limited that it can be difficult to locate the hawk.

A spotting scope can be handy for distant hawks, although scopes are more cumbersome to hold and use than binoculars, and the tripod is still more weight to be carried up the mountain. As a compromise, many serious hawk-watchers mount their scopes on wooden gunstocks, making them more stable and easier to hold steady.

Proper clothing is, if anything, even more essential. Windchill factors on the exposed rocks of a ridge overlook can be numbing, and there is usually at least a 10- or 15-degree temperature difference between the valleys and the mountaintops. Remember that several layers of lighter clothes provide better protection than a single, bulky garment. Wool pants insulate better than cotton jeans, and gloves and a hat are musts on cold days (if you have trouble focusing binoculars with gloves, try a pair without finger-tips). Also recommended are a soft foam pad on which to sit, a thermos of something hot to drink and lots of quick-energy food on which to nibble throughout the day.

HOTSPOTS

In many ways, the mountains south of the Mason-Dixon line are *terra incognita* for hawk-watching—poorly explored when compared with the Pennsylvania and New Jersey ridges, but with tremendous potential. New sites are discovered almost every autumn, while others, better known, attract most of the visitors.

Delaware is not known for its hawk-watching, but **Brandywine Creek State Park**, just a stone's throw from the Pennsylvania border, boasts the state's only ridge system—a long, gentle nub to be sure, just 500 feet high, but enough to attract migrating raptors, especially during the broad-wing flights of September. The park can be reached from Wilmington by following Route 100 North from Route 141 approximately 3 miles, or from Pennsylvania by taking Route 100 South from Chadds Ford. Either way, turn onto Adams Dam Road at the park sign, drive .4 mile and turn left into the park. Follow the entrance road past the toll gate and park at the top of the hill nearest the trees; the hawk-watch area is by the stone fence, with hawks following the low ridge across the stream valley.

Access is equally easy at **Washington Monument State Park** in central Maryland, where hawk-watchers sit in the stone tower itself. The park is on South Mountain, at the northern edge of the Blue Ridge, along which raptors move in good numbers. From the town of Frederick drive west 11 miles on Route 40; the park entrance is on the right. From the parking lot, a quarter-mile trail leads to the monument.

The Blue Ridge Mountains, including Shenandoah National Park, offer a multitude of hawk-watching possibilities. The area near **Rockfish Gap** at the southern end of Shenandoah National Park is especially popular (as well as regularly manned), with most of the activity centering on the parking lot and observation deck of a Holiday Inn at the intersection of the Skyline Drive and I-64. If wilderness hawk-watching is more to your liking, consider the summit of **Hawksbill Mountain** in the northern half of the park, Shenandoah's highest peak at 4,051 feet. There are two approaches, both strenuous, but the trail from the Upper Hawksbill parking area (milepost 46.7) is somewhat easier, a 2.1-mile round trip. Since the late 1980s, Hawksbill Mountain has been a release site for captive-bred peregrine falcons, so even if the migration is slow there may be a falcon or two in the air.

The narrowness of the Blue Ridge between Shenandoah and Roanoke helps to concentrate the flight, and the scenic overlooks along the Blue Ridge Parkway provide convenience and good views of the birds. Depending on the winds, virtually any overlook may be productive, but those that consistently produce good flights are **Harvey's Knob** Overlook (Parkway milepost 95.3), **Purgatory Mountain** Overlook (milepost 92), **Thunder Ridge** Overlook (milepost 74.7) and **Buena Vista** Overlook (milepost 45.6).

Two fire towers—one in southern Virginia, one in the north—provide hawk-watching possibilities. The **Linden Fire Tower** can be reached by taking I-66 to the town of Linden, then driving 8 miles north on Route 638 to the tower site. To the south, perched on Clinch Mountain between Russell and Washington counties, the **Mendota Fire Tower** has long been recognized as a fine lookout for migrants. Take Route 19/Alt. 58 North from Abington to the village of Holston, then go west on Route 802 for approximately 13 miles to Mendota. Turn right on Route 612, a small road that crosses Clinch Mountain; park at the summit and take the trail on the right to the tower, watching from the boulders below.

West Virginia has several well-known lookouts, although it seems likely that many good hawk-watching points remain undiscovered in this sparsely populated state. **Hanging Rock Raptor Migration Observatory** (formerly and better known as Hanging Rock Fire Tower), at the summit of Peter's Mountain near Waiteville, has been a focus of hawk-watching since the late 1960s. From Waiteville take Route 600 1 mile; at the crossroad turn left onto a dirt road marked Gap Mills and go 3.9 miles to the top of the mountain. Park and hike past the gate to the tower, about 1 mile uphill. In the Dolly Sods Wilderness, **Bear Rocks** provides flights on days of easterly winds, which concentrate the birds along this dramatic escarpment above the upper Potomac River. For directions to Dolly Sods see Chapter 23; from the intersection with Road 75, go 8.1 miles to the edge of the escarpment, park and walk north along the outcroppings. There may be no stranger surroundings for bird-watching in the East than the heathy balds and stunted spruce of the Bear Rocks area.

52

Rutting White-tails

White-tailed deer are almost supernaturally cautious, able to disappear like a puff of fog if they suspect danger is approaching. This is especially so of the biggest, oldest bucks, those who have survived many hunting seasons by relying on their wits and instincts.

The white-tail is by far the most common large mammal in the mid-Atlantic region; Pennsylvania alone has a herd estimated at 1.5 million, and the population in many areas continues to grow. But although they are common, deer can be difficult to observe at close range—anywhere, that is, except in Shenandoah National Park in Virginia's Blue Ridge Mountains.

Here, a herd of more than six thousand deer delight park visitors with their trusting attitude, a product of nearly sixty years of legal protection. The deer are easy to see all year, but they are at their best in November, at the onset of the rut, or mating season.

The biological preparations for the rut actually begin in early spring. The bucks, which had shed their antlers the previous winter, begin to grow a new set, which arise from the round pedicles at skin level between the ears. Covered in a fuzzy skin called velvet, the growing bone of the antlers is supplied with blood through a rich network of capillaries, as it sprouts and lengthens through the summer. Many factors contribute to the eventual size and span of the rack—age, genetics, diet. The number of points is not related to age in any but the most general terms, although younger bucks usually have smaller racks than mature animals 4 or 5 years old. This is not a hard-and-fast rule, however, and a yearling with good genes and a diet rich in minerals may sport a six- or eight-point rack.

By early fall, the antlers have reached their full development, and the blood vessels to the velvet shut off. The buck, which through the summer has been careful not to damage the growing rack, now seeks out a sapling or stand of shrubs and thrashes his antlers against them, rubbing off the velvet—and a good deal of the tree bark, leaving permanent "buck rubs" as a sign of his presence. It may take a day or two to remove all the skin, but when he is finished, the antlers will glisten like ivory at the tips, shading to gnarled, bumpy brown at the base.

Regardless of the number of tines, a white-tail's rack grows in a characteristic shape—rising from the pedicles and curving back, then flaring out and forward; the tines rise vertically from the main beams, including the small "brow tines" that grow closest to the skull. An eight-point rack with a 20-inch spread between the main beams is a large deer, although exceptional specimens may have fourteen or more points and a spread that exceeds 28 inches.

As the rut approaches, other physiological changes occur in the buck's body, spurred by a release of hormones—itself brought on by the diminishing amount of daylight. Most noticeably, the buck's neck swells which, coupled with his new, gray winter coat and freshly cleaned rack, make him a magnificent sight.

The bucks come into mating condition two weeks or more before the does; as the sexual tension builds, the males become increasingly irritable, fighting for dominance with other bucks and sparring with still more innocent saplings. At length, the females come into estrus, a condition the buck can smell by sniffing her legs and tail.

A buck does not leave encounters with the does to chance. Pawing away the leaves in an area the size of a small table, he may urinate on the ground, and he often slashes at low, overhanging branches. The result is known as a buck scrape, and it advertises his presence to any females in the vicinity. If they are in estrus, the does will often linger near the scrape, which the buck checks regularly, traveling a circuit from scrape to scrape through his territory, mating with the willing females he encounters. Sometimes a smaller, less dominant buck will linger near a bigger male's scrape, too, hoping to skim off a doe or two, but if the scrape's owner discovers him, a fight may ensue.

The rut lasts through early December, by which time most of the available females have been bred. The bucks, having lost up to a third of their body weight, are at a disadvantage in the upcoming winter, but even if they die of cold or starvation, their genes have been passed on to the next generation. By midwinter their antlers have dropped off at the pedicle, and their biggest concern is not sex, but survival.

HOTSPOTS

By far the best place in Shenandoah to watch the deer rut is **Big Meadows**, at milepost 51.2, and the surrounding woods. The only large, treeless area in the park, Big Meadows is a magnet for white-tails at all times of the year, especially autumn. In the nearby campgrounds, for example, at times there seem to be as many deer wandering among the tent sites as people.

The abundance of white-tails is not an illusion; like the tameness of the deer, the oversized herd itself is a product of the park's traditional no-hunting policy, and the lack of natural or human predators has led to a significant overpopulation problem in some parts of Shenandoah.

Deer are crepuscular animals, most active at dawn and dusk, and while the rut may cause them to be visible in midday more often than at other times of the year, your best chances of seeing a really big buck come in the first and last hours of daylight.

CAUTION: *While Shenandoah's deer are unusually tame and trusting, they are, like any wild animal, potentially dangerous. This is especially true during the rut, when the bucks become particularly aggressive. Their aggression is normally directed toward each other, but a human who approaches too closely or intrudes on a buck's doe may be attacked with hooves and antlers. Images of Bambi aside, a deer attack is serious business; many people have been injured and even fatally gored by both captive and wild white-tailed deer. The danger is worse with deer—like those in a park—that have lost their normal fear of humans. During the 1991 rut, an escaped, captive-raised six-pointer attacked a turkey hunter in northern Pennsylvania, knocking his gun away and goring him badly enough to require sixty stitches. The man may have saved his life by grabbing the deer's antlers, wrapping his legs around its neck and hanging on until a search team found him hours later.*

It is best to observe deer from your car, which provides a safe haven and reduces your impact on the deer's natural behavior, since many park animals do not view cars as a threat. If you come near a buck that has lowered his antlers, raised his hackles and laid his ears flat, begin walking quickly backward, while waving your arms and yelling loudly. The deer's body language is conveying a threat that should be taken seriously.

53

Autumn
Waterfowl

"In summer no place affordeth more plenty of sturgeon, nor in winter more abundance of fowl," wrote Capt. John Smith in 1612, speaking of the Chesapeake Bay. While the sturgeon were long ago fished to the vanishing point, Captain Smith's observation about waterfowl still holds true—the mid-Atlantic region is one of the continent's major wintering grounds for ducks, swans and geese.

Late fall and early winter, when the autumn migration has peaked but before the freshwater impoundments freeze up, is the best time of the year to see large numbers of waterfowl. The dominant species are Canada geese (currently enjoying a population explosion in the region), mallards, black ducks and lesser numbers of more than two dozen other species. (Two unique waterfowl spectacles— huge flocks of snow geese and brant—are treated separately in later chapters.)

The autumn migration represents the peak population for the ducks, which have just concluded their breeding season and are heading south with the year's production of young; if only for this reason—sheer numbers—the fall migration is spectacular. But there is also something perfectly *right* about the combination of ducks, brown fall leaves and a cold north wind, something that makes a naturalist glad to be alive and out in the marsh.

Each cold front that somersaults down from Canada brings a fresh wave of migrants, while those already on the wintering grounds are up and around when dawn is just a faint, pink smudge in the east. Before it is light enough to see more than silhouettes, the air is full of whistling wings, the disembodied quacks of hen mallards and the baying gabble of a flock of Canada geese engaged in preflight debate. As the sun comes up, the horizon is scribed with moving chevrons and snaky lines, massing and stretching, as the ducks move from the wide, safer waters where they spent the night to the quiet coves and backwaters to feed and rest.

As impressive as the late winter flocks may be, they are a shadow of the past, to judge from early accounts. Uncontrolled market hunting in the late nineteenth and early twentieth centuries exacted a heavy toll, but modern sport hunting, carefully regulated, has had no effect on duck populations overall. Sadly, the same cannot be said for habitat loss, which has seriously affected waterfowl. On a continental basis, the heaviest losses have been among wetlands in the north-central states and provinces—the so-called prairie pothole region that produces the bulk of North America's ducks.

The Atlantic Flyway, however, draws most of its waterfowl from eastern Canada, a region that has suffered much less habitat loss. Here, the biggest problems have been on the wintering grounds, with the destruction and degradation of coastal wetlands. This has forced the waterfowl into smaller and smaller areas, and focused increasing importance on the region's national wildlife refuges and state wildlife management areas.

Much of the money for the purchase and protection of such areas comes from the sale of hunting licenses and stamps, particularly federal and state "duck stamps," required (in addition to state hunting licenses) of all waterfowl hunters. Buying a duck stamp actually makes good sense for anyone interested in waterfowl conservation, whether one hunts or not—and as a bonus, a federal duck stamp serves as an admission pass at all national wildlife refuges, negating the need to pay an entrance fee.

While eastern waterfowl numbers have held roughly steady, there is one disturbing trend—the steady decline of the American black duck, a species endemic to the eastern United States and Canada, and traditionally one of the most important coastal ducks in the mid-Atlantic region. Black ducks of either sex closely resemble hen mallards, but with a darker, almost chocolate body and a plain yellow or olive bill, instead of the mallard hen's orange and black; adult blacks have bright red legs and a purple wing speculum, and in flight they show contrasting white patches on the undersides of the wings.

In the past thirty years, something has gone dreadfully wrong for the black duck. Once the most common coastal duck, its population has dropped in some areas by as much as 50 to 75 percent. No one is exactly sure why, although it is thought that fragmentation of the northern forests is allowing the mallard to expand north into what was once the exclusive breeding grounds of the black duck. Mallards and blacks are closely related and hybridize freely, as the large number of mallard-black crosses attests. It may be that mallards are simply swamping the black ducks reproductively, although some biologists believe mallards are only part of the problem. Other ills affecting the black duck include acid rain (which kills the small insects on which the ducklings feed), competition with snow geese on the wintering grounds, and a rise in logging and chemical spraying for spruce budworm. Most likely the trouble is a combination of these and other causes.

Another species in difficulty is the canvasback, once the king of the region's waterfowl. Regional populations have fallen from a quarter million in the 1950s to fewer than seventy-five thousand, a decline blamed on the widespread disappearance of such aquatic plants as wild celery, on which the cans once fed. Today, the ducks have shifted to a diet heavy in small mollusks, and are completely protected from hunting to spare them any further pressures.

HOTSPOTS

The national refuge system has always been geared toward waterfowl, but few duck aficionados will complain at this time of year. Almost every one of the region's refuges is a mecca for waterfowl and waterfowl watchers.

One important caveat for naturalists visiting in the fall: On most publicly owned refuges and management areas, at least limited waterfowl hunting is permitted, usually (but not always) in areas away from the main auto tours. Saturdays are always heaviest in hunting activity; better to visit on a Sunday (when many states do not permit hunting) or on a weekday. If this is a major concern, check the refuge address or phone number in the Appendix and call ahead—many permit hunting only on certain days of the week.

The first two weeks of November are the normal peak for waterfowl at the **Brigantine** unit of Forsythe NWR in New Jersey, with total counts exceeding one hundred thousand birds; black ducks, mallards, gadwall, pintails, wigeon and shovelers are common on the freshwater impoundments, while Turtle Cove and the surrounding salt water to the south holds rafts of scaup, bufflehead, scoters, mergansers and other diving ducks. For directions to Brigantine, see Chapter 6.

During the last part of October and the first several weeks of November, Shearness Pool at **Bombay Hook NWR** in Delaware (Chapter 11) hosts tremendous concentrations of puddle ducks, particularly green-winged teal and pintails, with counts of five thousand or more of each species routine. Brigantine and Bombay Hook are also two of the best places in the region for snow geese, which are covered in the next chapter.

At *Eastern Neck NWR* in Maryland, the waterfowl calendar is similar, with the peak coming in early November. Canada geese, the reigning monarchs of the Eastern Shore, are the dominant species here, along with such puddle ducks as mallards, black ducks, pintails and wigeon, and diving species like canvasbacks, scaup, buffleheads, scoters and oldsquaw on the Chester River and Chesapeake Bay surrounding this island refuge. For directions, see Chapter 12. Also on the Eastern Shore, *Blackwater NWR*, with its wide impoundments and proximity to the great salt marshes at Fishing Bay, attracts close to two hundred thousand ducks and geese each November.

The tidal rivers of the Eastern Shore serve as feeding and resting areas for huge numbers of ducks and geese in the fall. Particularly productive are *Pocomoke Sound* off Saxis, Virginia, and the *Choptank River* west of Cambridge, Maryland.

Other good waterfowl hotspots at this time of year are *Chincoteague NWR* (Chapter 27) and *Back Bay NWR* (Chapter 3), both in Virginia; Back Bay is especially productive for puddle ducks, and being farther south than most regional refuges, its peak does not come until late November or early December. Inland, both *Pymatuning* and *Middle Creek WMA* (Chapter 11) in Pennsylvania are good for puddle and some diving ducks, although most of Middle Creek's auto tour route is closed during the hunting season, since it passes through a controlled goose-hunting area. Still, the main road, which bridges the largest impoundment and several smaller ponds, is open and provides excellent views of Canada goose and duck flocks that often number in the tens of thousands.

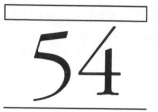

54

Blizzards of Snow Geese

No one is ever really prepared for the first sight of a huge snow goose flock. There is something almost magical about the way they blanket the salt marsh, pure white against the brown of the dead cordgrass, acre upon acre. And when they erupt into flight, black wingtips slashing the air, volleys of their high, yelping calls rolling across the flat landscape, it is an experience never to be forgotten.

Naturalists in the mid-Atlantic are fortunate, for the region is one of the most important wintering grounds in the East for the snow goose—specifically the "greater" snow goose, a geographic race once considered a species separate from the "lesser" snow goose that winters along the Gulf and Southwest. Today they are considered forms of the same species, *Chen caerulescens*.

The greater snow goose breeds in the eastern High Arctic, from western Greenland to Baffin and Devon Islands—the absolute ends of the Earth to human eyes, a wild land of muskox, white wolves and endless tundra. The geese arrive just as the snowpack is melting, females usually returning to the area of their birth. They may form large, loose colonies numbering in the thousands and also including Canada geese and brant. Biologists have found that snow geese have an affinity for nesting near snowy owl nests—the owls are no threat to a bird the size of a goose, but they aggressively drive away arctic foxes that would also endanger the geese.

Snow geese are all but unmistakable, and among wild birds can only be confused with the rare, smaller Ross' goose. The greater snow goose is marginally the larger of the two races, both of which have pure white bodies and black wingtips. The feet and beak are pink, and the beak has a black grin patch that looks like lips; the head and neck may be stained rusty from iron oxide in the Arctic water. Immatures are gray, with dark legs and beak. Occasionally a white domestic goose will go feral, but it lacks the black flight feathers of a snow goose. The "blue goose," a color phase of the lesser snow goose, has a dark body and white head, and is uncommon in the East.

In midautumn the snow geese begin arriving along the Atlantic coast, having flown down through Quebec and the Canadian Maritimes. They winter in a band from northern New Jersey to South Carolina, with concentrations at a number of national wildlife refuges in the region. The peak comes in November, when as many as a million may be found in Delaware and New Jersey; after that, local populations are determined by the weather, with a hard freeze driving the birds farther south. In mild years there are huge flocks as far north as Brigantine NWR, New Jersey, all winter.

Geese are primarily vegetarians, and snow geese are no different, feeding on grasses, sedges and weeds. But where Canada or white-fronted geese nibble at the leaves, snow geese have a more energetic feeding style, grubbing up the entire plant to get at the rootstock. On the wintering grounds they feed largely on the various species of cordgrass, the foundation plant of the salt marsh. With burgeoning snow goose populations (and a steady decrease in suitable wintering areas), many refuges have suffered serious damage to their marshes—so much so that some refuge managers have had to resort to scarecrows, noisemakers and an increase in sport hunting to keep the geese off some ravaged areas.

One tantalizing possibility for birders is the chance to find a Ross' goose among the snow goose flocks. Each year, a number of these diminutive white geese are spotted in the region, invariably flocking with their larger cousins. Ross' geese nest in a few scattered locations in the Northwest Territories, and most winter in central California, making them a prize for eastern naturalists. Finding them takes patience, since size is the only real difference, and you may have to search through thousands of snows to find the payoff. Look for a smaller goose with a shorter neck and quicker, snappier wingbeat. On the ground, watch for the Ross' rounder head, noticeably smaller bill and lack of a grin patch.

HOTSPOTS

Three national wildlife refuges offer the best snow goose viewing—the Brigantine unit of Forsythe in New Jersey, and Bombay Hook and Prime Hook in Delaware.

During the peak, snow geese may be anywhere along **Brigantine**'s wildlife drive, but most move back and forth between the fresh water of West Pool and the tidal marshes surrounding the diked impoundments. The observation tower near the cross dike, about three-quarters of a mile out the wildlife drive, is an especially good area to watch. It has views of geese loafing and bathing in the pool, and feeding in the marsh, with the high-rise casinos of Atlantic City providing an unusual backdrop in the far distance. In nearby Turtle Cove, snow geese may mingle with brant on the small, rough beach, which is closed to visitors. The birds are not feeding—they are swallowing sand and pebbles for grit to help them digest their food.

The north side of the wildlife drive (the "third side" of this giant rectangle, if you will) also usually holds many geese, but high phragmites reeds along the road can make viewing difficult. Look on the tidal marsh side for big swaths of bare mud—these are known as eatouts, areas denuded of cordgrass by the hungry geese.

Especially early in the month, when the grass is still growing, visitors may find flocks grazing in large fields at the northern corner of the drive, where the gravel road leaves the marsh and enters the upland. For general directions to Brigantine, see Chapter 6.

If anything, the snow goose numbers at **Bombay Hook** in Delaware are even greater than at Brigantine, although the wealth of feeding grounds in the farm country surrounding the refuge often lures the birds out during the day. Further, there is much back-and-forth movement of geese between Bombay Hook and Prime Hook just to the south. For this reason, both here and at Prime Hook, the best times for watching snow geese are the hours just after sunrise and before sunset. (Bear in mind that all refuges open and close with the sun.) Follow the 12-mile wildlife drive to Shearness Pool, the best bet for waterfowl of all sorts, and also watch Leatherberry Flats, the tidal marsh to the east of the road. For directions to Bombay Hook, see Chapter 11.

Prime Hook is an oddity among regional refuges, since it does not have a designated wildlife drive or loop road. A number of public roads cross the refuge, however, and the U. S. Fish and Wildlife Service has opened a few dirt roads and trails, but by and large the 8,800 acres are undeveloped—which suits the nearly sixty thousand snow geese that may be found here from November through late winter.

Snow geese may be seen in flight almost anywhere in or near the refuge, but the best spot for viewing is where Fowler Beach Road crosses Slaughter Canal near the refuge's northern end. Take Route 1 north from Lewes, Delaware, passing the refuge entrance sign at the junction of Route 16.

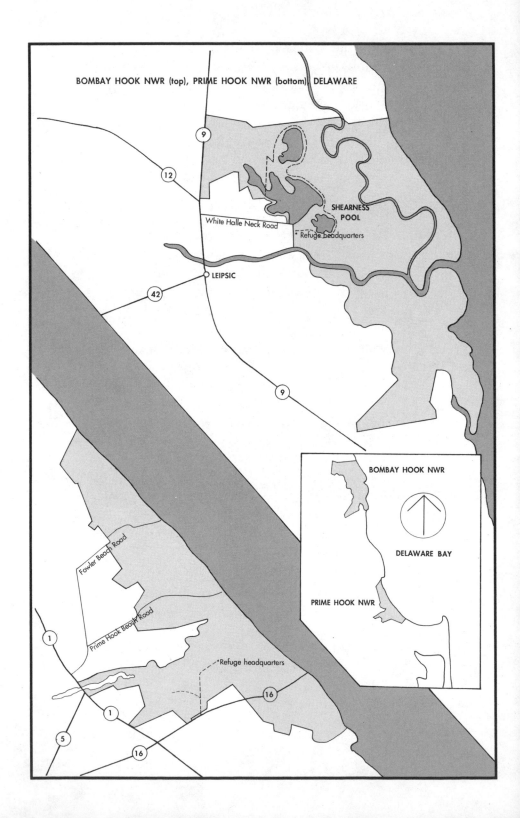

BOMBAY HOOK NWR (top), PRIME HOOK NWR (bottom), DELAWARE

9

12

White Halle Neck Road

SHEARNESS POOL

Refuge headquarters

LEIPSIC

42

9

Fowler Beach Road

Prime Hook Beach Road

1

1

5

16

16

Refuge headquarters

BOMBAY HOOK NWR

DELAWARE BAY

PRIME HOOK NWR

Just beyond Waples Pond (a marshy area on either side of the road), turn right onto Prime Hook Beach Road, then follow the signs for Fowler Beach. At 4.3 miles, make a right turn at a T-intersection, then go 1.7 miles to the canal, which flows through a wide marsh. Watch to the right, where a large pond is partly hidden by the reeds—at times, thousands of snow geese will form a huge, swirling flock as they circle in for a landing. The road dead-ends at the beach after another .5 mile.

CAUTION: *Bad weather, including exceptionally high tides, may temporarily close refuge roads, and a heavy snow may keep the roads closed long after public highways are clear and dry. If in doubt, call the refuges and check.*

Starkly white against the dead, brown cordgrass, snow geese feed along the edge of Turtle Cove at the Brigantine unit of Forsythe NWR in New Jersey, just north of Atlantic City.

Breakout: National Wildlife Refuges

They have been called the nation's wildlife jewels, the more than 450 national wildlife refuges scattered from the Florida Keys to Alaska's North Slope. More than two dozen lie within the mid-Atlantic region, places with names as familiar as Chincoteague or as unheralded as Supawna Meadows.

It is no accident that so many of the hotspot recommendations in this book feature the initials *NWR*. The refuges preserve some of the best (and in a few cases, the only) remaining wildlife habitat in their vicinities. Great Swamp NWR in north-central New Jersey would have been a jetport years ago if it hadn't been for local citizens, who bought the first 3,000 acres and donated it to the refuge system. Now, Great Swamp is one of the last large parcels of undeveloped land in a fast-growing maze of industry and housing.

Each refuge has a story behind it. Eastern Shore of Virginia NWR was a military air station until 1980, and still has the bunkers to prove it. Dismal Swamp NWR, across the Chesapeake, was surveyed by George Washington, and its swamps were ditched with slave labor. Each of the many refuges was recognized, early or belatedly, for its wildlife value and became part of the public domain.

The national wildlife refuge system is administered by

the U.S. Fish and Wildlife Service, a division of the Interior Department. Dating to 1903 and the administration of Teddy Roosevelt, the system has always been the poor cousin of the national parks, known to birders, photographers and hunters but not many others. That has changed, and each year more people are discovering these oases of life.

The refuge system is not without its problems and flaws, of course, and some of them are serious. Funded heavily through duck stamp sales, the refuges have always had a heavy slant toward waterfowl and wetlands—admittedly one of the most productive of ecosystems, but by no means the only kind of habitat deserving of protection. A glance at a map of the mid-Atlantic region's refuges shows the bias clearly. Every one is clustered along the coast, Chesapeake Bay or a major river, with one exception—Erie NWR in northwest Pennsylvania, which protects an abundance of glacial ponds, bogs and beaver swamps that are important for wood ducks. Landlocked West Virginia is the only state in the union without a single refuge.

Yet even if the refuge system seems designed for the betterment of waterfowl, a myriad of other species, plants and animals both, have ridden the ducks' coattails to protection. The refuges are strongholds for endangered bald eagles and peregrine falcons, for Delmarva fox squirrels, piping plovers and least terns, for diamondback terrapins and a host of rare plant varieties.

One of the recurrent controversies involving the entire national wildlife refuge system is that of *multiple use*—the administrative position that the refuges can be almost all things to almost all people. While their primary mission is to protect wildlife, refuges also allow such seemingly incongruous activities as grazing, logging, oil and gas drilling, recreational boating, fishing, hunting and trapping, even military bombing practice. A recent report by the General Accounting Office found that so-called secondary uses occurred at more than 90 percent of all wildlife refuges.

Refuges suffer from their neighborhoods as well as their neighbors. Great Swamp NWR, which encompasses a federally designated wilderness area within its 7,000 acres, suffers from serious water pollution problems, with an unsavory stew of agricultural chemicals and suburban sewage effluent tainting its wetlands; it has been called one of the ten most endangered refuges in the country. In southern Virginia, managers at Back Bay NWR can only shrug helplessly at the oversand vehicles that rumble down the length of the refuge's beaches, squashing tidal zone invertebrates and chasing away wildlife, including endangered piping plovers; by specific congressional fiat, certain North Carolina residents are allowed to drive through what is supposed to be wildlife habitat, and there is nothing the refuge can do about it.

Back Bay is also an example of a refuge beset by alien species. Walk one of the trails through the shrublands and reed beds, and you are as likely to surprise a feral hog as a native deer; their rooting, digging habits make them an ecological disaster. Nutria—South American mammals like large muskrats—are common in Back Bay and several other southern coastal refuges, where they have a significant impact on native plants. At Eastern Neck, Brigantine and most other regional refuges, European mute swans are a growing concern. While graceful and attractive, these huge waterbirds are extremely aggressive, defending large breeding territories against other waterfowl and raising concerns for native species as they increase in numbers. In some parts of the country, ecologists are advocating destruction of mute swan eggs to control the burgeoning flocks.

It is ironic that the best-known animals in the region's best-known refuge are the "wild" ponies at Chincoteague, which completely overshadow the refuge's native wildlife while degrading the habitat with their hooves and grazing habits (feral horses are a problem as well at Back Bay). Visitors to Chincoteague usually ooh and aah over yet another import, the diminutive sika deer, a spotted, Oriental elk that is more obvious here than the native white-tails.

Chincoteague NWR is a good example of a refuge that tries to please everyone. Assateague Island, of which the refuge is part, holds a state park, a national seashore and a national wildlife refuge within its 30-some miles, and must somehow reconcile the varied needs of wildlife and fun-loving humans. People come for the beaches, for the crabbing, for the birds, for the annual pony roundup—but for whatever reason, people come by the hundreds of thousands. In summer, the refuge is simply overwhelmed; traffic backs up on the narrow causeway to the island, snaking down Beach Road to the Tom's Cove visitors' center. Sitting in the traffic jam, people toss bread crusts to the mooching ponies while egrets and herons try to find the few places along Swan Pool that haven't been appropriated by picnickers. Down the beach from Tom's Cove, off-road vehicles make life miserable for ghost crabs and beach-nesting birds.

But there is another face to Chincoteague, as there is to all the refuges. Take a long walk away from the crowds, up the island a couple miles to Wash Flats, where the air is empty of the smell of sunscreen and yelling kids. In this solitude, alone with the laughing gulls, you find the heart of the refuge system.

For all their imperfections, the region would be much poorer without its refuges, the lands bounded by the sign of the flying goose. A sky-filling flock of snow geese taking wing, or a peregrine falcon coursing down the beach on its way south, or the arrowed reflection of a beaver's wake, are proof enough of that.

DECEMBER

December Observations

56

Songbirds in the Manure

Cow manure as a bird attractant? Certainly no one is going to stock feeders with the odious stuff, but experienced naturalists know that the surest way to find several species of unusual winter songbirds is to cruise farmland roads, looking for freshly manured fields. It may not be pleasant, but it works.

The birds in question are a trio of small songbirds—the horned lark, snow bunting and Lapland longspur. While the larks are fairly common in open country throughout the region (particularly in winter), the snow buntings and longspurs are much rarer.

Horned larks have an extremely wide range in North America. They are found in summer as far north as the Arctic Ocean, and year-round everywhere from the Canadian border down to the Deep South; they are completely absent only from Florida. Yet despite their relative abundance, horned larks are curiously little known. The color of dried grass, with a hint of yellow on the face and throat, a horned lark is not a flashy bird like an oriole; its call, a thin *tsee-tseetsee*, vanishes on the wind as soon as it leaves the bird's throat. Where some birds stand out against their surroundings, the lark disappears against its normal backdrop of grass fields and beaches.

At a distance, the best field mark on a horned lark is its distinctive facial and chest pattern: a dark line along the forehead (ending in two tiny, feathered "horns"), a dark stripe through the jaw and a black crescent on the chest. More often than not, though, the birds are invisible until the flock bursts into the air, flashing the white edges on their dark tails, twisting in a loose bunch just above the frozen ground.

The horned lark is probably the earliest-nesting songbird in the region; females are sitting on eggs by the beginning of March in many areas. This head-start strategy allows the larks to get off several broods each year, but obviously poses a serious risk if the weather turns sour. While the female may be able to incubate the eggs safely through a cold, snowy spell, it is much harder for the adults to garner insects for the newly hatched chicks, and many succumb to cold and starvation if spring comes a little too late.

In summer, horned larks inhabit golf courses, sod farms, airports, farm fields—anywhere with wide horizons and short grass. In winter they may stay in the same areas, but many migrate to the coast or to farming areas where manure is being spread.

Cow manure might not seem like a palatable diet to humans, but seed-eating birds like horned larks are able to glean a living from it, picking out seeds from the brown goo. Manure becomes a magnet for the birds, especially when the ground is frozen beneath a heavy layer of snow or ice, sealing off more natural sources of seeds.

The farmers don't spread manure for the benefit of the local songbirds, of course; the stuff piles up through the winter in dairy barns and has to go somewhere, so the farmers make regular trips to the fields, leaving wide, brown strips behind them. While this may seem a salutary reuse of natural fertilizer, manuring has become controversial, especially in the Chesapeake Bay watershed, which includes the

Susquehanna River and the fertile Pennsylvania Dutch farmland around it, where dairy herds are common. In winter, nothing percolates into the frozen ground, and much of the manure is simply carried into streams by snowmelt or a cold winter rain. This contributes little to the soil and, in turn, adds to the bay's already crushing nutrient load, endangering its fragile balance by causing algae blooms and other problems. One of the goals of the ongoing Chesapeake restoration project is to cut back on winter manuring.

In the meantime, birds and birders will continue to flock to freshly manured fields. While horned larks are the most common songbirds feeding there, snow buntings and Lapland longspurs are the real treat.

Buntings and longspurs are finches that have evolved for life in open country. The snow bunting breeds in the extreme reaches of the Arctic and is one of the few finches to undergo a drastic plumage change from season to season. In summer, the males are pure white, save for black wings, back and tail. As autumn approaches, both sexes molt into a similar pattern of white shot through with washes of buff, and black and brown on the wings and tail; in flight, each bunting becomes a semaphore code of dark and white patches blinking through the air, and the flock is a confusion of visual signals that makes it hard for a hawk to focus on just one.

Longspurs are close relatives of the snow buntings. There are four species in North America, but three—the chestnut-collared, Smith's and McCowan's longspurs—are strictly western in distribution. Only the Lapland longspur (also found in Europe, hence the name) can be found in the mid-Atlantic region, and then only in winter and in extremely limited numbers. Spotting a small flock of longspurs is a red-letter day for any naturalist.

Longspurs are so named for their elongated hind claws, but these are visible only at close range, and there are better field marks to look for. By winter, the male longspurs have lost their black face and chest feathers and have taken on a plumage that intricately mixes rusty brown on the upperparts with a tan face, dark cap and ear patch, and buffy eyebrow; females have a faint brownish chest band, while males have a darker band of scaly black feathers across the breast. They are roughly the same size as the buntings (about 6.5 inches) but are much darker, without white on the wings but showing white edges on the tail. This may lead to confusion with horned larks, but look for the rich, chestnut tones of the longspurs and the slimmer build of the larks.

HOTSPOTS

The extensive auto route in **southeastern Pennsylvania** suggested in Chapter 6 for winter raptors also goes through the middle of excellent lark, bunting and longspur country, especially the areas along Route 501 and to the north and south of Route 30 west of Lancaster. If there are no freshly manured fields along the main highways, head off onto the small side roads and do a little exploring.

Do not expect to see the songbird flocks from a moving car, unless the birds are flying—and even then, they may be hard to pick up against bare earth. Find a safe place to pull off onto the shoulder and scan with binoculars.

Generally the flocks will be small, just a few dozen to a few hundred, but occasionally a naturalist will hit a bonanza. In the mid-1970s, birders were stunned to find more than five thousand snow buntings along the auto route mentioned above, feeding in sorghum fields between Kempton and Hawk Mountain Sanctuary. The buntings stayed all winter, allowing regular visitors to see the gradual change of the males back into breeding plumage just before the flocks vanished north again.

In addition to farm fields, mixed lark, bunting and longspur flocks can be found on beaches and among dunes at most coastal sites. Some of the more productive spots include **Long Beach Island** (see Chapter 2, under Barnegat),

Higbee Beach WMA (Chapter 3) and *Sandy Hook* (Chapter 2), all in New Jersey; *Cape Henlopen* and *Delaware Seashore State Park* (Chapter 3) in Delaware; *Assateague Island* (Chapter 27), *Cape Charles* (Chapter 46) and the beaches at *Back Bay NWR/False Cape State Park* in Virginia (Chapter 3).

57

Watching
Winter Sea Ducks

The idea of ducks flying south for the winter is a sodden cliché. Not every species seeks warmer climates—and a few (to human eyes) go from a bad situation to a worse. They are the sea ducks, and they spend the winter on the open ocean.

There can be few more brutal environments in winter than the sea, where a bird must contend not only with the frigid air temperature, snow and sleet, but with the equally cold water. Because water conducts heat much more efficiently than air, the ocean can quickly sap the body warmth from any unprotected animal exposed to it. A human falling in 40° F. water has bare minutes to live, but a sea duck can spend months on and beneath the ocean, never stepping onto land.

The secret is insulation, coupled with a miserly circulatory system in the legs. The sea ducks, which include the eiders, oldsquaw, scoters and harlequin duck, are large and stockily built, an adaptation to a cold environment (most are Arctic or boreal species in the summer). They are heavily insulated with down, covered by lightly oiled, waterproof contour feathers that trap a layer of air next to the body, keeping the duck dry and warm. The freezing water holds no cruelties for a diving duck.

It is natural for shivering birders to sympathize with a duck in winter, imagining its "poor, cold feet" in the icy water. Actually, bird legs have only a bare minimum of soft tissue and blood vessels—most of the leg is bone, tendon or scaly skin, which loses very little body heat. Certainly, the ducks never seem to show any sign that the temperature bothers them.

The sea ducks are a varied group, both in shape and color, with some of North America's most bizarre waterfowl among them. The male king eider, a prized rarity that occurs in small numbers at regional jetties, has a black and white plumage pattern accented by a powder-blue head, greenish face and a large, orange bill plate that rises between the eyes. The surf scoter, or "skunkhead" as New England fishermen called it, is equally strange; the male is black with large patches of white on the forehead and neck, and sports a swollen bill splotched with black, white and orange.

The oddest of all may be the drake harlequin duck—blue-gray with chestnut flanks, black-edged bands of white on the neck and sides, and a complicated pattern of white, black and rust on the face. Native in summer to the turbulent rivers of Atlantic Canada, in winter the harlequin duck feeds on shellfish that cling to rock jetties, where the waves crash unendingly around it.

Sadly, the most enigmatic of the sea ducks has been lost completely. The Labrador duck, a study in black and white, was never common, although it wintered as far south as the Chesapeake. Because it tasted of fish it was not heavily hunted for market, but by the middle of the nineteenth century it was becoming quite rare, and the last specimen was shot in 1878. Experts theorize that it had a limited breeding range in coastal Canada and may have been wiped out by commercial egging.

Eiders and harlequin ducks can often be found close to shore, but surf, black and white-winged scoters, as well as oldsquaws, more often stay well beyond the surf line; for this reason, a spotting scope is almost an essential for any excursion to see these unusual birds of winter.

HOTSPOTS

Harlequin ducks, common and king eiders are the so-called jetty ducks, and several regional jetties are known for attracting these rarities each winter.

One of the best places in the region is the *Eighth Street jetty* at Barnegat Light, New Jersey. The abandoned jetty (replaced by a bigger, newer structure to the west) provides the kind of rocky habitat needed by mussels and other shellfish. They, in turn, attract the ducks, which dive in the frigid, turbulent water with what seems to be an astonishing degree of nonchalance—at least to a human bundled against the cold.

The harlequin duck is a much sought-after species, and the Eighth Street jetty is one of the surest bets for finding this unusual duck, with as many as a dozen or more present in good winters. Also seen regularly at Barnegat are common and king eiders. For directions to Barnegat see Chapter 2; park near the dead end on Eighth Street and follow the boardwalk to the beach. The jetty will be just ahead, although it may be submerged at very high tide. Check near the jetty for harlequins, eiders and oldsquaw, and farther from shore for scoters and loons.

Other regional jetties worth searching for sea ducks in December are the *Second Avenue jetty* in Cape May, the *Ocean City jetty* in Maryland and the *Indian River jetty* in Delaware (for directions to all three, see Chapter 3). The *Manasquan Inlet* in New Jersey and *Rudlee Inlet* in Virginia (both Chapter 14) may hold some jetty ducks, as may the islands of the *Chesapeake Bay Bridge-Tunnel* between capes Henry and Charles, and *Cape Henlopen State Park* in Delaware (both Chapter 3).

58

Christmas Bird Counts

Birding can be many things to many people—a solitary study of neighborhood species, a transcontinental search for rarities or a weekend ramble with friends. It can also mean competition, like the annual World Series of Birding each May in New Jersey, which pits teams of crack bird-watchers from around the country against each other, hoping to spot the greatest number of species in 24 hours.

The world series is a recent innovation, but its roots go back much farther—to a New England Christmas more than ninety years ago. At that time, it was considered traditional for teams of hunters to go afield at Christmas shooting anything they could find, with the group accumulating the biggest bag declared the winner. This repelled Frank M. Chapman, one of the early giants of American ornithology, who came up with a different variation. On Christmas Day, 1900, he and roughly two dozen other bird-watchers fanned out at scattered locations across the Northeast, each trying to accumulate the biggest "bag" of bird sightings. From this humble beginning, the Christmas Bird Count was born.

It is humble no longer. Now sponsored by the National Audubon Society, the CBC (as it is universally

known) annually attracts more than forty thousand participants in every state and Canadian province, and in locations
as far-flung as Guam, Colombia and the South Pole. Each of
the nearly sixteen hundred count sites encompasses a circle
15 miles wide; in one 24-hour period, sometime during the
last two weeks of December and the first week of January
and almost always on a weekend, the count circle is combed
and all species (and individual birds) are tallied. Some years,
the totals run as high as an astonishing 190 million birds for
North American counts alone.

The mid-Atlantic region, with more than 160 count
sites in the six states and District of Columbia, has one of the
highest densities of CBCs in the country; Pennsylvania alone
has sixty, Virginia has thirty-eight, and the number grows
each year as new areas are added.

All of the work is done by volunteers, either in the
field or watching home feeding stations. Many participants
start hours before daybreak, counting owls in parks and on
lonely backroads (and occasionally drawing the attention of
the police, who are often skeptical of the explanations
offered: Talking to owls? Really? Breathe into this balloon,
please). The count circle is usually divided into manageable
sections and volunteers assigned to each to ensure even
coverage. There is almost always room for more help, and
new counters are ordinarily welcomed with open arms,
whatever their level of expertise.

A CBC is competitive birding in its least offensive
form; the counters strive informally against others in their
state for the highest species count or the best list of rarities,
while trying to beat old records within the count itself. What
sets a Christmas Bird Count apart from most other competitive events is that the individual birds are recorded, as well
as species totals; this is no problem for, say, blue jays and
cardinals, but it becomes a chore for starlings and house
finches—and pity the counters who must quantify the winter
roosts of millions of grackles and blackbirds!

The traditional end to the day is the compilation dinner, usually a potluck affair at a local fire hall. Over mugs of hot soup and bowls of homemade chili, the day's findings are gathered and totaled; there is excitement over an unexpected discovery, perhaps frustration at not finding a normally common species.

CBC aficionados are statistics buffs, who look forward eagerly to the publication (by *American Birds,* the Audubon Society's scientific journal) of the results of the counts—a telephone book–sized volume, crammed with facts and figures from every one of the hundreds of CBCs.

Counters are not the only ones interested in the results. The Christmas Bird Count represents the longest continuous survey of North America's winter bird populations, and many scientists have mined the mountains of figures for clues to trends as disparate as range expansion in songbirds and the status of wintering red-tailed hawks. Because each count keeps meticulous records of the number of participants, hours in the field and miles covered, it is possible to interpret the tallies with surprising precision.

Science aside, though, the biggest merit of a Christmas Bird Count is fun—the chance to watch birds, meet friends and get outside during the bleakest months of the year.

HOTSPOTS

It is a rare count leader who does not welcome new, enthusiastic help, and there is a CBC site within reasonable driving distance of most parts of the mid-Atlantic region, although the majority are near the larger towns and cities.

A local birding club, nature center or science museum can usually put you in contact with the compiler for the nearest CBC, or you can write to the Christmas Bird Count editor, *American Birds*, National Audubon Society, 700 Broadway, New York, NY 10003, requesting a list of counts and compilers in your area. The Appendix contains a list of regional CBCs by state but, as already mentioned, the number grows annually as new counts are started. If there is no Christmas Bird Count in your area (and you enjoy organizing), ask National Audubon for help in starting one.

There is a fee ($5 at this writing) for participation to cover the cost of printing the annual CBC issue. Be prepared for an entire day outdoors, regardless of the weather; CBCers are fiercely proud of being undeterred by snow, sleet, rain or bitter cold. Be honest about your birding abilities— beginners are often teamed with experienced counters, which is a great way to learn. And if you are not up to fighting the elements all day, consider signing up as a feeder watcher, which allows you to participate while enjoying central heating.

Christmas Bird Counts are more than just fun—they provide valuable information on changing bird populations, like the explosive growth of winter Canada goose flocks in much of the region.

59

Brant
Concentrations

The smallest goose on the Atlantic Flyway (and the second smallest in North America), the brant looks more like a duck than any of its larger relatives. Nor is it nearly as well known as the Canada geese and snow geese that attract so much attention each autumn, even though spectacular concentrations of brant can be found along the New Jersey coast in December.

For years, scientists recognized two species of brant— the American brant of the East and the much darker black brant of the Pacific coast. More recently, biologists have come to believe that the two are simply forms of the same variety, and have lumped them (with "brent geese" from Europe and northern Asia) into one species, *Branta bernicla.* Those that winter along the mid-Atlantic coast average about 3.5 to 4 pounds in weight and are dark brown with light flanks and a large area of white around the tail; at close range, look for the brant's small bill and thin collar of white on the short neck, rather than the Canada goose's longer proportions and bigger cheek patches. In the air, the brant look almost black, and their throaty *ronk* call is noticeably different from a Canada goose's two-note *ha-RONK!*

Brant nest in water-soaked tundra along the coast of

the Arctic Ocean, a nasty environment where sudden storms can churn the sea to a frenzy, swamping the low-lying ground where the geese nest and wiping out the eggs and chicks. In other years, a late spring may mean no nesting at all, if the tundra is late in thawing. Those chicks that are raised then face a long flight over the Arctic archipelago, down the coast of Hudson and James bays, across southern Canada and New England (rarely stopping on the way) until they reach the mid-Atlantic coast.

The brant's traditional food has always been eelgrass, one of the few seed-bearing plants to thrive in salt water and an important food for many species of waterfowl. At one time, stands of it grew thickly in shallow salt and brackish water throughout the region, but a blight in the 1930s killed most of the eelgrass and sent the brant population into a tailspin as well, bottoming out at about fifty thousand birds in the 1970s. Interestingly, the blight hit Europe as well, with similar effects on that continent's brant flocks.

Since the worst days of the eelgrass blight, brant have switched to other food supplies, notably marine algae like sea lettuce, waste grain and even lawn grass; these new sources, coupled with a steady improvement in eelgrass stocks, make the brant's future hopeful.

Brant begin to appear along the coast in early October, with the number of arrivals building through November. The flocks usually peak between Thanksgiving and the second week of December, with the geese concentrated in sheltered bays and coves, and on the lee sides of barrier islands where they can find food in the shallow water. Throughout the winter, small, jumbled flocks of brant, jockeying constantly among themselves for position, are a common sight from the north Jersey shore south to Chincoteague.

HOTSPOTS

There is no better place to see brant in the mid-Atlantic region than *Barnegat Bay*, on New Jersey's central coast, where a significant portion of the eastern brant population usually spends the winter.

See Chapter 2 for general directions to the town of Barnegat Light at the north end of Long Beach Island; the best areas for seeing brant are the inlet and bay near the lighthouse, and from the many small side roads that dead-end west of Central Avenue/Long Beach Boulevard, the main north-south road on the island.

Brant are abundant as well at the **Brigantine** unit of Forsythe NWR, about 25 miles south of Barnegat (Chapter 6). The brant feed on eelgrass and bay lettuce on the saltwater bays to the east and south of the refuge, then move to the freshwater impoundments to bathe and drink; the observation tower near Turtle Cove is especially productive, and the brant can often be seen on the pebbly beach below, swallowing gravel for digestive grit. Likewise, brant are common in sheltered salt water at **Cape May** (Chapter 3) and **Sandy Hook** (Chapter 2) and on the **Manasquan River** just inland from Manasquan Inlet; see Chapter 14 for directions, then take Route 35 north of Point Pleasant to the bridge crossing the river. Other areas that support smaller wintering brant flocks are **Chincoteague NWR** and the north end of **Assateague Island** (see Chapter 27 for both).

60

Breakout: Feeding Winter Birds

It may be that no other form of nature study attracts so many people each year as feeding birds—by some estimates, fully a third of all American households have some sort of feeding station, ranging from the simply functional to the elaborate.

People have thrown crumbs to the birds since medieval days, but feeding winter birds did not begin to catch on in a big way until the late 1950s and 1960s, with the rise of the environmental movement. Today it is a multibillion-dollar industry, and years of experimentation and fine-tuning by bird enthusiasts have created a deeper understanding of what birds want and need in a feeding station. There is even a branch of ornithology that studies the effects of artificial feeding on bird populations; the northward expansion of mourning doves is thought to be linked with the boom in feeders, and there is no doubt that feeders are vital to the continuing invasion of the Northeast by house finches.

Whether you want a simple feeder or a fancy spread, there are several basics to keep in mind—choosing the right food and the right place and minimizing dangers for the birds.

Picking the right food is critically important. Each species of songbird has its own preferences, which you can exploit to attract exactly what you want, or to keep undesirables away.

Avoid bread crumbs, which have little nutritional value for birds, as well as the common seed mixes, which rely heavily on varieties like rape that birds do not like and so lead to a great deal of waste. The best overall choice by far is sunflower seed, particularly the small, all-black variety known as oil sunflower, which is more nutritious, results in less waste and can be handled by birds as large as cardinals and as small as siskins.

Sunflower seed is the preferred food of most of the common feeder species—cardinals, black-capped and Carolina chickadees, evening grosbeaks, house and purple finches, mourning doves, tufted titmice and white-throated sparrows. Goldfinches and pine siskins prefer niger ("thistle") seed when they can get it, but oil sunflower is a much more economical alternative to the hideously expensive niger and is eagerly accepted by the birds. For most sparrows, including dark-eyed juncos, the favorite food is white proso millet.

As important as knowing which seed to feed are choosing the right kind of feeder and placing it in the right spot. With the rising popularity of bird-feeding has come a bewildering array of feeder styles, some starkly functional, others ornately decorative. There are two major types of seed feeders—plastic tube feeders, which dispense seeds individually from a number of small feeding ports along the tube's length, and platform or tray feeders, usually fitted with a storage hopper and covered with a roof. Each has advantages and limitations. Tube feeders are cheap and can hang from a tree, clothesline or pole; because they attract smaller, more agile birds like chickadees, they are a good choice where starlings or blue jays are a problem.

On the other hand, cardinals, grosbeaks and many sparrows shy away from tube feeders, but can be enticed to the wider landing areas of a platform feeder. The drawback here is installation and cost, since these feeders are usually considerably more expensive and the larger models require a sturdy pole sunk well into the ground.

Most people who are serious about feeding the birds have several feeders, including tube and platform models; they may also have hanging globe feeders, which cater to small species, and a low, roofless tray feeder for ground-feeding species like doves. Suet feeders—plastic mesh bags or wire baskets—hold beef fat, or suet, and are an excellent way to attract woodpeckers, nuthatches, titmice and chickadees. The feeders need not be fancy; a length of tree branch, with 1.5-inch holes drilled into it and filled with suet or peanut butter, works as well as anything from the store. (Do not feed suet once the weather starts to warm up in spring, as the soft fat can mat feathers and rob the birds of insulation.)

Any time large numbers of animals gather in one place, the risk of disease increases greatly, so cleanliness becomes a major concern. Old seed, soiled by bird droppings and kept damp by rain or snow, becomes a breeding ground for mold, which causes a deadly respiratory infection in birds; clean up fallen seed regularly, and fit your tube feeders with plastic trays to keep the waste seed from dropping to the ground. The feeders themselves should be emptied and scrubbed with boiling water (no soap) regularly. The risk of disease becomes especially acute in early spring, when the warmer days permit the mold to spread rapidly.

The biggest mistake most novice bird-feeders make is in where they hang the feeder. Choose an area near trees or bushes, which will provide escape cover for the birds in case a hawk or cat attacks. At a home in the woods, feeder placement may be as simple as picking the best window from which to watch, but in new housing developments that haven't been landscaped, the paucity of cover becomes critical. If the best place for watching (outside the kitchen window, for instance) is too bare, consider planting a few evergreen shrubs and a small tree. One temporary solution is to drive a few 4-foot stakes into the ground before it freezes, then tie several discarded Christmas trees to them after the holidays.

With brand new feeding stations, patience can be as important as sunflower seeds. It may take the birds a while to learn about the free lunch, but when one discovers it, word usually spreads fast. If weeks pass without birds, take a critical look at the area and decide if there might not be another, more protected spot for the feeders.

Be prepared for some occasional trouble, which arrives most often in a gray fur coat with a large tail. Squirrels are the bane of many a feeding station—taking over the feeders, monopolizing the food and chasing the birds away. Not everyone finds their visits offensive, but if squirrels have outstayed their welcome at your feeder, try installing large plastic baffles on the poles and supports of all your feeders, which should be moved far enough away from tree trunks to keep the acrobatic squirrels from leaping across the gap. If coercion fails, try bribery; drive several spikes through a 2-by-4 and impale ears of feed corn on them, then put the corn somewhere between the squirrel's trees and your feeder. It may be enough to lure them away from the sunflower seeds.

Feeding stations often attract sharp-shinned and Cooper's hawks, which feed primarily on small birds. While it is an upsetting experience to see a hawk rush into a flock of "your" birds and grab one, bear in mind that this is as natural as a robin catching a worm or a trout eating a grasshopper. As with most predator-prey dramas, the song-birds killed are usually the sick, weak and infirm, and the hawks are doing a valuable (albeit unintentional) job of policing the health of the flock. And remember—no matter how angry it makes you, hawks and owls are completely protected by law and cannot be harmed.

Hawk attacks are rare, but window collisions are a

much more common danger, especially if the feeder is near a plate-glass window or sliding doors. Fortunately, most window strikes are not fatal. If you hear a thump and find a stunned bird, place it beneath a bush and check in half an hour; chances are it will have recovered and flown off. Unconscious or badly dazed birds can be brought inside and kept for a few hours in a dark box, then released as soon as they are moving again. You can also put the bird in a paper bag with the top loosely closed, then place it in a sheltered nook outside. Once it comes to its senses, the bird sees the light shining through the opening and takes off, but in the meantime it is hidden from prowling cats.

Evening grosbeaks are among the colorful birds that can be easily attracted to a home feeding station.

APPENDIX

Following is a list of addresses and telephone numbers for national wildlife refuges, parks, preserves and organizations mentioned in the text. Other nature centers in this mid-Atlantic region are listed in the section beginning on page 318.

NATIONAL WILDLIFE REFUGES

Back Bay NWR
4005 Sandpiper Rd.
P.O. Box 6286
Virginia Beach, VA 23456
(804) 721-2412

Blackwater NWR
Route 1, Box 121
Cambridge, MD 21613
(301) 228-2677

Bombay Hook NWR
RFD 1, Box 147
Smyrna, DE 19977
(302) 653-9345

Chincoteague NWR
P.O. Box 62
Chincoteague, VA 23336
(804) 336-6122

Dismal Swamp NWR
P.O. Box 349
Suffolk, VA 23434
(804) 539-7479

Eastern Neck NWR
Route 2, Box 225
Rock Hall, MD 21661
(301) 639-7056

Eastern Shore of Virginia NWR
RFD 1, Box 122B
Cape Charles, VA 23310
(804) 331-2760

Edwin B. Forsythe NWR
Great Creek Rd.
P.O. Box 72
Oceanville, NJ 08231
(609) 652-1665

Erie NWR
RD1, Wood Duck Lane
Guys Mills, PA 16327
(814) 789-3585

Prime Hook NWR
RD3, Box 195
Milton, DE 19968
(302) 684-8419

Great Swamp NWR
RD1, Box 152
Basking Ridge, NJ 07920
(908) 647-1222

NATIONAL PARKS, FORESTS AND RECREATION AREAS

Assateague Island
  National Seashore
Route 2, Box 294
Berlin, MD 21811
(301) 641-1441 or 3030

George Washington
  National Forest
USDA Forest Service
Harrison Plaza, P.O. Box 233
Harrisonburg, VA 22801
(703) 433-2491

Gettysburg National Military Park
Gettysburg, PA 17325

Great Falls Park
National Park Service
9200 Old Dominion Dr.
Great Falls Park, VA 22066
(703) 759-2915

Jefferson National Forest
USDA Forest Service
210 Franklin Rd., SW
Caller Service 2900
Roanoke, VA 24001
(703) 982-6270 or 6274

Monongahela National Forest
USDA Forest Service
Forest Supervisor
Elkins, WV 26241
(304) 636-1800

For information on
Cranberry Glades
Botanical Area:
In summer:
Cranberry Mountain
    Visitor Center
U.S. Forest Service
Richwood, WV 26261
(304) 653-4826

In winter:
District Ranger
U.S. Forest Service
Richwood, WV 26261
(304) 846-2695

For information on Dolly Sods
Wilderness or Spruce Knob Unit,
call the general Monongahela
number above or:
District Ranger
Potomac Ranger District
U.S. Forest Service
Route 3, Box 240
Petersburg, WV 26847
(304) 257-4488

Shenandoah National Park
Route 4, Box 348
Luray, VA 22835
(703) 999-2266 or 2229

STATE AGENCIES

Delaware Division of
  Fish and Wildlife
P.O. Box 1401
Dover, DE 19903
(302) 736-4506

Delaware Division of
  Parks and Recreation
P.O. Box 1401
Dover, DE 19903

Delaware Tourism Office
99 Kings Highway
P.O. Box 1401
Dover, DE 19903
(800) 282-8667 (in state)
(800) 441-8846 (out of state)

Maryland Department
  of Natural Resources
Tawes State Office Building
Annapolis, MD 21401
(301) 269-3761

Maryland Office of Tourism
Redwood Tower, Floor 9
217 E. Redwood St.
Baltimore, MD 21202
(800) 543-1036

New Jersey Department of
  Environmental Protection
363 Pennington Ave.
Trenton, NJ 08618

For tourism information:
New Jersey Department
  of Transportation
1035 Parkway Ave., CN600
Trenton, NJ 08625
(609) 292-3105

Pennsylvania Bureau
  of State Parks
Department of
  Environmental Resources
P.O. Box 1467
Harrisburg, PA 17105-1467
(800) 63-PARKS

Pennsylvania Fish and Boat
  Commission
P.O. Box 1673
Harrisburg, PA 17120
(717) 787-6487

Pennsylvania Game Commission
2001 Elmerton Ave.
Harrisburg, PA 17110-9797
(717) 787-4250

Virginia Commission of
  Game and Inland Fisheries
4010 W. Broad St.
P.O. Box 11104
Richmond, VA 23230
(804) 367-1000

Virginia Division of State Parks
203 Governor St.
Suite 306
Richmond, VA 23219
(804) 786-1712

Virginia Division of Tourism
Bell Tower on Capitol Square
Richmond, VA 23219
(804) 786-4484

West Virginia Department
  of Natural Resources
1800 Washington St.
Charleston, WV 25305
(304) 348-2764

West Virginia Division of
    Tourism and Parks
State Capitol Complex
Charleston, WV 25305
(800) CALL-WVA

STATE OR MUNICIPAL PARKS AND MANAGEMENT AREAS

Black Moshannon State Park
RD1, Box 183
Philipsburg, PA 16866
(814) 342-1101

Blue Ridge Parkway Information
200 BB&T Building
One Pack Square
Asheville, NC 28801
(704) 259-0779

Brandywine Creek State Park
P.O. Box 3782
Greenville, DE 19807
(302) 655-5740

Bull Run Regional Park
Northern Virginia Regional
    Park Authority
11001 Popes Head Rd.
Fairfax, VA 22030
(703) 278-8880

Canaan Valley State Park
Route 1-330
Davis, WV 26260
(304) 866-4121

Canoe Creek State Park
RD2, Box 560
Hollidaysburg, PA 16648
(814) 695-6807

Cape Henlopen State Park
42 Cape Henlopen Dr.
Lewes, DE 19958
(302) 645-6852

Cape May Point State Park
P.O. Box 107
Cape May Point, NJ 08212
(609) 884-2159

Cook Forest State Park
Cooksburg, PA 16217
(814) 744-8401

Delaware Seashore State Park
Inlet 850
Rehoboth Beach, DE 19971
(302) 227-2800

Fairview Fish Culture Station
Avonia, PA
(814) 474-1514

Hickory Run State Park
RD1, Box 81
White Haven, PA 18661
(717) 443-9991

Huntley Meadows Park
Fairfax County Park Authority
3701 Lockheed Blvd.
Alexandria, VA 22306
(703) 768-2525

Jennings Environmental
    Education Center
RD1
Slippery Rock, PA 16057
(412) 794-6011

Kettle Creek State Park
HCR62, Box 96
Renovo, PA 17764
(717) 923-0206

Middle Creek Wildlife
    Management Area
P.O. Box 110
Kleinfeltersville, PA 17039-0110

Presque Isle State Park
P.O. Box 8510
Erie, PA 16505
(814) 871-4251

Promised Land State Park
(including Bruce Lake
    Natural Area)
RD1, Box 96
Greentown, PA 18426
(717) 676-3428

Pymatuning State Park
P.O. Box 425
Jamestown, PA 16134
(412) 932-3141

Pymatuning Waterfowl Museum
(814) 683-5545

Pymatuning Wildlife
    Management Area
RD1
Hartstown, PA 16131

Riverbend Park Visitors Center
8800 Potomac Hills St.
Great Falls, VA 22066
(703) 759-9018

Sandy Point State Park
800 Revell Highway
Annapolis, MD 21401
(301) 974-1249

Seashore State Park
    and Natural Area
2500 Shore Dr.
Virginia Beach, VA 23451
(804) 481-2131

Trap Pond State Park
RD2, Box 331
Laurel, DE 19956
(302) 875-5153

Washington Monument
    State Park
Route 1, Box 147
Middletown, MD 21769
(301) 432-8065

PRIVATE PRESERVES AND ORGANIZATIONS

Brandywine Conservancy
P.O. Box 141
Chadds Ford, PA 19317
(215) 388-7601

Cape May Bird Observatory
P.O. Box 3
Cape May Point, NJ 08212
(609) 884-2736

Delaware Audubon Society
P.O. Box 1713
Wilmington, DE 19899
(302) 428-3959

Hawk Mountain Sanctuary
    Association
Route 2, Box 191
Kempton, PA 19529-9449
(215) 756-6961

The Nature Conservancy
1815 N. Lynn St.
Arlington, VA 22209

NATURE CONSERVANCY FIELD OFFICES

Delaware Field Office
P.O. Box 1324
Dover, DE 19903-1324

Maryland Field Office
Chevy Chase Metro Bldg.
2 Wisconsin Circle, Suite 410
Chevy Chase, MD 20815
(301) 656-8673

New Jersey Field Office
P.O. Box 181
17 Fairmount Rd.
Pottersville, NJ 07979-0181
(201) 439-3007

Pennsylvania Field Office
1218 Chestnut St., Suite 807
Philadelphia, PA 19107
(215) 925-1065

Virginia Field Office
1110 Rose Hill Dr., Suite 200
Charlottesville, VA 22901
(804) 295-6106

West Virginia Field Office
922 Quarrier St., Rm. 414
Charleston, WV 25301
(304) 345-4350

OTHER PRIVATE ORGANIZATIONS

New Jersey Audubon Society
790 Ewing Ave.
P.O. Box 125
Franklin Lakes, NJ 07417
(201) 891-1211

Shenk's Ferry Glen
    Wildflower Reserve
c/o Pennsylvania Power
    & Light Co.
Holtwood Land
    Management Office
RD3, Box 345
Holtwood, PA 17532
(717) 284-2278

Western Pennsylvania
    Conservancy
316 Fourth Ave.
Pittsburgh, PA 15222
(412) 288-2777

The Wetlands Institute
Stone Harbor Blvd.
Stone Harbor, NJ 08247
(609) 368-1211

APPENDIX

OTHER IMPORTANT ADDRESSES

*For permits to stop on
CBBT islands:*
Chesapeake Bay Bridge
   and Tunnel District
P.O. Box 111
Cape Charles, VA 23310-0111
(804) 331-2960

*For U.S. government topographic
maps:*
Eastern Mapping Center
U.S. Geologic Survey
12201 Sunrise Valley Dr.
Reston, VA 22042

DeLorme Mapping Co.
P.O. Box 298
Freeport, ME 04032
(800) 227-1656

PELAGIC BIRDING AND WHALE-WATCH OPERATORS

Atlantic Seabirds
Gene Scarpulla
7906-B Knollwood Rd.
Towson, MD 21204
(301) 821-0575
*Year-round pelagic trips from
Ocean City, Maryland, for birds
and marine mammals.*

Alan Brady
P.O. Box 103
Wycombe, PA 18980
(215) 598-7856
*Spring and fall trips from Barnegat
Light, New Jersey, for pelagic birds
and marine mammals.*

Brian Patterson
P.O. Box 125
Amherst, VA 24521
*Winter, spring and fall trips from
Virginia Beach, Virginia, for pe-
lagic birds and marine mammals.*

Ron Robbins
Route 109
Cape May, NJ 08204
(609) 898-0055
*Early spring through late autumn
dolphin- and whale-watches, plus
pelagic birds.*

BIRDING HOTLINES

Provided as public services by a variety of organizations and institutions, taped bird hotlines provide regularly updated information on rare bird sightings, as well as general reports on migration and population trends. Most tapes are updated weekly and rely on reports from listeners.

Cape May Birding Hotline
Cape May Bird Observatory
(609) 884-CMBO
Covers Cape May peninsula and surrounding region.

Delaware Valley Birding
    Hotline / Delaware
    Valley Ornithological
    Club & Academy of Natu-
    ral Sciences, Philadelphia
(215) 567-BIRD
Covers eastern Pennsylvania, New Jersey and Delaware.

Lehigh Valley (PA)
    Audubon Society
(215) 759-5754
Covers eastern Pennsylvania and surrounding region.

Voice of Audubon
Audubon Society of
    Western Pennsylvania
(412) 963-0560
Covers western Pennsylvania.

Voice of the Naturalist
Audubon Naturalist Society
(301) 652-1088
Covers Washington, D.C., and surrounding regions of Maryland and Virginia.

REGIONAL CHRISTMAS BIRD COUNTS

DELAWARE
Bombay Hook NWR
Cape Henlopen-Prime Hook
Middletown
Rehoboth
Seaford-Nanticoke
Wilmington

DISTRICT OF COLUMBIA
Washington, D.C.

MARYLAND
Allegheny County
Annapolis-Gibson Island
Baltimore Harbor

Bowie
Catoctin Mountain
Crisfield
Denton
Elkton
Jug Bay
Lower Kent County
Oakland
Ocean City
Point Lookout
Port Tobacco
Rock Run
St. Michael's
Salisbury
Seneca (MD-VA)

Southern Dorchester County
Sugarloaf Mountain
Tridelphia Reserve
Washington County

NEW JERSEY
Assunpink
Atlantic Ocean
(offshore of Shark River)
Barnegat
Belleplain
Boonton
Cape May
Cumberland County
Elmer
Great Swamp-Watchung Ridge
Hackensack-Ridgewood
Lakehurst
Long Branch
Lower Hudson (NJ-NY)
Marmora
Northwestern Gloucester County
Northwestern Hunterdon County
Oceanville
Pinelands
Princeton
Ramsey
Raritan Estuary
Salem
Sandy Hook
Somerset County
Sussex County
Trenton Marshes
Walnut Valley

PENNSYLVANIA
Audubon
Bald Eagle State Park
Beaver
Bedford County
Bernville
Bethlehem-Easton
Bloomsburg
Brushy Run State Park
Buffalo Creek Valley

Butler County
Central Bucks County
Chambersburg
Clarion
Clarksville
Culp
Dallas Area
DuBois
Elverson
Emporium
Erie
Gettysburg
Glenolden
Hamburg
Harrisburg
Huntingdon
Indiana
Johnstown
Lancaster
Lebanon County
Lehigh Valley
Lewisburg
Lewistown
Linesville
Lititz
Lock Haven-Jersey Shore
Lower Bucks County
Mansfield
New Bloomfield
Pennypack Valley
Pittsburgh
Pleasantville
Pocono Mountain
Port Barnett Bridge
Raccoon Creek State Park
Reading
Rector
Scranton
Southeast Bradford County
Southern Lancaster County
State College
Thompson
Upper Bucks County
Warren
Washington

West Chester
White Mills
Wild Creek-Little Gap
Williamsport
Wyncote
York

VIRGINIA
Augusta County
Back Bay NWR
Banister WMA
Big Flat Mountain
Blacksburg
Brooke
Calmes Neck
Cape Charles
Charlottesville
Chincoteague NWR
Clifton Forge
Danville
Fincastle
Fort Belvoir
Glade Spring
Gordonsville
Hopewell
Lake Anna
Lexington
Little Creek
Lynchburg
Manassas-Bull Run
Mathews

Newport News
Nickelsville
Nokesville
Northern Shenandoah Valley
Peaks of Otter
Philpott Reservoir
Roanoke
Rockingham County
Seneca (VA-MD)
Shenandoah National Park-Luray
Tazewell
Wachapreague
Warren
Waynesboro
Williamsburg
Wise County

WEST VIRGINIA
Charleston
Charles Town
Hampshire County
Huntington
Inwood
Lewisburg
Morgantown (WV-PA)
Oak Hill
Ona
Parkersburg (WV-OH)
Pipestem Area
Wheeling

OTHER NATURE CENTERS

NEW JERSEY

A. Morton and Elizabeth Cooper
    Environmental Center
1170 Cattus Island Blvd.
Toms River, NJ 08753
(908) 270-6960

Aeolium Nature Center
Seaside Park, NJ 08752
(908) 793-0506

Bernie Environmental
    Education Center
RD2
Port Murray, NJ 07865
(908) 832-5315

Cape May County Park
    Nature Center
Route 9 and Pine Lane
Cape May Court House, NJ 08210
(609) 465-5271

Cheesequake State Park
  Interpretive Center
Gordon Road
Matawan, NJ 07747
(201) 566-2161

Estell Manor Park
RD 20, Box 252A
Mays Landing, NJ 08330
(609) 645-5960

Great Swamp Outdoor
  Education Center
247 Southern Blvd.
Chatham, NJ 07928
(201) 635-6629

Hackensack Meadowlands
  Environmental Center
2 Dekorte Park Plaza
Lyndhurst, NJ 07071
(201) 460-8300

James A. McFaul
  Environmental Center
Crescent Avenue
Wycoff, NJ 07430
(201) 891-5571

John J. Crowley Nature Center
Lambert Castle
Paterson, NJ 07503
(201) 523-0024

Liberty State Park
  Interpretive Center
Morris Pesin Drive
Jersey City, NJ 07060
(201) 915-3409

Lorrimer Sanctuary
790 Ewing Ave., Box 125
Franklin Lakes, NJ 07417
(201) 891-2185

Marine Mammal Stranding Center
P.O. Box 773
Brigantine, NJ 08203
(609) 266-0538

The Morris Museum
6 Normandy Heights Rd.
Morristown, NJ 07960
(201) 538-0454

The Newark Museum
49 Washington St.
Newark, NJ 07101
(201) 596-6550

Ocean Institute at Sandy Hook
P.O. Box 533
Sandy Hook, NJ 07732
(908) 872-2284

Owl Haven Nature Center
P.O. Box 26
Tennent, NJ 07763
(201) 780-7007

Paws Farm Nature Center
1105 Hainesport-Mt. Laurel Rd.
Mt. Laurel, NJ 08054
(609) 778-8795

Pequest Natural Resource
  Education Center
389 Pequest Rd.
Oxford, NJ 07863
(201) 637-4125

Rancocas Nature Center
RD1 Rancocas Road
Mount Holly, NJ 08060
(609) 261-2495

Reeves-Reed Arboretum
165 Hobart Ave.
Summit, NJ 07901
(908) 273-8787

Scherman Hoffman Sanctuary
P.O. Box 693
Bernardsville, NJ 07924
(201) 766-5787

Scotland Run Park Nature Center
RD4, Box 775
Franklinville, NJ 08322
(609) 881-0845

Somerset County Environmental
   Education Center
190 Lord Stirling Rd.
Basking Ridge, NJ 07920
(908) 766-2489

Tenafly Nature Center
313 Hudson Ave.
Tenafly, NJ 07670
(201) 568-6093

Trailside Nature and
   Science Center
Coles Avenue
Mountainside, NJ 07092
(908) 789-3670

Washington Crossing
   Nature Center
RD1, Box 337A
Titusville, NJ 08560
(609) 737-0609

Weis Ecology Center
150 Snake Den Dr.
Ringwood, NJ 07456
(201) 835-2160

PENNSYLVANIA

Awbury Arboretum
Francis Cope House
Philadelphia, PA 19138
(215) 849-2855

Briar Bush Nature Center
1212 Edge Hill Rd.
Abington, PA 19001
(215) 887-6603

Churchville Nature Center
501 Churchville Lane
Churchville, PA 18966
(215) 357-4005

Four Mills Nature Reserve
12 Morris Rd.
Ambler, PA 19002
(215) 646-8866

Frick Nature Center
2005 Beechwood Blvd.
Pittsburgh, PA 15217
(412) 422-6538

Kings Gap Environmental
   Education Center
500 Kings Gap Rd.
Carlisle, PA 17013
(717) 486-5031

Monroe County Environmental
   Education Center
4225 Manor Dr.
Stroudsburg, PA 18360
(717) 992-7565

Montour Preserve
RD1, Box 292
Turbotville, PA 17772
(717) 437-3131

Nature Center of Charlestown
Route 29 and Hollow Road
Devault, PA 19432
(215) 935-9777

Peace Valley Nature Center
170 Chapman Rd.
Doylestown, PA 18901
(215) 345-7860

Pennypack Environmental Center
8600 Verree Rd.
Philadelphia, PA 19115
(215) 671-0440

Pocono Environmental
    Education Center
RD2, Box 1010
Dingman's Ferry, PA 18328
(717) 828-2319

Pool Wildlife Sanctuary
601 Orchid Place
Emmaus, PA 18049
(215) 965-4397

Powdermill Nature Reserve
Star Route South
Rector, PA 15677
(412) 593-2221

Richard M. Nixon Environmental
    Education Center
RD8, Box 438A
York, PA 17403
(717) 428-1961

Riverbend Environmental
    Education Center
P.O. Box 2, Spring Mill Rd.
Gladwyne, PA 19035
(215) 527-5234

Shaver's Creek Environmental
    Center
203 Henderson Building S.
University Park, PA 16802
(814) 863-2000

Silver Lake Nature Center
1006 Bath Rd.
Bristol, PA 19007
(215) 785-1177

Susquehanna Riverlands
RD1, Box 1797
Berwick, PA 18603
(717) 542-2131

Tinicum National
    Environmental Center
Scott Plaza 2, Suite 104
Philadelphia, PA 19113
(215) 521-0662

DELAWARE

Abbotts Mill Nature Center
Delaware Nature Society
RD4, Box 207
Milford, DE 19963
(302) 422-0847

Ashland Nature Center
Delaware Nature Society
P.O. Box 700
Hockessin, DE 19707
(302) 239-2334

Seaside Nature Center
Cape Henlopen State Park
42 Cape Henlopen Dr.
Lewes, DE 19966
(302) 645-6852

MARYLAND

30th St. Nature Center
4210 30th St.
Mt. Rainier, MD 20712
(301) 927-2163

Audubon Naturalist Society
8940 Jones Mill Rd.
Chevy Chase, MD 20815
(301) 652-9188

Battle Creek Nature Center
c/o County Courthouse
Prince Frederick, MD 20678
(301) 535-5327

Brookside Nature Center
1400 Glenallan Ave.
Wheaton, MD 20902
(301) 946-9071

Calvert Marine Museum
P.O. Box 97
Solomons, MD 20688
(301) 326-2042

Carrie Murray Outdoor
   Education Campus
1901 Ridgetop Rd.
Baltimore, MD 21207
(301) 396-0808

Clearwater Nature Center
11000 Thrift Rd.
Clinton, MD 20735
(301) 297-4575

Fairview Outdoor
   Education Center
Route 2, Box 120
Clear Spring, MD 21722
(301) 842-2151

Hard Bargain Farm
   Environmental Center
2001 Bryan Point Rd.
Accokeek, MD 20607
(301) 292-5665

Hashawha Environmental Center
300 John Owings Rd.
Westminster, MD 21157
(301) 848-9040

Hawk's Reach Nature Center
23701 Frederick Rd.
Clarksburg, MD 20871
(301) 972-9458

Irvine Natural Science Center
St. Timothy's School
Stevenson, MD 21153
(301) 484-2413

Maydale Nature Center
1726 Briggs Chaney Rd.
Silver Spring, MD 20904
(301) 384-9447

Meyer Station
1553 Meyer Station Rd.
Odenton, MD 21113
(301) 261-6996

National Aquarium in Baltimore
Pier 3
501 E. Pratt St.
Baltimore, MD 21202
(301) 576-3800

Patuxent River Park
1600 Croom Airport Rd.
Upper Marlboro, MD 20772
(301) 627-6074

Piney Run Nature Center
30 Martz Rd.
Sykesville, MD 21784
(301) 795-3274

Smithsonian Environmental
   Research Center
P.O. Box 28
Edgewater, MD 21037
(301) 798-4424

Watkins Nature Center and
Old Maryland Farm
301 Watkins Park Dr.
Upper Marlboro, MD 20772
(301) 249-6202

The Wildfowl Trust of
North America
Perry Corner Rd.
P.O. Box 519
Grasonville, MD 21638
(301) 827-6694

VIRGINIA

Hidden Oaks Nature Center
4030 Hummer Rd.
P.O. Box 236
Annandale, VA 22003

Hidden Pond Nature Center
8511 Greeley Blvd.
Springfield, VA 22152
(703) 451-9588

Laurel Ridge Conservation
Education Center
National Wildlife Federation
8925 Leesburg Pike
Vienna, VA 22184-0001
(703) 790-4437

Long Branch Nature Center
625 S. Carlin Springs Rd.
Arlington, VA 22204
(703) 358-6535

Mason Neck State Park
7301 High Point Rd.
Lorton, VA 22079
(703) 339-7265

Natural Tunnel State Park
Route 3, Box 250
Duffield, VA 24244
(703) 940-2674

Potomac Overlook Regional Park
and Nature Center
2845 Marcey Rd.
Arlington, VA 22207

Sky Meadows State Park
Route 1, Box 540
Delaplane, VA 22025
(703) 592-3556

Staunton River State Park
Route 2, Box 295
Scottsburg, VA 24589
(804) 572-4623

Twin Lakes State Park
Route 2, Box 70
Green Bay, VA 23942
(804) 392-3435

Virginia Living Museum
524 J. Clyde Morris Blvd.
Newport News, VA 23601
(804) 595-1900

Virginia Museum of
Natural History
1001 Douglas Ave.
Martinsville, VA 24112
(703) 632-1930

Vernon J. Walker Nature
Education Center
Reston Association
1930 Isaac Newton Sq.
Reston, VA 22090
(703) 437-9580

WEST VIRGINIA

A.B. Brooks Nature Center
Wheeling, WV 26003
(304) 242-6855

Oglebay's Good Children's Zoo
Oglebay
Wheeling, WV 26003
(304) 242-3000

NOTE: Nature center listings were drawn, in part, from "Directory of Natural Science Centers," with permission of its publisher, the Natural Science for Youth Foundation, Roswell, Georgia.

SELECTED BIBLIOGRAPHY

Bonta, Marcia. *Outbound Journeys in Pennsylvania.* University Park, PA: The Pennsylvania State University, 1987.

Boyle, William J., Jr. *A Guide to Bird Finding in New Jersey.* New Brunswick, NJ: Rutgers University Press, 1986.

Catlin, David T. *A Naturalist's Blue Ridge Parkway.* Knoxville, TN: University of Tennessee Press, 1984.

Clark, William S., and Brian K. Wheeler. *Hawks.* Boston: Houghton Mifflin Co.,1987.

Conners, John A. *Shenandoah National Park: An Interpretive Guide.* Blacksburg, VA: McDonald & Woodward Publishing, 1988.

"Directory of Pelagic Birding Trips in North America." *Winging It,* January 1991.

Dunne, Pete, David Sibley and Clay Sutton. *Hawks in Flight.* Boston: Houghton Mifflin Co., 1988.

Erlich, Paul, David S. Dobkin and Darryl Wheye. *The Birder's Handbook.* New York: Simon & Schuster, 1988.

Geyer, Alan R., and William H. Bolles. *Outstanding Scenic Geologic Features of Pennsylvania.* Harrisburg, PA: Pennsylvania Department of Environmental Resources, 1979.

Hamilton, W.J., and J.O. Whitaker, Jr. *Mammals of the Eastern United States.* Ithaca, NY: Cornell University Press, 1979.

Harwood, Michael. *The View from Hawk Mountain.* New York: Charles Scribner's Sons, 1973.

Heintzelman, Donald S. *A Guide to Eastern Hawk Watching.* University Park, PA: Pennsylvania State University Press, 1976.

Kaufman, Kenn. *Advanced Birding.* Boston: Houghton Mifflin Co., 1990.

Lawrence, Susannah. *The Audubon Society Field Guide to the Natural Places of the Mid-Atlantic States: Coastal.* New York: The Hilltown Press, 1984.

Lawrence, Susannah, and Barbara Gross. *The Audubon Society Field Guide to the Natural Places of the Mid-Atlantic States: Inland.* New York: The Hilltown Press, 1984.

Leopold, Aldo. *A Sand County Almanac.* New York: Oxford University Press, 1966.

Merritt, Joseph F. *Guide to the Mammals of Pennsylvania.* Pittsburgh, PA: University of Pittsburgh Press, 1987.

Murie, Olaus J. *A Field Guide to Animal Tracks,* Second Edition. Boston: Houghton Mifflin, 1974.

National Geographic Society. *National Geographic Society's Guide to the National Parks of the United States.* Washington, D.C., 1989.

National Geographic Society. *Our Federal Lands.* Washington, D.C., 1984.

Nelson, Bryan. *Seabirds: Their Biology and Ecology.* London: Hamlyn Publishing Group, 1979.

"The 90th Christmas Bird Count." *American Birds,* Vol. 44, No. 4.

Peterson, Roger T., and Margaret McKenny. *A Field Guide to Wildflowers of Northeastern and Northcentral North America.* Boston: Houghton Mifflin, 1968.

Pettingill, Olin Sewall, Jr. *A Guide to Bird Finding East of the Mississippi.* New York: Oxford University Press, 1977.

Riley, Laura and William. *Guide to the National Wildlife Refuges.* New York: Anchor Press, 1979.

Rue, Leonard Lee, III. *The Deer of North America.* New York: Outdoor Life Books, 1978.

Sundquist, Bruce, and Allen de Hart. *Monongahela National Forest Hiking Guide.* Charleston, WV: West Virginia Highlands Conservancy, 1988.

Tyning, Thomas F. *A Guide to Amphibians and Reptiles.* Boston: Little, Brown, 1990.

Welty, Joel C. *The Life of Birds.* Philadelphia: W.B. Saunders, 1982.

White, Christopher P. *Chesapeake Bay, A Field Guide: Nature of the Estuary.* Centerville, MD: Tidewater Publishers, 1989.

Wilds, Claudia. *Finding Birds in the National Capitol Area.* Washington, D.C.: Smithsonian Institution Press, 1983.

INDEX

NOTE: Boldfaced entries denote directions and italics indicate maps.

ABOUT THE AUTHOR

Scott Weidensaul is the author of more than a dozen books on natural history. Among his recent titles are *The Birder's Miscellany* and *A Kid's First Book of Bird-watching*. An award-winning newspaper columnist for fourteen years, he is currently outdoor editor for the Harrisburg, Pennsylvania, *Patriot-News.* He has written for national magazines such as

Photo: Rick Walters

Audubon and *Bird Watcher's Digest,* and his photography has appeared in many books and periodicals as well. Weidensaul has led guided natural history tours in the United States and abroad. A former investigative reporter, he lives in the mountains of eastern Pennsylvania, where each autumn he helps biologists run a hawk-banding station.